ACKNOWLEDGEMENTS

This book is a revised and enlarged version of a study prepared during my graduate studies at the Department of International Relations of Yale University under the direction of Dr. Arnold Wolfers with the advice of Dr. Samuel F. Bemis and other members of the faculty.

My concern about the problem of American support of free elections abroad was first aroused by discussions with Dr. Warner R. Schilling and Dr. Pamela N. Wrinch. Their interest and stimulus has been invaluable.

I am deeply indebted to the staffs of the Sterling Memorial Library of Yale, the Division of Manuscripts at the Library of Congress (particularly Miss Catherine Brand), and the National Archives in Washington, D. C., for their cooperation in granting me access to the various collections of papers in those institutions.

I wish to take this opportunity to express my gratitude to Dr. Bryce Wood, who introduced me to the study of international relations at Swarthmore College, and to Dr. Sydney W. Jackman, a colleague on the Bates College faculty who has helped sustain my interest in scholarly research. Last but not least, I am deeply grateful to my parents; without their help and constant encouragement this work could never have been completed.

Various chapters draw heavily upon articles of mine that originally appeared in the *Political Science Quarterly, Inter-American Economic Affairs*, the *Hispanic American Historical Review*, the *Journal of International Affairs,* and the *Western Political Quarterly.* To their editors I wish to express my gratitude for permission to incorporate in this book substantial portions of the articles.

THEODORE PAUL WRIGHT, JR.

Bates College,
Lewiston, Maine

CONTENTS

FOREWORD

The issue between the United States and Soviet Russia which above all others marked the opening of the cold war was the dispute over the holding of "free and fair elections" in Eastern Europe. It has continued to be the most persistent and publicized of Western demands in that struggle. As the conflict has spread to other areas of the world, our government has repeatedly expressed its objectives in the same terms. Thus American spokesmen have insisted on free elections not only in their efforts to dislodge the Soviets from control of Poland, Hungary, Rumania and Bulgaria, but also in negotiations for the reunification of Germany and Korea. As late as the summer of 1960, President Eisenhower challenged Chairman Khrushchev to a worldwide plebiscite in which all peoples would have the right to choose between communism and democracy.[1]

Probably the United States has emphasized this criterion for democracy in its negotiations and propaganda because its communist rival has adopted as its own and thereby rendered almost meaningless most of the more general slogans of American foreign policy such as "democracy", "anti-imperialism" and "national self-determination". Soviet resistance to free elections has suggested to us that they provide a sure test for distinguishing bogus communist "people's democracy" from the genuine form.

More recent experience with bona fide communist or front-group electoral successes in Guatemala, British Guiana, India's Kerala, Indonesia and potentially in Viet Nam has cast doubt upon the American premise that any truly free and fair election will inevitably produce victory for the democratic parties over all anti-democratic forces.[2] Even if this assumption were valid, it quite evidently does not follow that successful democratic parties in all states will necessarily be favorable to us in their foreign policies. Neutrality is the best we can hope for from many.

We might not have staked so much on free elections in the postwar period if our leaders had paid more attention to an earlier chapter of the nation's diplomatic history. For the Latin American policy of the United States in the first third of the twentieth century is replete with examples of unsuccessful intervention in support of free elections. At various times during the era from the Spanish-American War of 1898 to the inauguration of Franklin D. Roosevelt's Good Neighbor

1

Policy in 1933, our government interfered recurrently and in a number of different ways in the electoral processes of Cuba, Panama, Nicaragua, Mexico, the Dominican Republic, Haiti, Costa Rica, Honduras, Guatemala and El Salvador. These episodes in our relations with our small and weak neighbors of the Central American-Caribbean area might well have served as laboratories from which lessons about the efficacy of attempting to promote democracy abroad could have been drawn. That they were not was probably a consequence both of the discontinuity of top foreign policy-making personnel in the American political system and of the fact that the policy was not originally an end in itself, but rather a means to prior security goals.

In this book I shall examine eight case studies of United States electoral intervention in Latin America during the period 1898-1933 and then proceed to narrate and appraise the revival of the policy during the cold war since 1945. Since the circumstances of proximity and relative power dictated that the primary applications of the policy should be to our nearest neighbors in Latin America, the present work is devoted chiefly, but not exclusively, to intervention in the western hemisphere, but it should be borne in mind that these relatively minor affairs are to be regarded as precedents for policies of much wider relevance. In each case study I shall discuss the kinds of policy problems which elicited the support of free elections; the American policy makers who introduced, obstructed or qualified it; how they defined free elections in each situation; what methods they used; and what they achieved in terms of their objectives. The cases are subdivided chronologically into episodes, each focussed on a particular election, revolution or other event that raised a question for which free elections seemed to be the answer.

A principal theme that emerges from the work is that the United States, far from being the crusader for a "nationalistic universalism" of democracy which Hans Morgenthau has pictured her to be[3], has been most reluctantly involved in the domestic politics of her neighbors, usually for reasons of national security. Indeed, influential citizens of the states in question have themselves been instrumental in implicating us by urging us to guarantee a free poll in their countries.

During the first century and a quarter of our independence, most American citizens assumed optimistically that democracy was so self-evidently the best form of government that it would spread ineluctably over the globe with no more help from us than our shining example.[4] In fact, events of the nineteenth century did seem to point to a democratic trend of almost Marxian inexorability. Early in the twentieth century, as the first doubts about the automatic character of this process began to appear, paradoxically our capability of doing something to help the spread of democracy seemed to grow phenomenally. Yet by the second half of the century when we have become the most powerful state on earth militarily and economically, our predictions for the future of our form of government outside the North Atlantic area are gloomy except in official rhetoric. It is the communists who have inherited our earlier messianic expectations. Democracy is now regarded as a tender plant indeed, suitable only in very special conditions. A consideration of the case studies to follow will show one reason why we have become realistically pessimistic about our ability to foster free elections abroad by direct action even though we still talk about democracy as an objective in the cold war.

However, my conclusions need not lead us to an equally negative view of our chances of survival in competition with totalitarian communism. Nationalism has shown itself to be a potent barrier to Soviet control. If we cannot expect the new nations of Asia and Africa to achieve effective democracy immediately merely by adopting democratic constitutions, at least in the long run the democratizing effects of mass education and economic development may portend a better outcome than we can now foresee.

I

CUBA

The island of Cuba, which we conquered from Spain in 1898 during the Spanish-American War, was the first considerable area inhabited by a numerous and alien people to be occupied by the United States. As soon became evident, she provided us with the first foreign policy problems for which support of free elections might be adopted as a solution.

Previously we had been only a passive exemplar of democratic virtues. Now, with our own internal frontier of colonization closed, the territorial possessions of the United States included a small colonial empire—Cuba, Puerto Rico, and the Philippines. Would America pursue the same imperialist territorial objectives with the same forceful policies as many of the traditional autocracies and oligarchies had adopted? The paragon of peaceful democracy, in the words of Samuel F. Bemis, was projected into the arena of world politics and ever since has confronted the moral dilemmas of great power status.[1]

Following the Spanish-American War, the immediate problem in Cuba was what to do with the island. There appeared to be three alternatives: annexation, colonization and independence. Annexation, with ultimate admission to the Union on an equal footing with the other states was desired by some influential Americans and Cubans[2], but, since Cuba had a large Negro population, this was not politically feasible. Southern Congressmen, because of racial prejudice as well as their identification with the now "anti-imperialist" Democratic Party, opposed statehood for the new American possession on the ground that its racially mixed population was unassimilable.

The European powers expected the United States to reduce Cuba to the colonial status it had been subjected to by Spain, possibly with some vague and indefinite promise of future self rule. This outcome was not at all unlikely considering that the other conquered Spanish colonies, Puerto Rico an dthe Philippines, were receiving just such treatment. But the Spanish-American War had been fought specifically to free Cuba and a promise to that effect was embodied in the Teller Amendment adopted by Congress in a fine display of self-abnegating idealism at the very outset of the war on April 20, 1898. The Amendment proclaimed that "The United States hereby dis-

4

claims any disposition or intention to exercise sovereignty, jurisdiction, or control over said island except for the pacification thereof, and asserts its determination, when that is accomplished, to leave the government and control of the island to its people."[3]

American leaders like William McKinley, Theodore Roosevelt, General Leonard Wood and Elihu Root all felt bound to honor the pledge no matter what their private misgivings were as to Cuba's readiness for self government under a democratic constitution.[4]

Behind the self-denying Teller ordinance lay the deep-rooted anti-colonial sentiment of most of the American people and their consciousness that the United States, itself the product of a colonial revolt, could neither become a permanent colonial power nor actively support autocratic governments within its new sphere of influence.[5]

What brought about early American withdrawal from Cuba, more than anything else, despite the pleas of Cuban conservatives and the American military governor, was the existence of the Teller pledge to leave Cuba. Manifestly, political opponents could use it as a campaign argument to attack the administration if the promise were not fulfilled.[6]

The third alternative, immediate independence for Cuba, did not appear any more advisable than the proposal to annex the island, both because it was feared that a weak, poor and unstable Cuban government would tempt European states to intervene in her internal affairs to the detriment of U.S. security, and because of a nascent desire by some Americans to "uplift" their less fortunate neighbors.

The problem of what to do with Cuba was well summed up by Elihu Root: "We don't want Cuba ourselves; we cannot permit any other power to get possession of her, and, to prevent the necessity of one and the possibility of the other of these results, we want her to govern herself decently and in order."[7] With this purpose and only American domestic political experience to draw upon, "free elections" were the national operational criterion for "decent and orderly government." So it was that in 1899 President McKinley, who had always had moral qualms about the war with Spain over Cuba, instructed his new military governor, General Leonard Wood, "to go down there to get the people ready for a republican form of government . . . and to get out of the island as soon as we safely can."[8]

If European models for political control over dependent and unassimilable but civilized people were unacceptable in this connection, the experience of the United States in such matters offered no substitutes.[9] The settlement of the American West and the treatment of the American Indians could not be used for guidance because there the policy was one of extermination ("The only good Indian is a dead Indian") or concentration in "reservations" followed by white colonization of the land. The precedent of Northern military rule in the South after the American Civil War was inapplicable because the rebel states were destined for quick reentry into the Union.

Therefore, a wholesale transplantation of American political institutions, including our electoral process, took place almost automatically. As Governor Wood said in the same year, "ever since I have been in Santiago . . . I have prescribed liberal doses of the United States Constitution and the treatment has been remarkably efficacious."[10] In the following year he reported back to Root: "I am going to work on a constitution for the island similar to our own. . . . The leaders of (the Cuban parties) . . . are going to serve on the Commission for drawing up rules and regulations governing election. Our own people, however, will have to do most of the work, as they are the only members of the Commission who know much about election laws and details of elections."[11]

A formula for the steps by which Cuba was to be prepared for her promised independence was laid down in 1899 by Elihu Root, then Secretary of War: "The results of a census having been computed and tabulated, we shall be ready to provide for municipal elections, which will place all the local government of the island in the hands of representatives elected by the people, and when these local governments, thus elected, are established, they will be ready to proceed to the formation of a representative convention to frame a constitution and provide for (the election of) a general government of the island, to which the United States will surrender the reins of government."[12] Wood admitted that the result of this procedure was the adoption, without change, of the original proposals submitted by the Americans on the commissions only as working models.

The prescribed elections, held successively under Cuban direction without American observation or supervision, were reported to have been orderly and for the most part honest, but since the opposition withdrew from the contest beforehand both in the municipal election of 1900 and in the presidential election of 1901, there was little incentive for dishonest practices.

Although the United States found no acceptable guides in European colonial policy, its policy-makers did have constantly before them examples of what to avoid—namely, "the conditions which have subjected Haiti, San Domingo, and the Central American Republics

to continuous revolution and disorder."[13] Root showed a keen awareness of the necessary preconditions for democratic self-government.

Regarding literacy, intelligence, education and interest in government, he warned: "I do not believe any people, three-fourths of whom
are contented to remain unable to read and write, can for any very
long period maintain a free government."[14]

As for experience in self government and traditions of civic moral-
ity (including self control, respect for individual rights and acceptance
of majority decisions), Root pointed out that "all of our States have
the traditions of popular self government and respect for constitutional methods and principles continuing through centuries and perme-
ating the most ignorant social strata. These traditions with us amount
to a kind of unwritten Constitution which the most illiterate man has
taken in through the pores of his skin."[15]

Concerning national cohesion, mutual trust and the absence of
irreconcilably bitter class or factional divisions, Root warned that "the
bloody conflicts which raged so long (in Cuba) have necessarily left
behind bitter factional feeling (which) makes it necessary to proceed
somewhat more slowly in the formation of a government which is
to command universal respect and allegiance than would be necessary in a country accustomed to the discussion of public questions,
familiar with the problems presented, and trained to the acceptance
of the decisions reached by the ballot."[16]

Root and Wood were especially apprehensive about Cuba's high
percentage of Negro and Mulatto citizens, for it was an indisputable
fact that most of them were uneducated and, to all indications, unruly.

With such misgivings in mind, and without the political possibility
of putting into effect either of the logical alternatives to free elections:
annexation or non-intervention, the Secretary of War and the Governor turned to other ways of vitiating the full effects of majority rule.
If there had to be elections they might be restricted in such a way as
to prevent the colored population from bringing its full weight of numbers to bear. Five such restrictions were tried.

One method of cutting down illiterate or anti-American majorities
without openly flouting democratic principles was to restrict suffrage
by imposing literacy and property qualifications. Root, supported
by Wood, made the first attempt to secure conservative control through
suffrage restriction in Cuba in 1900. In refuting charges that the suffrage law of April 18, 1900 which the two men framed was racially
discriminatory, Root gave as evidence the fact that it enfranchised all
Cuban army veterans, many of whom were colored. Limiting the fran-

chise would, he contended, increase respect for it and stimulate the people to thrift and education: "With a sufficient system of free primary education, the entire people should acquire the suffrage on this basis fully as soon as they are capable of using it understandingly."[17] However, the Cuban Conservatives failed to take advantage of this opportunity and withdrew from the first election, much to the disgust of Wood.[18] Overwhelmingly Liberal, the Cuban Constitutional Convention adopted a provision for manhood suffrage.

If the United States could not eliminate disorderly elements from the electorate, it might at least foster parties and promote candidates favorable to its policies while it was in occupation of the country. At first, Americans as individuals found the Cuban Conservatives personally more congenial than their Liberal compatriots. The former were the Spanish-descended, the rich, the cultured, the landowners who "were alarmed lest the illiterate mass of the people get control of the elections." [19]   Some of the Conservatives even had been on the Spanish side in the sanguinary civil wars which preceded American intervention and they feared retaliation from their former enemies when the Americans departed. They persistently and unsuccessfully urged the United States to annex Cuba.[20]

Although Governor Wood resorted to everything short of open favoritism in order to encourage the outnumbered and politically apathetic "better elements" to organize for electoral purposes against the "lot of adventurers" in the Liberal camp, his efforts to "bring representative Conservative elements to the front" under the banner of the Union Democratic Party were unsuccessful. The Conservatives had the stigma of opposition to independence attached to them, and, as the historian of a comparable American puppet party in the Philippines wryly observed, "few people like to admit their incapacity for managing their own affairs . . ."[21]

Wood showed surprisingly little concern with the necessity of having at least two political parties to give meaning to elections. "Of course," he wrote Root in January, 1900, "the usual opposition party will gradually develop, but I shall endeavor to give them as slender a foundation as possible to stand on . . ."[22] In the following month he added: "I am preaching one policy and that is for all people to get together and unite for good government."[23]

Since the apparently pro-American Conservatives could not be brought to power by suffrage restrictions or tacit support, they could at least be assured enough legislative representation to be an effective check on the majority party. Wood proposed minority representation

in the Cuban constitutional convention of 1900 to obtain "a fair proportion of the delegates . . . for the conservative and intelligent classes"
which had abstained from voting.[24] Although this device was planted
in the Cuban constitution, it was subsequently perverted by the party
in power in a manner that made it possible for the majority to elect
the minority candidates as well as its own.

By another technique, coalition government, the performance of
at least the minimum legal forms of constitutional elections could be
assured while the full consequences of genuine political competition
might be avoided. The first example of the use of the coalition tactic
was in the Cuban presidential election of December, 1901—the final
preliminary to independence. Leaders of both major Cuban parties
signed a compact in which they agreed on a neutral candidate, Tomas
Estrada Palma. They correctly estimated that his long residence in
exile in North America before the Cuban revolution would make him
eminently fitted to extract favorable terms from the United States in
the liquidation of the American occupation and in the establishment
of normal diplomatic and economic relations.[25]

One radical leader, Bartolomeo Maso, refused to join the coalition
and ran against its candidate on a platform of criticism of the occupying power, thus foreshadowing the anti-Yankee tactics of Fidel Castro.
After the Platt Amendment, to be described below, was ratified, Maso
focussed his attack on it. Governor Wood in turn refused Maso's
group representation on the Central Board of Scrutiny for the election, whereupon the Cuban leader directed his followers not to go
to the polls. Wood was not a strong supporter of the two party system
in Cuba and probably thought that handing over the reins of government to a coalition regime would guarantee domestic peace for four
years anyway. He fully expected that the Cubans would ask voluntarily for annexation to the United States after a short trial of independence.[26]

When his attempt to secure conservative government failed, Root
shifted his attention to obtaining Cuban acceptance of a treaty giving
us the right to intervene in case the turbulent electorate should provoke political disorders which would endanger American lives and
property and therefore United States security. As a condition for
American evacuation of Cuba, Root obtained reluctant Cuban adherence to such a treaty. The proviso was also embedded in the Cuban
Constitution. Article III of the so-called Platt Amendment read: "The
Government of Cuba consents that the United States may exercise the
right to intervene for the preservation of Cuban independence, the

maintenance of a government adequate for the protection of life, property, and individual liberty, and for discharging the obligations with respect to Cuba imposed by the Treaty of Paris on the United States, now to be assumed and undertaken by the Government of Cuba."[27]

There was nothing in the Platt Amendment prohibiting the United States from helping a Cuban government to stay in power, even if the latter had been fraudulently elected. This assistance could include the suppression of insurrection, unless "individual liberty" were stretched so as to include liberty of franchise. Secretary Root emphatically denied that the "intervention described in the third clause of the Platt Amendment is . . . synonymous with the inter-meddling or interference with the Cuban Government",[28] and limited the conditions under which it would be applied to "just and substantial grounds." It was the Cuban opposition parties which converted what might have been an alternative to support of free elections into a means of achieving them by appealing to the American sense of justice.

The initial American experience with establishing democracy abroad through free elections appeared superficially, by the end of the American occupation in 1902, to be a great success. Cuba had been "uplifted" by four years of American education, sanitation and road-building, and at the same time the cynical predictions of Europe about the intentions of the United States were confounded. What seemed to be a democratic, stable Cuban government was installed. Our strategic interests were covered by the Platt Amendment.

Free elections in this first episode were a means rather than an end in themselves. American colonial rule as personified by Governor Wood was frankly paternalistic and dictatorial except insofar as the Teller Amendment obliged him to hold elections in preparation for American evacuation. By precept and example, he taught Cubans autocratic rather than democratic government. If later American statesmen had been equally willing to accept the form rather than the substance of democracy in the governments of their Latin American neighbors, the strategic goals of the policy could have been more cheaply secured, but other Americans valued free elections as a test of democracy which they were unwilling openly to forsake. Accordingly, the United States, vulnerable to appeals based on this ideal, was soon more deeply involved than ever in promoting free elections in Cuba.

The Cuban party pact of 1901 collapsed well in advance of the next presidential election. As soon as the Americans evacuated Cuba, the dominant faction began to manipulate the electoral machinery of the American-style constitution in such a way as to assure its own continuance in office. The Liberal party was eased out of the government and abstained from voting when it became apparent that the incumbent conservative or "Moderate Party" intended to carry the election by fraud and intimidation. Abstention was a familiar Hispanic-American maneuver indicative of an intention to organize a revolution and it was so understood in Cuba.

The Liberal candidate first demanded that the United States intervene and insist on an honest election. He pointed out that the Cuban government was using the threat of American military occupation on its behalf to silence Liberal protests against electoral fraud. His request was rebuffed by the American Minister to Cuba on the ground that the United States was interested only in preserving peace and order.

By August 1906 civil war broke out. The Liberals hoped they might force the protecting power to heed their earlier request to enforce free elections for they were confident they could win them. Alternatively, if the United States stood aside and let the two parties fight it out, the Liberals also stood a good chance of victory. At the worst, if American troops were sent in to support the Conservative government, the Liberals would be no less well off than if they did nothing and let their enemies stay in power by force and fraud. The cry "better the Americans than our opponents" was to be the root of many Latin American pleas for our assistance.

Thus the American government again had three alternatives from which to choose:

It could stand aloof from the civil war and simply warn European states whose subjects' lives and property were jeopardized by the conflict not to take action. Such a stand was far less feasible in the early 1900s when the American fleet was only the sixth largest in the world than later when it had grown to a strength such that no navy afloat could venture to challenge it in the Caribbean.[29] There is however no doubt that Secretary Root had had European life and property in mind when he helped frame the treaty. He had wanted a legal basis for invoking the Monroe Doctrine against European intervention in case of just such a breakdown of Cuban government as occurred.[30] A policy of non-intervention would also be untenable if the civil war were protracted and destructive, because American lives and property would be lost, with serious domestic political repercussions for the administration in Washington.

The second alternative was to aid the recognized government to suppress the insurrection. As the Cuban government began to lose the civil war in September, 1906, it too quietly requested American aid in the expectation that the aid would be unconditional. To support this plea U. S. Consul General Frank Steinhart in Havana endorsed the request by arguing that the civil war was jeopardizing Cuban independence.

The United States government would probably have followed this second policy were it not for the fact that Root, now Secretary of State, was away in South America on a good will tour and Secretary of War Taft was delegated to go to Cuba in his place to handle the matter.[31] Because of his judicial proclivities, Taft interpreted the treaty and his mission to permit not only renewed American occupation, but also reform of the Cuban electoral code and the supervision of new elections.

In these circumstances, the third alternative, support of free elections, was adopted in Cuba by an historic accident. One historian attributes this decision of the Taft Mission to the fear that the propertyless rebels would otherwise burn the valuable, highly inflammable and largely foreign-owned sugar-cane crop and mills.[32] It seems more likely that Taft used this strategic and economic argument to rationalize his own personal preference for revoking the fraudulent election of 1905. Taft himself admitted that the rebels were winning the civil war and would have taken Havana but for American interposition.[33] The winning side in a civil war would not be likely to encourage foreign intervention by such acts of desperation as burning foreign property. Moreover, those who, like Root and Assistant Secretary of State Robert Bacon, were most concerned about the alleged danger of European action, favored unqualified support of the established regime in Cuba rather than supervision of new elections.[34]

Several methods were employed by the United States to bring about free elections once the decision was made. First came the mediating commission, then military occupation and finally electoral law reform.

Taft was a different kind of lawyer from Root. A diplomat who served under Taft once described him as "a judge, a legalist rather than a leader . . . [who] believed a President should do nothing the Law had not specifically authorized him to do. . . . He was always thinking in set terms of Law. . . ."[35] For such a man, a partisan attorney's brief was insufficient justification for a policy or its application. He had to collect, sift and evaluate all the facts of a case as he found them with complete impartiality. When his colleague, Bacon, and Consul Steinhart were pressing him to help the Conservative government, Taft wrote President Roosevelt: "I should be willing to have [the insurgents] think that we come, as we really do, rather as arbitrators and compromisers than as desirous of directly suppressing the insurgents and putting them in jail."[36]

Taft conducted a full investigation into the causes of the revolt and asked for written and oral evidence and suggestions from both sides.[37] This procedure inevitably shifted the issue in dispute away from the question of whether the revolution itself was creating such anarchy as to require the American government to intervene on behalf of the Cuban government. Instead, the central question became the illegality of the last election which was the ostensible cause of the revolt. Once he had decided to judge the case on its merits, there was no alternative.

When all the evidence was in, Taft proposed as a compromise a coalition cabinet to conduct new elections. The infuriated Conservatives indignantly refused.[38] Thereupon Taft proclaimed a second American military occupation of Cuba in which he promised that "The provisional government . . . will be maintained only long enough to restore order and peace and public confidence and then to hold such elections as may be necessary to determine those persons upon whom the permanent government of the Republic should be devolved."[39] Thus, he contended, the Cuban government had only "gone into receivership".[40] The Cuban Congress was dissolved on the ground that part of its membership was fraudulently elected. New elections were necessary.

The frank admissions by the Cubans of electoral fraud and violence which Taft received during the course of his inquiry led him to conclude that the remedy for abuses of the law was more and better law. This was in keeping with the deep-seated American tendency to "make a law" as the answer to all social and political problems. The Cubans themselves urged on the Commission the necessity for the enactment of new electoral laws as a vital part of any solution to the political impasse of 1906.[41] Colonel Enoch Crowder, a lawyer from the United States Army's Office of the Judge Advocate General, was picked to frame the new electoral code during the second occupation. Like Taft, "his training and temperament were those of a jurist, of a judge rather than a lawyer".[42]

The Conservatives, with Taft's concurrence, pressed again for the incorporation of a literacy requirement into the new constitution, but Crowder, the chairman, advised that this was impossible because the constitution had been drawn up with special reference to securing manhood suffrage.⁴³ It was argued that in any case the Cubans would undoubtedly change the provision back again as soon as the Americans left if Crowder tried to dictate such a law. One critic of the latter's work commented "This legislation was drafted with learning and ingenuity. [It] was regarded as a masterpiece, 'a perfect electoral instrument, or at least proof against frauds and electoral abuses.' Cuba was equipped with governmental machinery that simply could not go wrong. Experience has shown the delusive character of this idea. Colonel Crowder's industry and the zeal produced a document which [U. S.] Minister Gonzales later declared he had not found more than four men able to understand. Its basic feature was a scheme of proportional representation, administered by bipartisan electoral boards, whose duty it was to count the votes and announce the persons elected from the party lists. It proved easier for the parties to decide who ought to be elected, and for the electoral boards to distribute the votes accordingly. Repeated tinkering has failed to make this democratic machinery work as intended".⁴⁴

To insure the completion of his plans for the second Cuban occupation, Taft secured the appointment of his protege, Charles Magoon, to the provisional governorship in place of General Leonard Wood, whom Roosevelt at first favored.⁴⁵ Chapman, the historian of Cuban-American relations, says of Magoon that he "was primarily a law student, interested more in legal abstractions than in the direct practice of his profession. . . . It was expected at the time that some purely legal questions had to be solved, such as those of the proposed electoral and municipal laws. . . . Perhaps no man in America was better acquainted with Cuban law at this time than Charles E. Magoon. . . . He was not a natural leader and administrator like Wood; he was rather the hard-working clerk who tries faithfully to execute superior orders, without much initiative of his own".⁴⁶ Magoon had achieved some success as American Minister to Panama by acting as an impartial umpire between the contentious parties.⁴⁷ He was to repeat the role in Cuba as provisional governor.

The new governor wrote back to his patron in Washington that the new Cuban government to be established must necessarily be bi-partisan so that one party might act as a check on the other.⁴⁸ During the second occupation this was accomplished by filling official vacancies with qualified Liberals until the distribution of offices was equal.⁴⁹ During the preparatory period for the new elections in 1908, Magoon encouraged the Conservatives to reestablish their party

which had been shattered by the civil war and American intervention
of 1906. His motive, different from Wood's blatant partisanship, was
simply a desire to stimulate the quarreling Liberal factions to reunite
so that the people would have a clearcut choice between two parties
in the election. In the outcome, a relatively free, contested election
was possible largely because both parties were convinced that they
were going to win and therefore neither abstained in the usual way.[50]

When Taft had proclaimed the second occupation in 1906, he
wrote of "giving another trial at self government" to this country which
had "stumbled on the hard road to democracy", but he cautioned that
"three times is out" and that annexation would be the cost of another
failure.[51] The good character of the election of 1908 as a test of Cuban
capacity for self government was further illustrated in President Roosevelt's message of congratulation to the Liberal President-elect, Gomez:
"The conduct of this election shows in impressive fashion the serious-
ness with which the Cuban people have now prepared themselves
once more to assume the duties of a free and independent Republic".[52]

Secretary Taft had come to Cuba in 1906 with a bias in favor of
the party in power, the conservative "Moderates". He asserted "There
is nobody in the Liberal Party fit to be President. . . . It is not a government, but only an undisciplined horde of men under partisan leaders".[53]
Yet so deep was his revulsion from the bland admissions of fraud
by the Moderates and so strong his feeling that the United States
could not morally support a fraudulently elected government that his
sympathies were alienated from them.

Like many Latin American leaders in later years, the Moderates
had wanted American intervention without the onus of publicly asking for it. The revelation of their request at Taft's hearings caused
much patriotic indignation among Cubans. Taft was dismayed to
find that his painstakingly neutral mediation was widely understood
by Cubans as a Liberal victory.[54] This interpretation probably contributed to the Liberal triumph in the American sponsored election at
the end of the occupation.[55]

Thus, impartial mediation to bring about free elections established
a dangerous precedent when it amounted to rewarding the party out
of power for resorting to armed insurrection to remedy electoral
abuses.[56] Senator Joseph Foraker (Rep., Ohio) had predicted that
this would be the result of the Platt Amendment when he opposed it
in 1901. Consul General Steinhart had also warned in 1906 that we
must act solely on behalf of the recognized government so as to uphold its dignity in the interest of future stability.[57] Taft, whose respon-

sibility it was to resolve the dilemma of stability versus free elections, acknowledged the danger but chose the latter.

After the Cuban civil war of 1906 established regimes in the Caribbean area could never be sure of unqualified American support against revolutionaries. Consequently they were wont to give their manipulated elections some greater semblance of legality when the State Department protested, lest the unpredictable Yankees should seize upon domestic disorders as the excuse for another impartial mediation.

The danger of the precedent set by Taft became apparent in the next Cuban electoral crisis a decade later. Typical of Latin American parties in office, the victorious Liberals of 1908 split in 1912. The Liberal President, Gomez, disgruntled because debarred by his party from succeeding himself and unsuccessful in naming its candidate, threw the election to the Conservatives.[58] So by 1916 the pendulum had swung full cycle; all the elements of the 1905 crisis were present again. A Conservative president showed every sign of intending to force his own reelection by fraud. The Liberals, confident that they could repeat their success of 1906, were threatening revolution if the United States did not step in to assure free elections.[59] The American Government faced anew the old dilemma of how to interpret the Platt Amendment.

The situation was further complicated by the fact that the First World War was monopolizing the attention of President Woodrow Wilson. As early as May 1916, Secretary of State Lansing recommended that "It would have a wholesome effect should the President of the United States . . . state that the international situation demands, as never before, that constituted authorities be upheld and law and order be maintained at all costs".[60] Both Lansing and our Minister to Cuba, William Gonzales, personally sympathized with the efforts of President Menocal to win reelection because he was American-educated, well disposed and had close relations with American businessmen in Cuba. The Liberals, on the other hand, were accused of being pro-German and hostile to our interests.[61] This became a serious matter as the entry of the United States into the war drew closer and the Cuban sugar crop increased in importance for the prospective war effort.

Nevertheless, after the election, Washington gave diplomatic support to the holding of new elections in certain provinces where the Cuban Supreme Court had voided the ballots for flagrant fraud. Gonzales even offered to send the American military attaché to observe these provincial elections. Possibly Lansing was moving carefully lest he attract the attention and arouse the moral indignation of President Wilson.

Providentially for Lansing and for Menocal, the Liberals made the grievous error of launching their long threatened revolt *before* the new elections could be held, thereby putting themselves beyond the pale of legal respectability. Lansing had our Minister announce on February 13, 1917 that the United States had given its confidence and support only to Governments established through legal, constitutional methods. The armed revolt against the Constitutional Government of Cuba was considered as a lawless and unconstitutional act and would not be countenanced. The leaders of the revolt would be held personally responsible for any injury to foreign nationals and for destruction of foreign property.

The Liberals then asked for American supervision of the elections, but too late. Lansing did make half-hearted efforts to procure amnesty for them, a restaging of the partial elections and an invitation by the Cuban Government to General Crowder to investigate the whole affair. But the Conservatives now knew that in the last resort they had the United States behind them even to the extent of landing more American troops at Guantanamo; so they quietly and skillfully parried Lansing's proposals and snuffed out the demoralized rebellion.

In the end Lansing made an even stronger statement in favor of the government regarding the remnants of the revolutionary forces: "As Cuba has now declared war against Germany and has aligned herself with the United States, the people of Cuba should set aside their political differences in the face of international danger. . . . The United States will be forced to consider as its own enemies those persons in revolt against the Constitutional Government unless they immediately return to their allegiance."

This episode offers a striking parallel to the conflict of choices the United States has encountered in the Cold War since 1945. Our absorption in a wider world conflict has caused us to be impatient of local political quarrels and inclined to support the "ins" however justified the complaints of the "outs".

A letter from the Cuba Company, one of the American sugar interests, to Assistant Secretary of State Frank Polk indicates that there may have been more behind all this than the war needs of the Allies.[62] The letter charges that Menocal and one of his chief Liberal opponents were financially interested in rival sugar companies and may have been not averse to seeing each other's mills and cane destroyed in the civil war to raise the value of the product of their own mills.

If this were so, then the United States government was being used to benefit one side over another in a commercial rivalry under the guise of supporting constitutional government and the Cuban war effort.

As soon as the First World War was over, the State Department began applying pressure on President Menocal to ask for American supervision of the 1920 election. Polk now warned that "In its support of constitutional governments the United States must take into consideration their attitudes in regard to the freedom of elections . . . the only attitude which the Government of the United States can conscientiously support." At first Menocal balked, but later he reluctantly accepted an electoral reform mission, possibly as a delaying tactic.

The Liberals having learned a lesson painfully from the events of 1916-1917, now openly invoked American supervision. Alternatively they begged that the United States stay neutral in case of revolution. The sympathies of our naval and military attachés in Havana were won over and also American businessmen and lawyers were employed to lobby for them in Washington, to try to discredit both the Cuban President and the American Minister to Cuba.

Gonzales, Polk, and Crowder all agreed that electoral reform alone would not suffice. "It makes no difference what the laws are, unless we administer them it will do no good," the General said.[63] Gonzales resisted the pressure for ever greater American involvement in Cuban elections with a prophetic prediction: "If we intervened in an election in Cuba on the score of preventing fraud, the only way in which we could make good our guaranty of honesty would be to conduct the elections with our agents or managers in control of the booths, polling-lists—everything. A marine or two standing around would mean nothing. If we are going to indorse elections in Cuba as honest we have to *conduct* them, or be ourselves guilty of moral fraud. To conduct elections every other year, for our obligation would be permanent, would make the country's independence such a farce that complete and permanent occupation would in my opinion be much more desirable".[64]

However, Crowder, like the good soldier he was, went to Cuba again to help amend his own incomprehensible electoral code in the light of the intervening decade's experience. He found widespread padding of the voting lists, ballot-box stuffing and collusion in fraud between the major parties and concluded that ". . . the electoral administration of Cuba has been a failure . . . not because of weakness of the law, but because of absolute disregard and narrow interpretation

of its provisions by those executing it." Nevertheless, he doggedly recommended a new electoral code which would, in the words of Gonzales, "be as fraud-proof as it seems possible to construct".[65] The chief
reform of Crowder's new code was to provide orderly procedures for
the appeal of disputed elections to an impartial judiciary. Another
was to forbid party alliances whereby dummy third parties had been
used to split opponents' ranks. The oligarchic control of party conventions was to be broken. Finally, a new census and registration
was to be made. An expert on the problem later commented that "In
the end, the number and character of the guarantees in the new law
against fraud, all based on previous Cuban experience, were such as
to constitute an indictment of the nation".[66]

The State Department continued to resist involvement in the Cuban election and refused to settle intra-party disputes even though
they had a vital bearing on the outcome of the election. When the
Liberal Party split again in 1920 as it had in 1912, and the defeated
Liberal candidate of 1916 made a coalition with the Conservatives on
condition he would be candidate of both, Bainbridge Colby, the Secretary of State, rebuffed proposals to mediate the dispute with the
opinion that no good purpose would be served by a conference in
Washington with the representatives of the Liberal party. He added
that any attempt to transfer the forum of political activity from Cuba
to Washington was harmful to the best interests of Cuba and fruitful
of endless misunderstandings. As to the perennial Liberal threat to
withdraw from the electoral campaign if their demands were not met,
Colby stated the withdrawal of any element from the national elections would in no way influence the policy of the United States to
regard the result of a fair election as expressive of the national will.
Our government would therefore expect all citizens of Cuba to accept
and abide by the results. Again and again it was reiterated that Cubans must exhaust the remedies provided by their reformed election
law before applying to Washington for relief.

The ambiguity of the Department's interpretation of the Platt
Amendment was most clearly illustrated by Colby's final statement
of August 25, 1920: "The sole interest of the United States in the approaching presidential elections in Cuba is that these elections shall
be conducted in such a way as to secure the freest and fairest expression of the popular will. . . . The responsibility for (this) . . . rests with
the Government and people of Cuba. The Government of the United
States does not propose actually to supervise the elections. However,
it is by treaty pledged to 'the maintenance of a government in Cuba

adequate for the protection of life, property and individual liberty.'
It is, therefore, unalterably opposed to any attempt to substitute violence and revolution for the processes of government. I am desired
to emphasize the fact, however, that it is no less opposed to intimidation and fraud in the conduct of elections. . . ."

The Conservatives again took advantage of the American refusal
to act and called the bluff of the Department. The laboriously elab-
orated safeguards of Crowder's code were flagrantly disregarded.
Many of the elections were contested in the courts so the Department
sent Crowder, this time uninvited, on a third mission to Cuba. He
obtained new elections for the Liberals in some districts just as in
1917, but this time the Liberals withdrew from the contest at the last
minute, thus affording the Department an excuse for evading the
choice of treaty interpretations again.

Crowder stayed on for eight years, first as a special commissioner
and then as ambassador, in a forlorn effort to impose electoral purity
on the recalcitrant Cubans. Initially he succeeded in getting the
incoming President, Zayas, to promise further changes in the electoral
code. Zayas had to take his advice for several years because he
wanted an American loan, but the electoral reforms he promised were
never undertaken except in a way that made matters even worse than
before. The technique of using American economic aid as a weapon
to force political reforms was ineffective, a lesson which the planners
of the Alliance for Progress in our own time ought to bear in mind.

Soon Crowder was "muzzled" by the incoming Republican administration in Washington because of domestic criticism in the United
States.[67] "If Cuba insisted upon taking a downward path," the new
Secretary of State, Charles Evans Hughes, self-righteously told the
Cuban Chargé d'Affaires in 1923, "the United States would not fail
to give her caution and advise her in her own interest, and if she still
persisted, she could not in any way hold the United States responsible
for the inevitable disaster that would follow . . ."[68] By this time the
sense of danger from European intervention in case of Cuban civil
war had vanished and the Platt Amendment policy was probably continued more out of inertia and a vague sense of moral obligation to
our ward.

Zayas' Liberal successor, Machado, amended the Crowder code
in 1927 to make it even less effective. U. S. Ambassador Harry Guggenheim forced him to restore the code in 1930, but by that time, as
the Ambassador had to admit, the real desire of the opposition was for
a coup d'état, not reform. Both Ambassadors Crowder and Guggen-

heim did conduct a running battle with Machado over free elections, but with little or no support from Washington. Crowder considered Machado's plan of 1927 to extend not only his own term of office, but also that of the Congress, "highly objectionable since it defies the most elemental principles of representative government".[69] The Latin American Division and Hughes' successor refused to raise objections.

Guggenheim later asserted that Machado's action was one of the two underlying causes of political resentment against him in the turbulent years that followed. By 1931 the Ambassador painted a dark picture for Cuba: "The Liberal Party [has] been in power for five years; all the politicians without power and without jobs [are] in a desperate financial situation, and the Liberal Party is giving them no hope of returning to power for many years to come. . . . The opposition to the Government, always very bitter, consists of the combined forces of all the defeated candidates . . . who are not in agreement except in their opposition to Machado." He proposed a coalition government and other reforms to satisfy the opposition but Secretary Henry Stimson stressed the return to the Root interpretation of the Platt Amendment.

The same unsatisfactory relationship between Washington and its representatives in the field was repeated between the succeeding Democratic Secretary of State, Cordell Hull, and Sumner Welles, Ambassador to Cuba during the prolonged civil strife which accompanied Machado's overthrow in 1933. Hull instructed Welles: "Under this [Root] interpretation, it will be evident to you that conditions in Cuba, highly unsatisfactory and even alarming as they may be, do not constitute a just basis for the formal action of the Government of the United States looking towards intervention".[70] Welles succeeded in ousting Machado by bluff, but was unable to maintain the moderate government of Cespedes which followed. Radical students and non-commissioned army officers bent, like Castro's followers a generation later, on social revolution rather than just the restoration of order and free elections, displaced Cespedes with Grau San Martin. President Roosevelt blocked Welles' attempt to oust Grau San Martin by direct American intervention, but in the end Welles and Jefferson Caffery, his equally conservative successor as U. S. Ambassador to Cuba, achieved this objective by the indirect means of American nonrecognition of the new Cuban government. Caffery insisted that Grau San Martin was supported only by the army and "ignorant masses" who had been misled by utopian promises and was opposed by "the better classes". He accused the Cuban President of relying on Communist elements.

Bryce Wood in his study *The Making of the Good Neighbor Policy* comments that Caffery was making an external, normative judgment about the quality of the will of the Cuban people thus placing the issue of the representativeness of the radical government "beyond empirically verifiable judgment."[71] Wood intimates that Welles also confused the "better classes" of Cuba with the will of the majority of the Cuban people and speculates that the new Assistant Secretary of State's principal objective in this episode was the suppression of the social revolution. If so, it is more understandable why Fidel Castro was so suspicious in 1959 of American intentions as conveyed to him by Ambassador Philip Bonsal who, like Welles and Caffrey, was a member of the American social elite. In both epochs the demand for free elections became a device in the hands of socially conservative American officials to stifle needed social reform. The contrast with American policy toward the social revolution in Mexico is striking.[72]

Caffery managed to wean away Sergeant Fulgencio Batista, the leader of the non-commissioned officers, from support of Grau San Martin, who was then replaced by a less revolutionary executive in January 1934. In the same year the treaty embodying the Platt Amendment was abrogated as part of President Roosevelt's Good Neighbor Policy.[73]

II

PANAMA

The story of how President Theodore Roosevelt "took Panama" in 1903 is a well-known chapter of American diplomatic history.[1]

The United States had wanted an interoceanic canal in Central America for strategic and commercial reasons for many years. The choice of the Panama route over the Nicaraguan route was maneuvered by representatives of the unsuccessful French New Panama Canal Company to recover their financial investments. Colombia, of which Panama was then a state, rejected the treaty negotiated with the United States for the building of a canal. Thereupon a "revolution" of the local Colombian citizenry at the Isthmus of Panama seized control and ships of our Navy prevented Colombia from landing troops to regain possession.

Roosevelt had to justify this scarcely concealed act of imperialism, so in his hasty recognition of the new state he argued that the revolution merely "reasserted the right of self control and . . . [was] an unopposed expression of the will of the people of Panama.[2] The policy problem was how to prove the validity of this assertion and at the same time so bind the new state to its North American sponsor that it could be protected from Colombian designs of reconquest or European encroachments.

Since annexation was out of the question for the same reasons that applied in Cuba, Secretary of War Root urged that an election be held as soon as possible for delegates to a constitutional convention to confirm the declaration of independence and ratify Panama's new canal treaty with the United States.[3] Philippe Bunau-Varilla, who had been representative of the French canal company and architect of the revolution, was now Foreign Minister of Panama. "I must say," he advised Secretary of State John Hay, on January 6, 1904, "that this expression of opinion [of the municipal elective bodies of the treaty] is in harmony with the satisfaction of the whole country which was made conspicuous at the recent election where, for the first time in the history of the State of Panama, every citizen has been at liberty to perform his duty according to his conscience."[4]

Root sent William Buchanan, our Minister in Panama, documents relating to the formation of new governments in Cuba and the Philip-

pines as a guide in drafting the constitution.[5] Presumably the treaty
was to be modelled on the Platt Amendment treaty with Cuba. Although the key articles of both treaty and constitution granted an
explicit right of intervention to the United States, they contained a
significant difference in wording which opened the way to divergent
interpretations of our rights and duties with respect to freedom of
elections in Panama.

The Hay - Bunau-Varilla Treaty of 1903 states in Article VIII: "The
. . . right and authority are granted to the United States for the
maintenance of *public order* in the cities of Panama and Colon and
the territories and harbors adjacent thereto in case the Republic of
Panama should not be, in the judgment of the United States, able to
maintain such order." [6] However, the Constitution of Panama de-
clares in Article 36: "The Government of the United States of America
may intervene in any part of the Republic of Panama to reestablish
public peace *and constitutional order* in the event of their being
disturbed, provided that that nation shall, by public treaty, assume
or have assumed the obligation of guaranteeing the independence and
sovereignty of this Republic."[7] (Emphasis added in both quotations.)

In scarcely a year's time, Panamanians were posing a dilemma to
Secretary of War Taft, i.e., whether the United States was not morally
obligated to intervene to guarantee free elections as a part of the
"constitutional order".

The Panamanian situation developed very similarly to that in Cuba
for the Republic of Panama too was launched with a coalition government.[8] Yet within a year of receiving independence at the hands of
the United States, the Liberal faction was using Uncle Sam as a
whipping boy to garner popular support and plotting with the commander of the Republic's tiny army to overthrow the government.
The Liberals feared that their minority position in the coalition would
enable the Conservatives to win complete control in the coming election despite the assumed popular majority of the former.

One of the Liberal leaders, Belisario Porras, sounded out the U.S.
Chargé d'Affaires on Washington's attitude toward a revolution. He
was informed firmly that we would countenance no revolutionary activities and that changes in the Panamanian government should be made
either at the ballot box or by voluntary resignations. Soon after the
army was disbanded, at American behest, in favor of a "guardia
rurale" and some U.S. Marines were kept in the Canal Zone near the
city of Panama to suppress disturbances.[9]

While visiting Panama, Taft took the occasion to lecture his hosts

on the dangers of both majority and minority tyranny, either of which
would produce a government in Panama "not worth supporting" because "If [your government] must depend upon election, . . . it must
depend upon honest election. It is to be understood that if the men
in power can control the elections so that the vote of the people
amounts to nothing, then you have a tyranny, and you have a government that is not by law, and it ought to go down. . . . A government
in which the minority upon the election of the majority, retires from
the borders of the country in exile only to await the result of the next
successful revolution, is not a government at all." [10]

Taft undoubtedly intended his little homily primarily for Liberal
perpetrators of the recent military sedition. He confided to President
Roosevelt that "the only danger . . . of any trouble will be the acces-
sion to power of the Liberal Party because it will mean the introduction of a large Negro influence into the Government." [11] But in the very
next year, 1905, the Liberals quoted Taft's words back to him in a
statement in which they asked him:

"1. Does the American Government guarantee public order and constitutional succession in this Republic?

"2. Is a government which violates the constitution and laws and
attacks the first right of the citizens—that of suffrage—within the pale
of such protection?

"3. Granted the possibility—to us an absolute certainty—that in the
coming elections all manner of outrages will be committed against the
people, will the Government of the United States look on with indifference at the spectacle of a defenseless people at the mercy of those
who trample on their rights?

"4. Is it not preferable for the United States to adopt while there is
yet time such a course as to avoid appearing before the eyes of the
world as the champions of outrage and oppression?" [12]

Pointing out the logical connection between the Hay - Bunau-Varilla
Treaty guarantee and their plea for an American guarantee of the
election, the petitioners posed the same policy dilemma for the U.S.
that the Cuban Liberals raised a year later: "Should in the opinion
of the illustrious Government of the United States, the violation of free
suffrage on the part of the Panama Government not be considered an
attempt against constitutional order, what remedy remains there for
the people of the Isthmus to protect their rights and to prevent usurp-
ation of their sovereignty?"

Taft's lieutenant, Canal Zone Governor Magoon, and Root came to
opposite conclusions about this policy choice. "I did not understand,"

Magoon wrote to his chief, "that [you] intended to advise the Liberals that they were at liberty to judge for themselves as to whether or not fraudulent methods were adopted as to the elections and declaring the result. The danger lies right there. [I] suggest in answer to the [Liberal] memorial you disabuse their minds in that regard and assure them that the United States will assist them in bringing about a fair ballot and an honest count, and in the event of a controversy arising, the contest must be determined by some tribunal other than the defeated party and settled in some way other than by revolution." [13]

But Root, who was by now Secretary of State, interpreted the treaty restrictively as he had the Platt Amendment and vigorously rejected the idea of preventive interference. "The first of [the Liberals'] four questions," he said, "is to be answered in the negative. This practically disposes of the remaining three questions and of much of the arguments of the statement presented. . . . In my opinion these [Treaty] provisions do not contemplate relieving the Republic of Panama from all responsibility for the maintenance of public peace and constitutional order, nor do they place the onus of such maintenance in the first instance upon the United States. . . . The United States will exercise its rights under the treaty for the maintenance of public order in Panama, Colon, and upon the canal strip . . . and it will not go beyond its treaty rights." [14]

At the same time Root sought to evade the dilemma of conflicting policy aims—i.e., the goals of security and democracy—by arguing that the decision and responsibility for free elections or revolution lay in Panama, not Washington. He insisted that those who charged they would be defrauded in the election should pursue the legal remedies provided by the laws of the Republic. Prophetically he lectured the Panamanians on the perils of inviting intervention: "The day when the Government of the United States appoints citizens of this country as its agents in the territory . . . of Panama and pays them from its Treasury and gives them instructions to intervene in whatever debates about the electoral or civil right the Panamanian citizens may have, in order that such agents may solve them, on that day you will have lost your sovereignty." [15]

However, Root apparently felt obliged by Taft's unwitting commitment of 1904 to make the concession of suggesting to "the Government of Panama that, in view of the charges made in advance by the Liberal party, which are liable to be reiterated after the election, it is desirable to secure the most unimpeachable and satisfactory evidence of the

fairness of the election by means of observation of competent wit-
nesses during the conduct of the election." [16]

President Amador of Panama accepted Root's offer and invited the
United States to send observers, although he candidly admitted that
"it is quite impossible to change in a day a people who have for
years been practicing the election methods heretofore prevailing under
the Colombian administration of affairs." [17]

William F. Sands, an American diplomat who was delegated to watch
the election, commented in his memoirs that even by "old-fashioned
Tammany standards, it was a pretty crude affair." [18] The American
refusal to intervene other than by observing the election encouraged
the Conservatives to use official pressure and discouraged the Liberals, many of whom refused to vote. The government won by a land-
slide. After the election, Magoon affected a more or less satisfactory
compromise in the form of a new coalition administration. [19]

In 1908 the United States faced the same policy problem as earlier:
whether simply to maintain order in Panama, even if that amounted
to supporting a fraudulently elected government, or to intervene on
behalf of the "out" party and thereby submit to the blackmail of
threats of revolution. Although Roosevelt was still President, Root
Secretary of State and Taft Secretary of War—the outcome was different. The inconsistent *Norte americanos* did not react as could have
been logically assumed.

No sooner was the 1906 election out of the way than the Liberal
leaders presented another memorial, this time to President Roosevelt
while he was inspecting the progress of work on the canal. [20] Contemporary events in Cuba had been followed with an unhealthy interest by the "outs" and the possibility of a repetition of the Cuban situation was discussed publicly. [21] Roosevelt replied to the memorial with a
speech in which, like Root, he chastized both factions, but promised no
action. "Progress and prosperity," he admonished, "can come only
through the preservation of both order and liberty; through the observance by those in power of all their rights, obligations and duties to
their fellow citizens, and through the realization of those out of power
that the insurrectionary habit . . . ultimately means the destruction
of the republic." [22]

Because of the Cuban experience, many thought Roosevelt bluffing. [23]
In any case, the Liberals were in no mood to submit to fraud again. [24]

United States Minister Herbert Squiers, a military proconsul of the
Leonard Wood stamp, had thought to head off further agitation by

proposing suffrage limitations like those Wood and Root had tried in vain to persuade the Cubans to adopt, and with equal ill success.[25]

The 1908 election might have proceeded to the same conclusion as that of 1906, for however much the Liberals might bluster, the overwhelming strength of the American forces in the adjacent Canal Zone made it obvious that there could be no successful revolution without at least our tacit consent. But Roosevelt decided to send Taft down to Panama to investigate the situation, possibly to help build up his chosen successor's prestige for the approaching presidential campaign at home. Whatever the motive, Root found himself powerless to resist this time.

Taft reacted with indignation to the evidence of fraud and force just as he had in Cuba two years previously. President Amador, like some of his Cuban fellow Conservatives, misjudged the temper of the American jurist and told him frankly that he "did not expect that it was possible to get along without a fraudulent election." [26] Thereafter Taft's former aversion to the Liberals changed to an attitude of studied impartiality between the parties. He pleaded with Roosevelt to end the ambiguity of the Hay - Bunau-Varilla Treaty and forecast: "The question is one which will not down, and we must expect to be confronted with fraudulent elections and the threat of a revolution every two and four years unless we take some decided steps through a treaty to assume ourselves control over the elections, in case we deem necessary to secure a fair expression of the popular will." [27]

Taft justified this proposal on the ground that "it is certainly contrary to the interests of the United States to have a succession of elections in which fraud is present, and which give rise each time to ground for insurrection by the defeated party. The thing of all others which must be avoided, if we are to construct the canal, is disturbance of any kind in Panama and Colon, and nothing is more certain to engender this than the bitterness of a party defeated by fraud at the polls. . . . We should be given direct control over the elections so as to permit us . . . to determine who is fairly elected. This I agree detracts from the independence of the Republic, but as the Republic has not shown itself competent in this regard we are justified in insisting that we be given greater control to protect our own interests which are so closely involved with the peaceful continuance of the Panamanian Government."

Pending the treaty revision, he suggested that we reserve to ourselves the right, if palpable fraud were committed, to install the opposition candidate as the fairly elected President. Two Americans in each

polling place would watch proceedings to determine the fairness of
the election. President Roosevelt authorized the latter course, though
not the treaty revision, in an instruction which stated that "the Government of the United States will consider any attempt at the election
of a successor by fraudulent methods . . . which deny to a large part
of the people opportunity to vote, constitutes a disturbance of public
order which under Panama's Constitution requires intervention. . . .
This Government will not permit Panama to pass into the hands of
any one . . . elected . . . by fraudulent methods . . ."[28]

Taft promptly relayed the message to President Amador [29] who had
no choice but to accept observation again though he protested that he
could not legally vest the observers with official authority.[30] A Committee consisting of Squiers, Canal Commissioner Blackburn, Chief
Engineer Col. Goethals and Counsel Rodgers was set up to superintend the observation with the aid of two hundred Spanish-speaking
men supplied by Goethals.[31] The opposition candidate asked that
Marines be employed as observers, probably because that would lend
credence to his claim that the American observation of the election
proved that the United States favored him.[32] This request was refused,
but the claim of American partiality was widely enough believed that
the opposition won the preliminary municipal election and the government candidate withdrew before the presidential election.[33] The
different outcome from the 1906 election which was also observed can
only be attributed to the earnestness with which Taft went about his
mission. Consequently Panamanians reversed their attitudes now that
it appeared that he was serious about his threat of further action if
the observers detected fraud.

A curious sidelight on this election is the shadowy role played by
William Nelson Cromwell, an American lawyer who, it is claimed, had
shared with Bunau-Varilla the engineering of the Panamanian "revolution" of 1903 and had maintained a paternal interest in the republic since. He accompanied Taft on his electoral mission to Panama in
1908, and was apparently instrumental in persuading the Conservative candidate to withdraw lest there be revolution followed by American occupation damaging to his and other business interests.[34] The
American Minister reported the next spring that the New Yorker was
repaid for his financing of the election campaign of the Conservative's
Liberal opponent by deductions from the pay of government officials.[35]
Perhaps he was only "hedging his bets" by helping both parties.

The death of the President of Panama, José Domingo Obaldia, in
1910 produced an instructive example of a conflict between Washing-

ton and its representative in the field over American policy toward free elections.

The Panamanian Constitution, like others in Latin America, deviated from its American prototype in that there were three vice-presidents or "designados", elected annually by the legislature instead of by popular vote. Therefore the United States had an opportunity in 1910 to undo the anti-American results of the Liberal victory in the 1908 election by securing the election of a Conservative vice-president to succeed the deceased chief executive.[36] In this case, the problem was one of whether to prevent free elections rather than of how to promote them.

George T. Weitzel, an influential officer of the Latin-American Division of the State Department, suggested that the temporary incumbent of the Presidency, Mendoza, be given the opportunity to withdraw gracefully from the race on technical grounds of ineligibility. Then our preference among the other candidates to succeed Obaldia would be discretely intimated to him. The favored candidate, one Lewis, "would have the advantage of being not only a compromise between the administration and the opposition, but would also place at the head of the Government a man best qualified for the position both because of his interest in the welfare of Panama and his friendliness to Americans and their canal.[37]

Marsh, United States Chargé d'Affaires in Panama, not only echoed Weitzel's sentiments but went much further in his partisanship with an astonishingly frank plea for American paternalism: "As Lewis is a Conservative his election would pave the way to the breaking up of the Liberal party—which party I consider a menace to American interests. . . . [It] would be most gratifying to the Canal Zone authorities as he would never go against the clear wishes of the American Government or Canal Commission. . . . In my opinion, where American influence has dominated in Latin America, there prosperity has followed and those countries have been lifted out of the medieval ages. . . . To me it seems a high and stern duty of the United States . . . to civilization and Providence . . . to exercise an ever-watchful and ever-increasing control over Central America. . . . The United States should not hesitate to express its opinion or even intervene in the affairs of Central America . . . for the good of [its] influence and prestige . . ."[38]

Having disposed of the incumbent, Mendoza,[39] Marsh began to malign the other Liberal candidates, Porras and Arosemena, to the Department. The source of some of his prejudices can easily be seen in his observation that "American businessmen . . . including the manager of United Fruit . . . tell me that they have been so subjected to persecution by the authorities during the last year that unless present Liberal control is broken up in the coming election they will have to ask the official aid of the United States Government. . . . A large proportion of the respectable element of Panama are openly desirous of American annexation. . . . I consider Lewis' election especially necessary for comparatively honest government, reform of the courts and police, and . . . revision of the land laws to favor foreigners."[40]

Acting Secretary of State Huntington Wilson tried to curb his tactless subordinate by warning him that the "Department does not approve of your unnecessary continued mixing in local politics and supporting of particular candidate. . . . You must not nullify your good work by sowing the seeds of hostility on the part of Mendoza's following or antagonizing Porras who is likely to be President two years hence if not now . . . and who, with skillful handling should be made thoroughly friendly to the United States."[41]

It was then discovered that our aggressive representative had threatened the Panamanian Acting President that if Lewis were not elected, the United States would declare the National Assembly spurious, occupy Panama and send a military governor to rule.[42] This effrontery produced a nationalistic reaction which led to the defeat of the pro-American Lewis and the election of one of the Liberals, Arosemena.[43]

By this time the matter had come to the attention of Taft, who was now President of the United States. He indignantly repudiated the machinations of Marsh and recommended his dismissal for insubordination, while revealingly admitting that Marsh "may be right that Lewis is the best man . . . but I am distinctly opposed to bringing pressure to bear for any particular candidate. Mendoza's withdrawal in view of his Constitutional ineligibility was all right and it was all right to secure it . . . [but] we have such control in Panama that no government elected by them will feel a desire to antagonize the American Government. I am particularly anxious to avoid the charge of undue meddling because of its effect in Central and South America."[44] Taft would not involve the United States in the cause of free elections, but neither, on the other hand, was he willing to perpetrate the fraud of unfree elections.

American observation of the elections of 1906 and 1908 in Panama was often referred to as "supervision", but the first actual participation by Americans in the electoral proceedings of an independent state occurred in Panama in 1912.

President Taft and his Secretary of State, Philander Knox, tried to rule out a repetition of the observation of the 1908 election,[45] but both "ins" and "outs" requested American supervision this time because the "outs" controlled the election boards, so the advantages of the two were about equal. The conservatives controlled the police, President Arosemena having switched to their party since 1910. Both United States Minister Percival Dodge and Acting Secretary of State Huntington Wilson recommended supervision to Taft to "avoid serious disturbances." The President was impressed by the argument of precedent when his own words of 1904 and 1908 were quoted back to him, and consented. He appears to have been under a mistaken impression about the extent of the intervention, probably because of the terminological confusion just described.

The Committee of Dodge, Col. Goethals and the Commander of the American garrison in the Canal Zone, which was appointed to superintend the work, decided to use thirteen American officers to supervise the registration of voters and nearly 200 soldiers and Canal Zone employees were provided for overseeing the voting.[46] The "outs" tried unsuccessfully to get the Committee to take over control of their opponent's chief remaining weapon, the police. When the "outs" won the preliminary, municipal elections, the "ins" accused the supervisors of partiality and tried to restrict their powers during the forthcoming presidential election, or to postpone the balloting altogether. Failing that, they tried to arrange a "deal" with the "outs" by which they would not contest the final election, but the United States would take control of the police and finances permanently and reform the electoral laws. As a last resort, in accord with Latin American tradition, they withdrew from the election.

Dodge summed up the whole episode this way in his dispatch of July 20, 1912: "Though it seems almost incredible, in view of the repeated unequivocal declarations of our Government, President Arosemena's Government has up to the last deluded itself with the idea that by insistence . . . it could at last be able to secure the support of the United States. . . . It did not expect that this supervision would be effective and prevent it from making use of its official powers. The committee believe that both of the recent elections have been as fair and free from fraud as the circumstances admit, and that the candidates favored by the great majority of the voters have been elected. What frauds have been perpetrated have been unavoidable under the present election laws, which should be changed, and have probably been perpetrated equally by both parties . . ."

In his memoirs Huntington Wilson related that one supervisor told him afterwards that of the illiterate Negroes, Indians and half-breeds who were brought in by local bosses to vote, not half knew the names, parties or policies of the persons for whom they were voting.[47]

In 1916 the current "outs" (the "ins" of 1912) asked for electoral supervision similar to 1912, but the Panamanian government politely refused to accept the subsequent American offer.[48] The Liberal administration called attention to the charges of partiality against the American supervisors of 1912, even though the putative favoritism had been on behalf of its own candidate! The new Secretary of State, Lansing, persuaded President Wilson not to make an issue of the refusal by suggesting that "should no necessity arise for our supervision of the elections and the present party continue in power, we may shortly attain the reforms so earnestly desired and which have already been discussed with the Panamanian representatives near this Government."[49] As with Cuba in the same year, the President's attention was riveted elsewhere, and he accepted the word of his Secretary of State.

Opposition leaders again brought about American supervision of the election of 1918 by citing the Hay - Bunau-Varilla Treaty, but they failed in 1920 and thereafter.[50] Subsequent American activity on behalf of free elections in Panama was limited to ineffective diplomatic representations. One indignant "out" candidate of 1928 said sarcastically, "The expression of Your Excellency of an 'earnest wish that there should be a free, fair and honest election in Panama next year' is most laudable, but it is hardly more than a pious vow which might be appropriately formulated in respect to elections in free democracies everywhere."[51]

Hoover's Secretary of State, Stimson, refused to invoke the American treaty right of intervention when Panama's first successful revolution broke out in 1931. The original treaty itself was replaced in 1936[52] as part of President Roosevelt's Good Neighbor Policy.

Years later, in November 1949, Arnulfo Arias came to power by coup d'etat in Panama. He had caused the United States some concern by his unfriendly attitude when he was president just before our entry into World War II. The Truman administration consulted the other Latin American governments with a view to joint nonrecognition of Arias, but the consensus of opinion favored recognition which the United States thereupon granted.[53]

It must be recognized that American interest in free elections in Panama was almost entirely a by-product of concern lest revolutionary disturbances there should disrupt the construction and operation of the Panama Canal which was of immense strategic importance to us.

The differences between Secretaries Root and Taft about American policy were more differences over the means of securing peace and order in Panama than over the ends to be pursued. Root was more skeptical about the feasibility of democracy where its necessary prerequisites were absent, so he preferred to look on the problem of disorder in Panama as a military question to be dealt with by the American military authorities in the Canal Zone.[54] Taft was more strongly influenced by the moral aspect of the situation, but his basic assumption, as we have seen, was that the indignation of the losers in fraudulent elections was the real cause of revolutions harmful to American interests, and that therefore the cure for revolution was to take progressively more stringent measures to guarantee free elections. The ingratitude and inconsistency of those who benefited from American electoral intervention should have warned Taft that his basic premise was false.[55] Revolutions were threatened and launched by men who were hungry for office, power, money and revenge. Frustrated by the United States in their resort to the usual Latin American technique of winning power, they learned to appeal to the consciences of Americans like Taft. Thereby many came to power, NOT by free elections in our sense of the term, but rather by using the fact of American electoral interference to make the power-conscious populace think that the United States supported their party rather than the opponents' and thus causing a voter stampede to their own side.

Finally, what did we accomplish by the free elections policy in Panama? It preserved comparative domestic peace during the vital periods of the construction of the Canal and World War I by giving the parties out of power some hope of winning office by a means other than revolution. Considering the immense disproportion between American military power and any force a Panamanian revolt could have raised, it is probable that this same result could have been achieved simply by supporting a pro-American dictator or oligarchy as Root evidently proposed to do. But that might have had just as deleterious an effect on our reputation in Latin America as the continual intermeddling in elections eventually did. Perhaps the greatest fault in American policy was rather lack of consistency which left both friend and foe puzzled and uncertain as to what we wanted and would do next.

III

NICARAGUA

To understand how we became involved in supporting free elections in Central America, and especially in Nicaragua, it is first necessary to relate how American recognition policy was changed by the Central American Treaty of 1907, for the treaty created the immediate policy problem which accounted for the most frequent American intervention in that area.

Late in 1907, the United States and Mexico called a conference of the Central American Republics at Washington to devise some means of ending the constant wars, revolutions and international intrigues which convulsed that region so near to the vital Panama Canal site. Apparently Secretary of State Root and President Roosevelt feared that the constant strife and frequent debt-defaulting would bring about European intervention as it had in Venezuela in 1902 and had threatened to do in Santo Domingo in 1904.[1] Root wished to make whatever action the Conference prescribed multilateral in order to prevent a repetition of our occupation of Cuba in 1906 which had damaged American relations with South America.

Earlier American efforts at creating stability in Central America consisted of the traditional diplomatic methods of good offices, conciliation and mediation, as exemplified by the conferences of 1906 aboard the *U.S.S. Marblehead* and at San Jose, Costa Rica. The breakdown of those agreements led Root to say in his opening address to the Washington conference that "some practical methods" were needed to execute the new agreements reached there. More paper promises of non-aggression and non-intervention seemed futile.

"If we in the Washington Conference," the Foreign Minister of Costa Rica replied to Root, "turn our eyes toward liberty, if we make provision here to insure that our countries, free from past errors, will start a new life of real democratic solidarity, if we could obtain that the governments of our five countries do not remain indefinitely in power but be both in origin and in their acts a free expression of the will of the people, if we obtain that the rights of man . . . become effective . . . in short, should we enter in all sincerity into a constitutional life, we should have done great good to our countries, and the generous intent of Presidents Roosevelt and Diaz would be materialized." [2]

The "practical method" selected by the delegates to "insure that their governments be an expression of the will of the people" was the device of the non-recognition of revolutionary regimes. This had been proposed for application to all of Latin America earlier in the year by an Ecuadorian diplomat, Dr. Carlos R. Tobar.[3] His intention was to discourage the innumerable revolutions and *coups d'etat* which plagued the continent.

Article II of the General Treaty of Peace and Amity which the Central American Conference now drew up stated: "Desiring to secure in the Republics of Central America the benefits which are derived from the maintenance of their institutions and to contribute at the same time in strengthening their stability and the prestige with which they ought to be surrounded, it is declared that every disposition or measure which may tend to alter the constitutional organization in any one of them is to be deemed a menace to the peace of said Republics." [4] An additional Convention to the treaty provided that "The Governments of the High Contracting Parties shall not recognize any other Government which may come into power in any of the five Republics as a consequence of a *coup d'etat*, or of a revolution against the recognized Government, so long as the freely elected representatives of the people thereof have not constitutionally reorganized the country."

The United States had traditionally followed the practice of recognizing any new government which was in effective control of its country, enjoyed the acquiescence of its people, and showed promise of fulfilling its international obligations, without regard to the manner in which it came into power.[5] Although we were sensitive about too quick an acceptance of "effective control" because of our own experience with civil war, by and large our recognition policy followed the doctrines of classical international law until 1907. The similarity of the non-recognition clause of the 1907 treaty to the doctrine proposed by Dr. Tobar and the radical departure it marked from the previous policy of the United States identify the origin of the clause as Latin American. As the historian Robertson concluded, "Whether they were aware of it or not, in the first of those articles as well as in certain articles of the general treaty, the Central Americans had embodied the essential principle of the Tobar Doctrine." [6]

Root himself later denied authorship of the articles,[7] but they appeared to fit his purposes by focusing the condemnation of the signatories on the fact of revolution rather than on the legality of elections.

They "pan-Americanized" the sanction and reduced the likelihood of American military intervention. Therefore, though the United States was not itself a party to the treaties which the conference it sponsored signed, it adhered to their provisions in practice. The Central American rulers were ready to accept the doctrine because it meant a guarantee of the *status quo*, and a perpetual leasehold on office, punctuated at most by the periodic controlled elections traditional in the region.

The treaty, then, by no means obligated us or any of the signatories to insist on genuinely free elections before recognition of a new government. If American statesmen had been content to accept without question the assertions of revolutionary governments in Central America that "the freely elected representatives of the people had constitutionally reorganized their countries", in the words of the Treaty, recognition need never have been withheld, but then the treaty would have been rendered meaningless by removing all disincentive to both revolutions and controlled elections. Actually, therefore, the treaty-makers by trying to combine two incompatible purposes: stability and free elections, only compounded the problems of both. They jeopardized the former by making more difficult the acceptance of stable but unconstitutional revolutionary governments, and thus inviting counterrevolution. At the same time they failed to assure the latter condition, free elections, by neglecting to provide any method for forcing constitutional governments to give up the many subtle forms of pressure at their disposal to influence voting.

The Central American Treaty of 1907 explicitly forbade interference by the signatories in each other's internal politics. Zelaya, the dictator of Nicaragua, openly flouted the treaty. Furthermore, it was charged that he was sounding out Great Britain, Germany and even Japan on the possibility of granting one of them a concession to build an interoceanic canal through his country since the United States had in 1902 spurned the Nicaraguan route for Panama's.[8] The dictator's anti-American attitude and actions forced the State Department to withdraw our minister in 1908.[9]

At this juncture, a new administration came into office in Washington. Philander Knox replaced the cautious Elihu Root as Secretary of State. His aggressive, new Latin American Division recommended that he obtain a treaty right to take action in Central America *in advance* of *internal* disturbances.[10] Knox tried to get Mexico, the cosponsor of the 1907 conference, to join in compelling its observance. He advised President Taft that "there should be some conventional right to intervene in Central American affairs promptly, without waiting for outbreaks and with a view of averting rather than quelling disturbances." [11]

Taft, who was sensitive to the legal contradictions of the 1907 treaty, replied that he was "not content until we secured some formal right to compel peace between those Central American Governments, . . . to have the right to knock their heads together until they should maintain peace. . . ." [12] Failing to obtain that, Knox embarked nevertheless on a direct intervention in Nicaraguan domestic affairs to get rid of the dictator.

The means of overthrowing the dictator were ready to hand. Nicaraguans plotting revolution against him were able to look to Washington for at least tacit support for their filibustering expeditions. The technique is the same used successfully in Guatemala in 1954 and unsuccessfully in Cuba in 1961. [13] One of these dissidents wrote years later to Secretary Stimson: "I think that the policy of approaching my country to the United States was due to me who came to Washington in June, 1909 as a private citizen to ask the help of the United States, and have had with Mr. Huntington Wilson (Assistant Secretary of State) several talks over that matter, from which started the revolution against Zelaya." [14]

J. Butler Wright, a State Department official, stated bluntly in 1915 that "Zelaya was ousted from the Government of Nicaragua in 1909 by the direct action of this Government." [15] The method was the same as in Panama in 1903: American naval interposition prevented Nicaraguan governmental forces from suppressing the revolution when it was weak. [16] This action was taken under the guise of "protection of American life and property", but was a manifest violation of the spirit if not the letter of the 1907 treaty.

On December 1, 1909, not long after the rebellion broke out, Knox ruptured diplomatic relations with Zelaya. Possibly to appease President Taft's conscience, he charged among other justifications for his action that "republican institutions have ceased in Nicaragua to exist except in name. . . . The Government of the United States is convinced that the revolution represents the ideals and will of a majority of the Nicaraguan people more faithfully than does the Government of President Zelaya . . ." [17]

By using the lack of real democracy in Nicaragua as an excuse for helping to overthrow the dictator, Knox made it logically impossible to carry out Root's apparent purpose of using the 1907 treaty simply to discourage revolutions regardless of how undemocratic the regimes

thus kept in power were. All that Knox intended was to duplicate in
Nicaragua our successful customs control convention with the Dominican Republic and to make a loan to shift the ownership of the Nicaraguan debt from European to American hands. In this way he hoped
simultaneously to eliminate the incentive for revolutions and the pretext for European intervention. But after he had gone so far as to
break relations with an existing, if beleaguered, government on the
ground of its undemocratic character, the United States had no good
argument to resist the appeals of Central American "outs" that it investigate the actual honesty of elections staged by new governments
before recognizing them.

The next three years witnessed a prolonged struggle over what
meaning should be attached to the "republican institutions" and the
"will of a majority of the Nicaraguan people" specified in Knox's note
of December 1, 1909. Soon after the note was delivered, Zelaya resigned. The Liberal Party, of which he was the leader, thought to
placate the United States by having the dictator's designated successor, a distinguished lawyer named Madriz, unanimously approved by
the Nicaraguan Congress.[18] This artifice impressed Admiral Kimball
who had been sent to mediate the civil war, but it failed to appease
Knox who refused to recognize Madriz. The State Department claimed
he was ineligible on technical grounds requiring a detailed knowledge
of the Nicaraguan Constitution to understand.[19] Knox saw that the
Congress was a mere tool of Zelaya's. What he was really intent on
was not so much a constitutionally legal election as the success of the
revolution so a government could be installed which would put into
effect his program of economic reform for Nicaragua.[20]

This purpose was demonstrated the next Fall in 1910 when the
American-backed revolutionaries finally won control of the country.
They promised Knox all his economic demands: reparations and a loan,
as well as that "a general election will be held within one year, the
date to be fixed by a constitutional convention convoked for that purpose."[21] The Secretary then sent a special Commissioner, our Minister
to Panama, Thomas C. Dawson, to facilitate compliance with these
promises.

Dawson got the victorious rebels to sign a pact in which they promised to support one of their number for the provisional presidency and
to agree among themselves in the future on a candidate for his
successor. "They obligated themselves to take into consideration that
the one chosen must represent the revolution and the Conservative
Party . . . and that the Government to be established in Nicaragua

must not permit, under any pretext, the Zelayista element in its administration." [22]

The agreement was probably conceived, at least by its Nicaraguan
signatories, as a means of preventing free elections by eliminating any
real contest. Given the fraudulent election practices habitually resorted to by Central American governments, the effect of the pact, as
one observer noted in 1934, was bound to be that "its signers and
prominent leaders of the Bluefields (*i.e.*, the 1909) revolution have
held the presidency practically continuously since 1910." [23]   Dawson
reported that "a popular presidential election is at present impracticable and dangerous to peace," [24] so the new President *ad interim* was
elected by the Assembly and not by popular vote, although that had
been one of Knox's legal objections to recognizing Madriz!

The election of the Assembly itself was perfunctory since all opposition had been made practically impossible by the exclusion of the
defeated "Zelayista" Liberal Party. A later commentator remarked
that the U.S. Consul's reports show that he was either naive about the
pressure brought to obtain a Conservative majority or uninterested. [25]
Clearly "free elections" meant very little by then despite the American
assertion that "formal diplomatic relations between the Washington
and Managua (Nicaragua) Governments were not restored until after
the people of Nicaragua had passed on the merits of the revolution by
holding a general election." [26]

Knox's policy of condoning and even encouraging uncontested elections while his envoys concentrated on putting Nicaraguan finances in
order [27] might well have succeeded had the loose coalition of Conservatives and anti-Zelaya Liberals who carried out the revolution stayed
faithful to the Dawson Pact. But the ambitions and jealousies of the
various leaders soon plunged the country back into violent political
conflict.

First, the provisional president, an ex-Liberal, launched an abortive
coup d'etat against his Conservative colleagues and fled. Then the
Conservatives fell out among themselves. Two of them, the new provisional president and the commander of the army, forced the third,
General Emiliano Chamorro, into exile. They then bargained to win
the State Department's tacit consent to the election of the army commander by the Assembly instead of popularly in return for approval
of Knox's loan plan. President Adolfo Diaz explained that "free
elections are hopelessly impracticable for several years in Nicaragua,"
by which he probably meant that a free election would produce an
anti-American Liberal majority.

The State Department steadily refused to budge from its position that while the economic program was primary, the Dawson Pact must be carried out to the letter, including the popular election of a president for the regular term. The American Minister now threatened non-recognition in case of a violation of the pact, but the Assembly went ahead anyway and elected Mena, the army commander, for the full term in the Fall of 1911.

At this point, General Chamorro returned from exile to demand his rights under the Dawson Pact. He was far more popular than either Provisional President Diaz or President-elect Mena, so he threatened that unless the latter's election were invalidated and a popular election held he would start a revolution. Except for reminding Mena peremptorily of his obligations, the State Department took no decisive action on the controversy in the hope that "if matters are allowed to take their regular course the unfriendly factions will soon exhaust themselves and thereafter become more receptive to reason." Knox revealed the chain of reasoning behind his policy in a speech he himself made in Nicaragua in the Spring of 1912:

"The full measure and extent of our policy is to assist in the maintenance of republican institutions upon this hemisphere, and we are anxious that the experiment of a government of the people, for the people, and by the people shall not fail in any republic on this continent.

"We have a well-known policy as to causes that might threaten the existence of an American republic from beyond the sea. We are equally desirous that there shall be no failure to maintain a republican form of government from forces of disintegration originating from within; . . . the progress already made . . . by Nicaragua . . . depends almost entirely upon the preservation of peace and contentment in the country and the surest means of reaching this end is the faithful observance of the pledges made by the leaders of all parties. . . . We are especially interested in the prosperity of the people of Nicaragua . . . [because it] means contentment and contentment means repose."

After six more months of contention between pro- and anti-election factions, General Mena himself broke into revolt. He mistook the rejection by the U.S. Senate of the Knox-Castrillo loan treaty for evidence of the repudiation of Knox's whole Nicaraguan policy. The reaction of the United States was quick and effective: Marines were landed on the pretext of protecting American lives and property and the revolt was suppressed in August, 1912.

Acting Secretary of State Huntington Wilson explained the American action by declaring that "In discountenancing Zelaya . . . the Government of the United States opposed not only the individual, but the system, and this Government could not countenance any movement to restore the same destructive regime. . . . Under the Washington Conventions [of 1907], the United States has a moral mandate to exert its influence for the preservation of the general peace in Central America, which is seriously menaced by the present uprising. . . . The revolt of General Mena in flagrant violation of his solemn promises . . . and of the Dawson agreement . . . give to the revolt the attributes of the abhorrent and intolerable Zelaya regime." Now "Zelayaism" had contaminated not only the whole Liberal party, but a leading Conservative as well. The candidates for election to the presidency had narrowed down to Diaz and Chamorro.

When it came to nominating a Conservative candidate after the revolt, Minister George Weitzel quietly induced General Chamorro to withdraw to "remove the appearance of militarism in the new administration" and because Diaz would be more palatable to the anti-Zelaya Liberals. Weitzel had to veto the amazing suggestion of President Diaz that he be reelected by indirect vote of the Assembly, the very proposal which had caused Mena's downfall!

The Department of State inquired if Weitzel thought the election should be supervised. "It would be unwise," he replied, "for the United States to supervise the election; the Panama precedent is hardly applicable (because the right of the United States to interfere in that country is recognized by treaty and by the constitution of the Republic, notwithstanding which, the defeated party charged fraud.) . . . Neither party would willingly acquiesce in an adverse result, however, fair, and we should have to bear the burden of criticism without the power to justify our course by assuring the honesty of the administration after it enters office. The fact is the cry of fair elections just now is not sincere." [28]

Naturally, the Liberals refused to put up a candidate in an unsupervised election and Diaz won by default. [29] To charges that the elections of 1910 and 1912 were unfair, Weitzel disingenuously replied that "the candidacy of Diaz was passed upon twice . . . it is hard to understand therefore why there should be any necessity for an American supervision of the election in Nicaragua. . . ." [30]

The story of these two years in Nicaragua, 1910-1912, shows that the meaning Secretary Knox attached to free elections in Nicaragua was very narrowly defined to include only popular elections in accord with a party compact which in effect prevented all competition. He insisted on even this inadequate minimum almost entirely out of a desire to maintain the peaceful conditions necessary for his economic program to take effect.

We have already had occasion to refer to the unsuccessful attempts of the Taft administration to regularize its political and economic intervention in Nicaragua by formal treaty. The Wilson administration which followed Taft's in 1913 dropped the distasteful Knox-Castrillo Loan Convention with its odor of "dollar diplomacy" in favor of a treaty to purchase an option on the Nicaraguan Canal route. This would provide public money to stabilize the Nicaraguan economy without the need for further recourse to private loans. At the same time it would pay off still-menacing European creditors, thereby eliminating any future danger to the Panama Canal from non-American competitors.[31]

Judge Charles A. Douglas, a friend of William Jennings Bryan, the new Secretary of State, acted as counsel for the Nicaraguan Government, and drafted the treaty with a "Platt Amendment clause" like Cuba's.[32] Bryan admitted to President Wilson that "the Platt Amendment provision is asked for by the Nicaraguan government, and is intended for the benefit of that government, still I think that it is of advantage to us, in that it will give us the right to do that which we might be called upon to do anyhow. We cannot escape the responsibilities of our position."[33] One biographer of Wilson concluded from this that the idea of making Nicaragua a protectorate of the United States was conceived by certain American bankers, Douglas, and the Diaz regime, chiefly as a means of keeping an unpopular government in power.[34] Diaz had asked for a protectorate before in 1911, but had been rebuffed by Knox.[35]

The proposed treaty ran into a storm of opposition in the U.S. Senate from Democrats and Republicans alike who raised both moral and practical objections.[36] Senator Borah of Idaho stressed the former with arguments invoked in many a later debate over American aid to dependent foreign governments: "I do not believe . . . that we are dealing with Nicaragua at all; we are not dealing with the Nicaraguan people, nor with the public officers whom the Nicaraguan people have set up or elected; we are dealing with ourselves; . . . with the puppets which we put in power; we are making a treaty with those men who do not represent the Nicaraguan people at all."[37]

Ex-Secretary Root, now Senator from New York, made the same point from a more pragmatic perspective: "I am troubled about the question whether the Nicaraguan government which has made the

treaty is really representative of the people of Nicaragua . . . I find
. . . in the report of the commanding officer of our marines in Nicaragua . . . the following: 'The present government is not in power by
the will of the people; the elections of the House of Congress were
most fraudulent' and a further statement that the Liberals, that is to
say the opposition, 'constitute three-fourths of the country.' It is
apparent from the report . . . that the present government . . . is really
maintained in office by the presence of United States marines. . . .
*It is highly probable that if we were to withdraw our force after mak-
ing such a treaty there would be a revolution and the treaty would be
repudiated."* [38] (Emphasis added.)

Bryan's problem, then, was "to show that we have no ulterior designs" [39] and revise the treaty in such a way that political opponents of
the Nicaraguan government would have no valid excuse for revolution or repudiation.

The Secretary therefore told Wilson that he was inclined to think
that it would be well to have the securing of free elections emphasized
in the treaty. He cited American experience in Mexico where such a
treaty was lacking to illustrate the importance of his point. [40] In proposing the Platt Amendment feature he denied that the United States
had in view the support of any particular Nicaraguan government, but
rather that we wished to aid the people there in securing a fair election so that they could select such officials as they pleased. [41] Bryan
believed that free elections were sufficiently implied if Nicaragua
agreed to American intervention for the purpose of "maintaining a
constitutional government," for "such a government must rest upon
the constitutional right of suffrage and *suffrage is not suffrage at all
unless it is free and fair*," but "Minister Chamorro would like the Platt
Amendment to cover free elections." Therefore Article VI was added:
"The Government of Nicaragua consents that the United States may
exercise the right to intervene for the preservation of Nicaraguan independence, the maintenance of a constitutional government adequate for
the protection of life, property and liberty, *and free and popular elections* and for the discharging any obligations if may assume or con-
tract." [42] (Emphasis added.)

It is possible that Chamorro, as a prospective rival of his fellow
Conservative, President Diaz, in the 1916 election, wanted the United
States to guarantee a fair ballot because, as in 1912, it would be to his
advantage since he enjoyed greater popularity.

Bryan even offered to have the United States supervise an election in
Nicaragua as it had in Santo Domingo to prove its good faith, [43] but the

U.S. Senate was adamant and eventually, on February 18, 1916, the Bryan-Chamorro Treaty was passed without either the explicit right of intervention or the guarantee of free elections. Ex-Minister Weitzel observed acidly, "One who is not a 'deserving Democrat' may, perhaps,
be permitted to say in justice to Mr. Bryan that if the Senate had
accepted his amendment to the treaty the Nicaraguan problem would
have been settled without bloodshed." [44]

By 1916 Bryan had been replaced as Secretary of State by the more
realistic Robert Lansing and the Latin American Division was again in
control of Nicaraguan policy.   These experienced professional diplomats approached the ordeal of another Nicaraguan election with utmost
scepticism.   J. Butler Wright, the Chief of the Division, recommended
without enthusiasm: "Personally, I do not see how we can do otherwise, in accordance with democratic principles and in fairness to all
concerned, than to supervise the elections,[45] but only on condition that
all factions agreed."   The Liberals, who were "out" and probably
could count on the support of a majority of the populace, assented with
alacrity,[46] but President Diaz declined the assistance on the startlingly
frank ground that he "did not consider free elections advisable at
this time." [47]

Wright later observed that from the experience the United States
had had in attempting the supervision of the election registration in
Panama he was of the opinion that effective supervision would not be
feasible even if the Government of Nicaragua had not objected.[48]
Now he recommended with relief: "A course influenced solely by
logical consideration would appear to demand that a Government
whose disinclination to accept the proposal of the United States to
supervise its election implied fear of their result should not receive even
the tacit support of the presence of United States marines at the
time of the election. . . . [but] the exigencies of the situation . . . the
manifest necessity for the continuance of a settled policy as regards
Nicaragua and the patent advantages to both countries . . . in securing . . . a Government in that country actuated by proper motives
toward . . . this country, appear strongly to indicate that we can
well afford to dispense with logic in an illogical situation and by tact-
fully and discreetly expressing the opinion of this Government that
General Chamorro is the most desirable candidate . . . to eliminate,
until such time as Nicaragua may become more stable, the menace of
the Liberal Party and for the sake of peace . . . in Central America
to lend the great force of our support to the installation of a government which appears . . . to be the most popular and beneficial." [49]

The Department still considered the Liberal Party to be tainted with the stain of Zelaya, particularly after it nominated one of the former President's chief ministers, General Irias. Benjamin Jefferson, U.S. Minister in Nicaragua, bluntly told Irias that no candidate would be recognized by the Department *"even if elected"* [50] unless "he could give a satisfactory proof of not having taken an active part in the administration of President Zelaya; . . . and should give proof to the Department that he has not participated directly nor indirectly in any of the revolutionary movements against the Government established in Nicaragua since the downfall of the Zelaya regime. . . ." [51]

The Department claimed to be impartial among the non-Zelayaist candidates, but in fact it carefully assessed their attitudes toward the United States and the chances that their election would provoke a revolution. [52] Jefferson worked behind the scenes to compose the differences within the Conservative Party and to prevent Diaz from maneuvering his own reelection unconstitutionally or from making common cause with the Liberals against Chamorro. In both these objectives he succeeded, [53] but only at the cost of the withdrawal of all other candidates and the holding of another uncontested election. [54] With no effective observation of the election in prospect, and therefore no opposition candidates, it was a futile gesture for Secretary Lansing to warn Diaz that he would not recognize any person elected President if there were evidence that the election was not absolutely free. [55] In effect, the State Department had named Diaz' successor, but it had avoided a revolution this time and assured the continuation of the American economic program.

As another quadrennial Nicaraguan election approached inexorably in 1920, the problem for the Department remained one of assuring enough popular acquiescence to the government to prevent a counter revolution like that of 1912 from breaking out. [56] But Americans were also awakening to the anomalies of the 1907 Central American Treaty and the insufficiency of a policy based on it to preserve the peace necessary to Nicaragua's permanent economic rehabilitation.

In 1918, a young American scholar, Dana G. Munro, wrote a book, *The Five Republics of Central America,* based on field research he had done there under the auspices of the Carnegie Endowment for International Peace. Shortly afterward he joined the State Department's Latin American Division which put him in a position to influence policy in accord with his theories. [57]

Munro argued that it was not revolution itself which was the great evil in Central America, but rather the causes of revolution and the refusal of parties to accept adverse verdicts at the polls. Among these, he asserted, were the threats to personal liberty and property which a rival party's rule meant for politicians which created a vicious circle of revenge. The corruption of elections meant that "there was no means of changing officials in power, and consequently no recourse against bad government, except revolution. Civil war had thus become an indispensable part of the political system." [58] In this kind of a situation, he concluded that the mere discouragement of revolutions offered no solution. Therefore, Munro was striking at the heart of the 1907 treaty: "The policy of refusing to recognize any forcible change of government . . . is a very difficult one to carry out consistently. . . . The ousted authorities, if they themselves secured office, like almost all Central American administrations, as the result of a successful revolution or an election controlled by the government, can hardly lay claim to a higher degree of legality than their successors . . ."

Munro demonstrated equally the futility of Root's and Knox's solution: "Even an intervention to protect foreign life and property often determines . . . the outcome of a civil war. . . . It is impossible to intervene merely to prevent disorder, and then leave to the people the choice of their own rulers, for elections, . . . are nothing more than a form for putting into effect the choice of the government already in office."

It would be difficult to convince the Central Americans of the sincerity of our good will and the disinterestedness of our intentions, he warned, so long as we continued to uphold a minority administration in Nicaragua by force of arms. "It is unthinkable that the United States, in the name of constitutional government, should permanently identify itself with any one faction or that it should continue indefinitely to use its power to exclude from all share in the administration the party to which a majority of the people of the Republic profess allegiance. Ultimately, an attempt must be made *either* to hold a fair election *or* to effect an agreement between the various parties by which a president accepted by all can be placed in office."

The policy problem thus assumed a different character. The same ultimate end was in view: the security of the United States by the prevention of unsettling revolutions, but now it was a question of how to achieve that end by a specific means: free elections. This shift in emphasis set the stage for what had been purely a means becoming almost an end in itself.

Despite the extensive experience of American officials with faulty electoral procedures in Cuba and Panama, the State Department made no effort to investigate or reform the election laws of Nicaragua until 1920. The Liberals claimed to represent a majority of the people in all their attacks on the American intervention after 1909 but without a careful census and registration there was no way to disprove this charge.[59]

As early as January, 1910, Judge Advocate General George B. Davis had recommended to the Department that Colonel Crowder be sent to Nicaragua to do the same work he had in Cuba: to make a census and registration for election purposes.[60] Nothing came of this because the State Department was bent on a policy of purely economic reform. It so openly favored the Conservative Party and excluded the Liberals in the elections of 1910, 1912 and 1916 that the latter did not contest the elections and there was no need for the party in power to have recourse to much abuse of the electoral machinery. The lack of an explicit treaty right of intervention also differentiated United States policy toward Nicaragua from that in Cuba and Panama with respect to free elections.[61]

In 1920, the Liberals decided that the only way to escape the taint of "Zelayaism" which had ruined their chances in 1916, was to form a coalition with a dissident splinter of the Conservative Party. Thus, the election of 1920 promised to be closely enough contested to make questions of electoral administration crucial to the outcome.

The State Department at last referred Nicaragua's electoral code for analysis to General Crowder who was by now the established authority on the subject. He rendered the opinion that "the Electoral Code . . . seems to me to be almost totally lacking in the usual safeguards.[62] Secretary Bainbridge Colby tried to induce President Chamorro to invite Crowder to Nicaragua to revise the law in conformity with "modern standards," but the President politely declined the Department's proffer, giving the excuse of the proximity of the election. Colby did not insist, but he did send a note of public protest to Chamorro on August 26, 1920, similar in intent to his note of the day before to President Menocal of Cuba: "The Department of State has received with the *deepest concern* reports showing that disturbances have arisen . . . incident to the registration of voters. . . . While the Department does not presume to form any judgment as to the reasons . . . it cannot but *view with the gravest apprehension* the imprisonment of the leaders of one of the political parties. . . . [This] action . . . is bound to produce the most *unfortunate impression* upon the people of the United States. The Department . . . *trusts* that the reports . . . are incorrect. . . . It *hopes* that the Government of Nicaragua will realize that elections cannot be held in such a manner as to permit a candidate for the Presidency to be chosen by the full and free expression of public opinion if acts of intimidation are now undertaken. . . . It therefore *feels confident* that the Government . . . will take steps immediately to dispel the impression created . . . and will take no further action which will cause this Government to feel that the people of Nicaragua will not be able to vote freely . . . in the coming elections." (Emphasis added.)

Since, however, no clear threat of non-recognition or other sanction was made, Chamorro, like the president of Cuba, called the bluff of the Americans and proceeded to win the election for the Conservative candidate, his uncle, by the usual methods.

The Secretary also sent a special military attaché, Major Jesse I. Miller, to observe registration and election practices as a basis for future action. Miller discovered heavy padding of the registration lists by the Conservatives and the exclusion of supporters of the Liberal-Coalition Party. On the other hand, his investigation also showed that the Liberals had by no means the overwhelming majority they claimed. In lieu of a reform of the electoral law, he made several practical suggestions such as the marking of voters with indelible ink to prevent multiple voting, the opening of the polls to all previously registered voters, and the appointment of bipartisan election boards.

Colby thereupon reprimanded Major Miller for exceeding his assignment. His words show that the Department's main concern was still the prevention of revolution: "Please inform Major Miller that the Department's sole interest in the revision of the laws relating to elections is that every enlightened and *reasonable* measure shall be taken to see that the result of the election is an expression of the popular will and is *accepted* by the people as such. In this way only will the resentment that is sure to be occasioned by any unfairness of method be avoided and public order and security protected against disturbances which may result from any *well-founded* dissatisfaction with electoral methods."

After the election, Minister Jefferson warned that revolutionary disturbances of a serious character were liable to occur unless radical measures were adopted at once to placate the disappointed Liberals. Acting Secretary Norman Davis proposed a coalition cabinet, but this met with the approval of neither side. The United States did succeed in extracting from the new president a written promise to request an expert from the Department to frame a new election law, and Chamorro in return received assurances that the new law would not be applied retroactively to his own election as had been demanded by the opposition. Here we see electoral law reform and coalition government playing the parts of temporary alternatives to free elections instead of means to that end.

A small "legation guard" of marines had symbolized the power of the United States in Nicaragua since the suppression of the 1912 revolution.[63] There were, of course, persistent demands by the Liberals that these men be withdrawn and just as steady pressure by the Conservatives to keep them, because their presence enabled the "in" party to perpetuate itself in power.

In the American presidential election of 1920 the Republican Party reversed its previous predilection for expansion and criticized the Democrats for their imperialism in the Caribbean. The isolationist mood which swept the country after World War I thus had repercussions in Latin American policy as well as European. The Latin Americans themselves began to demand the application to their own countries of President Wilson's ringing wartime declarations about self determination.

In this kind of an atmosphere the incoming Republican Secretary of State, Charles Evans Hughes, felt obliged to fulfill his party's campaign promises and prepare the way for the evacuation of Nicaragua lest the same charge of imperialism be turned on the Republican Administration in 1924.[64] He therefore informed the American Chargé d'Affaires in Nicaragua: "The Department for some time has been giving serious consideration to the question of the withdrawal of the Marines from Managua [Nicaragua] . . . [Their] continued presence . . . has at times given rise to the assertion . . . that the United States Government is maintaining in office a government which would otherwise perhaps not be strong enough to maintain itself against the attacks of its political opponents. On the other hand . . . should the Marines suddenly be withdrawn there appears to be reason to believe that political disturbances might ensue. . . .

[Therefore], the Department considers that the success of the whole plan of withdrawal depends upon the Government coming into office as the result of the next elections having the support of the majority of the people in order that it will be in such a strong position that when the Marines are then withdrawn there will be no occasion for political disturbance. To bring this about free and fair elections are essential . . . [so] that the Government which may result from the elections will have the support of the majority of the people of Nicaragua."[65]

Hughes, like Taft and many other Americans, seemed to be harboring the delusion that revolution, or at least "justified revolution," could come only from majorities frustrated by unfree elections, or that if the majority did decide the outcome of the election, there would be no justified excuse for revolution. Then the United States could support the incumbent government without the embarrassment of charges that it was supporting a minority government against its justly rebellious citizens.

The first step toward evacuating the Marines was electoral reform. Hughes' policy had three other related measures: nonrecognition, disarmament and the creation of a nonpartisan constabulary. Nonrecognition would forewarn potential rebels of United States' disapproval of revolution; electoral reform would assure free elections and thereby remove the incentive for revolution; disarmament would deprive the professional revolutionists of their weapons; and the "Guardia Nacional," the constabulary, would suppress what revolts did break out and would police the elections impartially.[66]

We have seen that the most the State Department could or would do with respect to electoral reform in 1920 was to extract a promise from President Chamorro that he would invite an American expert in to revise the Nicaraguan electoral law. He had probably consented to do this only to win recognition and as a delaying tactic. The incoming Republican administration in Washington, he had hoped, would revert to former Secretary Knox's indifference to the niceties of electoral procedures.[67] However, Secretary Hughes, for the reasons just discussed, continued his Democratic predecessor's plans after a slight delay. Accordingly, the Nicaraguan Government engaged Dr. Harold W. Dodds of the National Municipal Council in December, 1921, to draft a new electoral code which he modelled on Crowder's in Cuba.[68] The Conservative majority in the Nicaraguan Congress first procrastinated and then amended the "Dodds Law" in such a way as to leave the "ins" some loopholes for corrupting the elections, but the State Department accepted the law as the best obtainable under the circumstances.

The Department then eliminated the unconstitutional candidacy of the incumbent president for reelection in 1924, as it had in 1916 and 1920, by a threat of nonrecognition. Secretary Hughes informed him that "The Government of the United States . . . would regard his election as unconstitutional and upon the expiration of his present term would be highly indisposed to extend its recognition to him as the Constitutional President." [69]

We have noted before the ambiguous character of coalition government as a method for promoting free elections. Ex-Minister Weitzel's verdict on the Dawson Pact of 1910 was decidedly negative in words equally applicable to Laos in our own day: "The new Government [1910-1911] was in the nature of a coalition such as has been tried numerous times in Nicaragua, but has never succeeded. . . . As soon as a member of an opposing faction is given an important office in the administration, he at once begins to use it to overthrow the Government in the interest of himself and his faction. . . . A division of power in Nicaragua, as elsewhere, means lack of efficiency, absence of responsibility, and utter confusion." [70]

Nevertheless, Munro had reached the opposite conclusion in 1918: "The United States," he warned, "can hardly assist one party in securing and holding the control of the government without assuring itself that the men whom it thus keeps in office are acceptable to the people under their rule. . . . This can only be done by establishing an administration which fairly represents the best elements in the community. It should not be impossible to secure such an administration by an agreement between the party leaders. . . ." [71]

Harold Dodds, although he was the framer of the new Nicaraguan electoral law, also believed that "Peaceful entrance into the presidency is more by negotiation and arrangement among the leaders of the party than by election." [72]

A fortuitous event opened the door to another experiment with coalition government. President Diego Chamorro (1921-1923), uncle and successor of President General Emiliano Chamorro (1917-1921), died in 1923 and was succeeded by Vice-President Martinez—a man with ambitions of his own. Although the latter was prevented by the United States from running for the next full term, he refused to assent to the candidacy of the younger Chamorro for a second term of office. Instead, like the dissident Conservatives of 1920, he created a coalition of anti-Chamorro Conservatives with the moderate (i.e., non-Zelayist) Liberals. The situation of 1920 was reversed in that this time the Coalition Party held the reins of power. Chamorro's legal representative in Washington, Chandler Anderson, afterward charged bitterly that "The new coalition party both before and after the (1924) election had all the encouragement which a sympathetic attitude on the part of the Latin American Division of the State Department could give it because Dr. Dana G. Munro, in charge of Central American Affairs in the Department . . . naturally desired to utilize the opportunity offered by the coalition party to find out how his theory would work in practice. The views expressed in his book no doubt had an important influence upon the origin of the coalition party movement. . . ."[73]

The experiment was no more successful than the Dawson Pact had been because it excluded Chamorro, the most forceful Conservative leader, and because it was headed, as such coalitions tended to be, by a weak compromise candidate. Since the coalition was not all-inclusive, we may regard it as a means toward free elections rather than as an alternative to them as in other cases.

The State Department this time prevailed upon President Martinez to accept Dodds' supervision of the registration of voters under his new law in the Spring of 1924. The registration showed that neither party had a clear majority which again exploded the myth that the United States had been keeping the leaders of a huge Liberal majority from office.[74] But when the Department proposed that Dodds supervise the election as well, it met with flat refusal.

Munro then recommended observation as a "by no means satisfactory" alternative to supervision[75] and Hughes authorized the Marines to carry out this task. President Martinez agreed but only on condition that the Marines should wear civilian clothes because otherwise the Conservatives would make political capital out of the presence at the polls of American forces. However, since the Marine commandant took clear exception to this requirement, the proposal came to nought.

Needless to say, the Coalition ticket, backed by the incumbent president, won the election, though it was agreed that the election of 1924 with all its defects was by far the best that had ever been held in Nicaragua up to that time.[76] The defeated Chamorro Conservatives were naturally not mollified by the relative honesty of the poll and they demanded a new balloting as the defeated Liberal-Coalition had in 1920. Hughes' reply on December 10, 1924 shows both a growing awareness of the conditions for a free election and the considerations working against further American involvement:

"The Department has very carefully considered the whole Nicaraguan electoral situation. It feels that it is not feasible to demand new elections because it is not in a position to take the strong measures necessary to insure compliance with the demands and even should the Government readily consent to new elections they would be valueless unless very closely supervised by this Government which would also mean armed intervention which is not to be contemplated. The Department has also given consideration to the question of suggesting the appointment of a *designado* (Vice-President) and a coalition cabinet in which all parties will have a voice, this provisional government to hold new elections. This also is impracticable for the reasons mentioned above and because it does not seem likely that a coalition government in Nicaragua, should the suggestion meet with the support of all factions, would have any more chance of success than did a similar attempt in Honduras. The Department is therefore disposed to raise no question regarding the validity of the elections and to continue normal diplomatic relations. . . ."

Instead of a new election or an all-inclusive coalition, the new President, Solorzano, was urged to make a written engagement that the 1928 elections would "be carried out in full freedom and fairness for all parties and strictly in accordance with the provisions of the Dodds electoral law", that the long-deferred constabulary would be set up, and that the economic program would be pursued to completion. Solorzano readily complied as Diego Chamorro had in 1920. Emiliano Chamorro, who knew the worthlessness of such paper promises, was bluntly warned not to revolt.

The most noteworthy occurrence of the 1924 election was the change in attitude of the State Department toward the two major parties of Nicaragua comparable to Taft's in Cuba and Panama. Hughes turned against the Chamorro Conservatives for their blatant expediency in demanding American electoral supervision in 1924 when they were "out" although they had refused it in 1920 when they were "in".[77]

Furthermore, the pressure for real impartiality in keeping with repeated American protestations rose as the fear of Liberal anti-Americanism fell. The Department began to differentiate moderate Liberals from diehard "Zelayistas". Munro, it was alleged, had been a personal friend of Sacasa, a leading moderate Liberal whom he had met while gathering material for his book.[78] Summer Welles, another official with great influence on Latin American policy, told Conservative representatives in Washington in 1924 that the United States would not be disturbed particularly if the Liberals should come into power, and that, in fact, "it would be convenient for Nicaragua to have a Liberal president from this election."[79] In vain did the Conservatives plead that "their defeat would necessarily be a disaster for Nicaragua" and that their party during the twelve years it had been in office had been uniformly favorable to the United States.[80] Acting Secretary Joseph Grew announced emphatically that we had no party preferences, and, as in Cuba in 1920, we regarded attempts to transfer the center of Nicaraguan political activities to Washington as detrimental to Nicaraguan interests.

Despite the ominous dissatisfaction of the Chamorro Conservatives with the election, the Marines were finally withdrawn on August 3, 1925. A mere two months later the ex-President executed a *coup d'état* against the Coalition Government. Hughes' policy of promoting free elections to enable the United States to liquidate its occupation of Nicaragua without inviting revolution had failed.

The October *coup* need not have caused a repetition of the earlier American intervention, certainly not of its electoral aspects, were it not that Secretary Hughes had adhered in 1923 to a renewal and reinforcement of the Washington Conventions of 1907. We must go back therefore to the second Central American Conference of Washington (Dec. 4, 1922-Feb. 7, 1923) to understand the source of the policy problem of recognition for the solution of which free elections were again a criterion.

The Conference met in the wake of the most recent of Central America's periodic, unsuccessful attempts to form a federation. The United States was distinctly cool to any efforts to impose such a union by force.[81] The Bryan-Chamorro Canal Treaty had become a bone of contention between Nicaragua and her neighbors, Costa Rica, Honduras and El Salvador, so the campaign for unification had taken on an anti-Yankee complexion.[82] However, we were anxious to sponsor some substitute for the 1907 treaty, now expired, to keep the peace in Central America.

The most significant act of the Conference was to reaffirm the non-recognition clause of the 1907 treaty with the addition of even more restrictive conditions for recognition of revolutionary regimes:

"The Governments . . . shall not recognize any other Government which may come into power in any of the five Republics as a consequence of a *coup d'état* . . . against the recognized Government, so long as the freely elected representatives of the people thereof have not constitutionally reorganized the country.

"And even in such a case they obligate themselves not to acknowledge the recognition if any of the persons elected as President, Vice-President, or Chief-of-State-Designate should fall under any of the following heads:

"1) If he should be the leader or one of the leaders of a *coup d'état* or revolution, or through blood relationship or marriage, be an ascendent or descendent or brother of such leader or leaders.

"2) If he should have been a Secretary of State or should have held some high military command during the accomplishment of the *coup d'état* or the revolution, or while the election was being carried on, or if he should have held this office or command within the six months preceding the *coup d'etat*, revolution or the election.

"Furthermore, in no case shall recognition be accorded to a government which arises from election to power of a citizen expressly and unquestionably disqualified by the Constitution of his country as eligible to election as President, Vice President, or Chief-of-State-Designate."[83]

These amplifications read like a codification of American experience with nonrecognition since the 1907 treaty and a conscientious rectification of oversights in it. For instance, it deals with the problem of what to do with the revolutionary regime which has staged mock elections to legitimize itself.

Although Hughes still believed that "the chief danger of strife among our neighbors on the south lies in internal dissensions and in the tendency to have revolutions instead of fair elections",[84] he, like Root, later denied categorically authorship of the proposal. "It was their own policy, desire, and expression. The United States, or its delegates, did not initiate this provision in any way. We simply did not oppose the proposal, and thus expressed ourselves as being in accord with it."[85]

Further evidence that the new provisions were of Central American inspiration is provided by a contemporary editorial from a Honduran newspaper which stated on October 31, 1922, that "The way to assure peace consists in guaranteeing compliance with law, beginning by making the (Central American) Governments respect free elections."[86]

Subsequently Hughes defended his adherence to the nonrecognition convention on grounds which clearly show his reluctance. "It has not," he declared, "been fully appreciated what a difficult situation. . . . Secretary Hughes was placed (in) by the proposal of this provision by the Central American Republics. The question whether . . . the policy . . . is a good one is very debatable. In these . . . countries revolutions and *coups d'état* are often about the only reform measures available to the people . . . to dislodge corruption. Elections there frequently don't mean much . . . (Therefore) these people are entitled to their revolutions. . . . But . . . it would have been impossible . . . to take the position that they must not take this step to make revolutions less likely; that we wouldn't agree to it; and that we insisted that they have revolutions (because) revolutions in Central America . . . are not advantageous to *us*. We cannot tolerate much disturbance in the Caribbean region, because of the vital importance to our self-defense of the Panama Canal. . . . If the disturbances are of such character in injuring life and property that foreign Governments would take control if we were supine, then it is absolutely essential that we intervene." [87]

So it was that when ex-President Chamorro engineered his *golpe d'estado* shortly after the Marines departed, the State Department had to thread its way through a legal thicket of treaty interpretation to decide whom to recognize as president of Nicaragua.

Chamorro, if not an architect of the 1923 treaty, had signed it because it protected his party while he was "in". His lawyer, Chandler P. Anderson, offered a dubious defense of the principle of nonrecognition as "based on the recognized right of the people of each country to have a government elected freely and fairly in accordance with their Constitution and laws. [88] So the Conservative leader did not usurp the Presidency outright, but carefully set about preparing the way for his own succession in a legal enough way to satisfy the treaty requirements. He did not depose the coalition President, himself a former Conservative, but forced him to purge his cabinet of Liberals, claiming that he was only trying to undo the "fraudulent elections" of 1924 [89] which he therefore sugested be nullified. After that he offered to call a constituent assembly. When the State Department refused both of these gambits, he had the Conservative majority in the Congress "disqualify" enough of the Liberal members so that Sacasa, the Liberal-Coalitionist Vice-President, could be impeached. Then Chamorro was quickly and successively elected Senator, and First Designate; the helpless Coalition President was compelled to resign and the First Designate automatically became president.

The Department's reaction to all this maneuvering was to deny the usurper recognition permanently on January 7, 1926 the way it had Zelaya in 1909: "The Legation in Managua [Nicaragua] has been instructed to inform Chamorro that the United States would not recognize any Government headed by him since such a government would be founded on a *coup d'état.* . . ." In other words, we would not consider any election "free" if the leader of an immediately preceding revolution won.

At the same time that it refused Chamorro recognition, the United States made it known that it would not use armed force to put Vice-President Sacasa in power, but the Liberals took the matter into their own hands and launched a counter-revolution. This presented the Department with the perplexing legal problem of whether a revolution against an unrecognized revolutionary government disqualified the former's leaders from recognition if they were victorious and one of them were subsequently elected president!

The ensuing civil war developed into a destructive stalemate which soon threatened the economic health and political independent of the country which the policy of nonrecognition was designed to preserve so the State Department resorted to mediation. At a conference aboard a United States warship the Conservatives offered the Liberals a return to the political *status quo ante bellum* and a promise of free elections, if Sacasa would resign his claims to the presidency and accept former President Diaz (1911-1916) as a compromise substitute for Chamorro. The Liberals were confident of winning the civil war now with Mexican aid so they declined the offer.

The State Department extricated itself from this snarl by accepting a series of steps almost as tortuous as those by which Chamorro had tried to legalize his position. First, Chamorro resigned in favor of a Conservative henchman. The United States refused to recognize this man any more than it had Zelaya's immediate successor, Madriz, in 1909. It insisted that the Nicaraguan Congress be reconstituted to its pre-coup membership of 1925. The restored Congress elected ex-President Diaz and the United States promptly recognized him, thus leaving the Liberal claimant, Sacasa, a mere rebel. Diaz could be accused of having been a party to Chamorro's *coup d'état,* but he had held no office under him so the Latin American Division concluded that: "It would be impossible to interpret the Central American Treaties as barring out (sic) from office in the reorganized government the entire membership of a party. There was only one real leader of the Chamorro *coup d'état* and that was Chamorro."[90]

Clearly, our dogged pursuit of constitutional legality was largely self-defeating in terms of the aims of the policy. Even the belated victory over Chamorro came to nought. The Liberals persisted in their campaign to win control by force and United States Minister Charles Eberhardt warned Washington of a possible uprising behind the lines on the Conservative side. That top American officials still did not realize what both sides wanted primarily was power and not free elections is illustrated by the Department's plaintive reply to Eberhardt on December 18, 1926: "It was the understanding of the Department from the Legation's reports that President Diaz could count upon the support of a substantial majority of the people of Nicaragua and that his designation by Congress seemed to confirm this understanding. For this reason the Department cannot understand your reference to a possible general uprising against the Government . . . which would result immediately in (its) . . . speedy collapse . . ."

Another result of this episode was that it finished the public career of Emiliano Chamorro as far as the United States was concerned. His Washington lobbyist, Anderson pleaded in vain that "the whole policy [of impartiality] was wrong . . . because the Department really should concern itself to assist in keeping in power the party which was friendly to the United States instead of assisting the Mexican intrigue to destroy that party, and that although naturally they could not openly take sides, skillful diplomacy could easily have produced the desired result without open partiality."[91]

People in the State Department are reported to have said that they had "bet on the wrong horse."[92]

Nonrecognition had driven Chamorro from office and installed a more or less legally elected successor in his place, but it had not restored peace to Nicaragua. President Diaz promptly repeated his requests of 1911 and 1914 for an American protectorate. Under the treaty he proposed in February 1927, Nicaragua "would empower the United States to intervene in order that there be maintained a constitutional government adequate for the protection of lives, property and individual liberty *which would have its origin in a vote of the people in a free election . . ."* (Emphasis added)

Secretary Frank Kellogg replied to this transparent act of desperation that the fact the United States had recognized the Diaz Government and not the rival Liberal government didn't mean that it was obligated or prepared to lend armed assistance in protecting it against revolution. Assistant Secretary Grew added that it was extremely doubtful that the U. S. Senate would consent to such a treaty anyway. The Department was no more willing to keep Diaz the Conservative in power by force than it had been to put Sacasa the exiled Liberal Vice-President in power the year before. But if the Liberals went on now to win the presidency by force of arms, the prospect was one of another long period of nonrecognition which hurt the country's economy, aroused anti-American sentiment and encouraged counterrevolution. Most of all, the war was arousing American fears of intervention by other powers. Great Britain requested that the United States protect her subjects in Nicaragua and sent a warship to the scene as a hint that if the United States didn't take action she would.

Even more important as a threat to American prestige if not security was the military support revolutionary Mexico was giving to the Liberals. Conservatives and their North American friends had been warning the Department since 1924 that a Liberal victory would mean the expropriation of American property in Nicaragua as had happened in Mexico.[93] Douglas H. Allen, a lawyer for the mahogany companies, made a trip to Nicaragua in January, 1927 to see what he could do to protect their properties from destruction in the civil war. "Intervention," he reported, "is absolutely necessary to afford adequate protection to American and foreign interests. . . . If the revolutionists, aided by Mexico, succeed in overthrowing the present Government, the resulting regime cannot be recognized by the United States without disregarding the terms of the five power Treaty of 1923 . . . and the people of Nicaragua will have to face several years of revolution . . . similar to Mexico. . . . Mexico has directly challenged the prestige of the United States in Latin America and our stand must be maintained."[94]

If one were to substitute Cuba for Mexico the last sentence would sound like part of a brief for overthrowing Fidel Castro in 1961! Even the spectre of communism was raised to induce us to intervene in Nicaragua. Under pressure of this sort, President Coolidge announced to Congress on January 10, 1927 that the United States would intervene militarily to protect foreign lives and property.

Kellogg immediately warned Diaz that forceful measures on the limited basis of the "protection of lives and property" formula were inadequate for a permanent solution of Nicaraguan unrest and that he should not lose sight of the main problem. "No matter how constitutional its title may be, a government cannot be expected to maintain itself indefinitely in the face of serious internal dissension by relying upon indirect support derived from measures which the Government of the United States must take to protect its own nationals and interests. . . ."

Douglas Allen had already pointed the way to a "permanent solution" in his report on a conference with the Liberal "President", Sacasa: "I believe that if the matter is properly handled the Liberals could probably be induced to request intervention by the United States . . . provided the United States would be willing to keep a small force at Managua and also to take over the supervision of the elections in 1928. In this way the Liberals believe that they would have a fair show in the elections as otherwise they are afraid that Diaz will sway the elections . . . Neither party can trust the other or any other Nicaraguan to oversee the coming elections. . . . If the Liberals did win in the elections of 1928 (under United States supervision) their success would not (then) be due to Mexico's support and their coming into power would not be of any grave concern to the prestige of the United States."

Eberhardt also gave his opinion that one of the first demands of the

Liberals in case of a new mediation would be that the 1928 election be adequately supervised by the United States. With evident reluctance he recommended that he be instructed to encourage that solution, carefully stressing that even a supervised election could not be "guaranteed fair", because of "the usual cry of fraud which is sure to follow any Nicaraguan election no matter how or by whom conducted." Kellogg agreed if both parties would request supervision.

The solution had yet to be negotiated and that required a man of greater prestige than our Minister in Nicaragua. Therefore in April, 1927 President Coolidge sent Henry L. Stimson, former Secretary of War, to Nicaragua "to straighten the matter out." [95] Stimson read Allen's memoranda to Assistant Secretary of State Olds and talked to the lawyer personally. [96] Afterwards he wrote that Allen was "the gentleman whom I found most helpful in giving me fair and intelligent information when I was going to Nicaragua." [97] It seems reasonably certain that Stimson got most if not all his ideas for his mediation of the civil war from Allen: the necessity of political intervention to protect American interests and the Central American treaty policy; the danger of allowing the Liberals to win with Mexican aid, but the feasibility of letting them win an election under American auspices if they could be tied down by continued financial control; the impossibility of a coalition government pending the election because of the mutual mistrust of the two parties; the idea of the United States supervising the election to prevent the Conservatives from controlling the election machinery; and finally the notion of threatening the Liberals with the "permanent antagonism" of the United States if they didn't agree to a settlement. Thus we can see that American supervision of the 1928 Nicaraguan election had its origins, at least partly, in the concern of private business interests to stop a destructive civil war and in the willingness of the Liberal Party to do so only under that condition.

Stimson's contributions to the agreement were his prestige as a personal emissary of the President and his enthusiasm and forcefulness compared to the equivocation of the State Department officials. Throughout the negotiations the latter repeatedly manifested their reluctance to engage in another electoral supervision. Assistant Secretary Grew cautiously cabled Stimson on April 15, 1927, that "The Department hopes . . . you may eventually discover a way to avoid our assuming the responsibility of supervising an election."

In briefing Stimson before he left, State Department personnel advised him only that a supervised election in 1928 was "the best way out." [98] Even Coolidge who seldom meddled in foreign affairs had misgivings about this method because of his bitter experience with the abortive Tacna-Arica plebiscite between Chile and Peru the year before.[99] Kellogg bowed to Stimson's adamant position on "the absolute necessity of (the) 1928 election being supervised by (the) United States . . . (because) (the) Washington Conferences of 1907 and 1923 have made (the) question of free elections the very heart of the Nicaraguan problem." But the Secretary insisted that if Stimson's negotiations with the disputants were broken off, "the United States would not stand committed even to supervise the 1928 elections."[100]

Our Government executed its pledge to oversee the 1928 election with a single-minded determination that bespoke the feeling that American honor and prestige were at stake. The operation required far greater manpower and experience in large scale organization of a foreign population than the State Department could muster. Perforce, the Department turned to the military men who were already present in Nicaragua to the number of some 5,000 Marines. Brigadier General Frank R. McCoy, a veteran of American occupation administrations in Cuba and the Philippines, was nominated on Stimson's recommendation to be Chairman of the Electoral Board. His role paralleled Crowder's in the 1908 election in Cuba except that McCoy had an indigenous government to deal with. The General was ably seconded by the two American civilians most familiar with the technicalities of Nicaraguan electoral law and practice: Dodds and Munro.

The inadequate Dodds Law of 1923 had to be amended, although McCoy was already dubious of the too extensive machinery it provided.[101] The Conservative Congress refused to pass "la ley McCoy" just as an earlier Conservative Congress had mangled "la ley Dodds", but the General put it into effect as an *ad hoc* administrative decree. In an Executive Memorandum of September 7, 1928, the American Electoral Mission listed thirty-five unfair or illegal practices resorted to in past elections against which supervisory personnel were warned to be on guard.[102]

With the discovery of each new technique for exerting power illegally to influence the voters, the supervisors were driven to demand control over more governmental functions. "I believe," Munro reported, for instance, "it would be advisable to have the Collector of Customs [American] take over the collection of internal revenues at once . . . for political reasons. The Liberals complain that the Conservatives' tax officials are treating them unfairly and they fear, with much reason, that discrimination in the assessment and collection of taxes will be used as a means of coercing voters in the elections."[103]

The same logic that pushed the supervisors to increase the area of control forced them toward an extension of the duration of control. Stimson had talked of supervision of "several successive elections", but Assistant Secretary Francis White cautioned him later that "Our commitments are only through the next election. . . . After all, we are in Nicaragua to carry out elections and not to change either permanently or for any length of time the character of the Nicaraguan Administration."[104] However, as the election approached and the tension mounted, it appeared that the only way to get both parties to participate and accept the results peaceably was to reduce the importance of this one election by getting both candidates to promise that whichever won would ask for American supervision again in 1932. In fact, the plan was originally broached by the Nicaraguan Liberals and the State Department as late as October 1928 warned that it could not commit the next administration in Washington.

The problems the American electoral mission encountered reproduced those that the supervisory commission had met with in Panama in 1912. They soon discovered that even the most earnest declarations of impartiality didn't dispel intrigues or prevent accusations of American bias from being made. Neither Nicaraguan political party wanted a free election as an end in itself. The Conservative "ins" accepted supervision only as a last extremity in the face of imminent military defeat and the Liberal "outs" accepted it only in the face of Stimson's threat to disarm them forcibly if they didn't. Neither side really believed that the United States was interested only in the process of free elections and not in the outcome. The American partiality to the Conservatives in the elections of 1910, 1912 and 1916 and the refusal of the State Department to exert sufficient pressure to assure free elections in 1920 and 1924 were hardly auguries of impartiality this time. Besides, neither party could afford to believe in American impartiality because up until the last-minute agreement on American supervision of the 1932 election just referred to, too much was at stake for the Nicaraguans, as individuals and as party members.

Consequently, the prospective candidates sought American endorsement. In the end, emphatic denials to the contrary notwithstanding, the State Department predetermined the victor by pronouncing the ineligibility of Chamorro, the strongest Conservative, while permitting the candidacy of Moncada, the victorious Liberal Commander. This result was brought about by means of a casuistical interpretation of the 1923 convention. Chamorro had been given to understand at the time of his resignation in November, 1926 that he was eligible to run in the 1928 election,[105] but the Department later disqualified him for candidacy and recognition on the ground that "unless we interpret . . . the Nicaraguan Constitution to mean anybody holding the office of President during any presidential term is debarred . . . during the next succeeding term, it would open the way for the President to resign just before the elections, taking good care to see that a friendly person succeeded him, and then run for reelection. . . ."[106]

The same reasoning presumably barred Sacasa as he too had been a president, though unrecognized as such, in the preceding term. But Sacasa's leading general, Moncada, had become a favorite of Stimson's, and his candidacy was admitted with the specious argument that no recognized government had been overthrown by the Liberal revolution in which Moncada had held a "high military command".

Stimson's continued warm personal relations with the Liberal leader precipitated an unintended bandwagon movement toward the latter's party. The Conservatives were helpless because Diaz had been stripped of the powers which ordinarily gave victory to the "ins". We have noted that McCoy even bypassed the Conservative majority in the Nicaraguan Congress to get his amended version of the Dodds electoral code instituted. The Liberals rejected Conservative overtures for a coalition, as the "outs" had in the Panama supervision, and McCoy stopped the Conservatives' plan to throw the election into Congress by turning down all splinter party applications for a place on the ballot. He argued that 'The people of the United States believe it is to the advantage of every country to have two equally great and influential parties. . . ."[107]

Secretary Kellogg added that "there should be but two candidates, each representing one of the principal parties. It is such an election that the Tipitapa Agreement (Stimson's which ended the civil war) clearly contemplated, and not an election involving a free-for-all contest among party factions, with the probability of throwing the result for determination into the Nicaraguan Congress, the membership of which is only partially involved in this supervised election."[108]

McCoy, despite the vigor with which he carried out his assignment, warned his men on the electoral mission just before the 1928 election: "Though both parties invited the United States to supervise the election . . . it is anticipated that the losing side will charge personal bias, fraud, etc. against the American Electoral Mission. *No matter how impartial the work and attitude of every member, these charges will be made* and must be accepted philosophically . . . the election itself, however important as an example of fair and peaceful settlement of

Nicaraguan issues, is but one detail of the country's problem. . . . All Americans connected with the Mission are counselled . . . to guard against the unduly optimistic belief that a fair election is a panacea for Nicaragua's troubles or will even relieve her most pressing necessities." [109] (Emphasis added)

Five flaws in the supervision may be observed: 1. the cost was disproportionate to the value; 2. there was no anti-American third party and so the main issue, American intervention, was excluded; 3. Nicaraguans gained no real experience in democracy from the election because it was all done for them; 4. the effect of the presence of American troops and the imputed preference of the American government on the voters was unavoidable. 5. Finally, while the supervision did end the civil war, was the threat to our security for the avoidance of which it was undertaken a real one? None other than ex-Secretary Elihu Root advised Stimson out of his retirement: "The difficulty of invoking (the Monroe) Doctrine is the difficulty in saying that (United States) safety is imperilled by anything that has yet happened in Central America. . . . The more I reflect on this affair, the more clear it seems to me that the real and serious mistake was made when Knox began to meddle with what was none of his business." [110]

How long would the electoral intervention continue? Assistant Secretary White wrote McCoy, just after the 1928 election, "I fervently hope we will have no more elections in Latin America to supervise." [111] But the party compact of 1928 whereby both candidates promised that whichever won would invite the United States to superintend the 1932 election, was now an obligation of honor for us because we had agreed to the pact.

Stimson had suggested during his mediation mission that "such supervision could be continued . . . in subsequent years . . . for several electoral periods . . . and thus be made the means for gradual political education of Nicaraguans in self government through free elections." [112] After he himself became Secretary of State in 1929, he took a less sanguine view of the missionary aspects of the intervention. Despite the acceptance of the verdict of the ballot box by both parties, one of Moncada's subordinates, Sandino, refused to acquiesce in the American supervision and conducted guerrilla warfare against the Marines. The rebel seemed to enjoy some popular support and to many Latin Americans he became a symbol of defiance of North American imperialism much as Castro of Cuba did a generation later. [113]

Probably more important, though, in deciding Stimson to make 1932 the last electoral supervision were economic and political pressures generated by the Great Depression which struck the United States after 1929. He felt compelled to notify President Moncada on November 24, 1930, that "the time is rapidly approaching when it will be necessary for the United States Government to withdraw its Marine forces from Nicaragua . . . I cannot see how they can remain later than to assist you in carrying out the elections of November 1932. . . . Public opinion in this country will hardly support a further continuance of that situation."

Even the outlay for the election was fought by a Democratic Congress in Washington which attached a rider to the Naval Appropriation Act forbidding the use of funds in it to send Marines to supervise the elections.[114] Acting Secretary Castle therefore refused the request of Admiral Clark Woodward, the Chairman of the Electoral Mission for 1932, for more marines by replying that "The feeling in the United States as represented in Congress and by the public in general (is) growing stronger all the time that these steps (of withdrawal) were necessary and that the United States Government must not be drawn into the position of policing Nicaragua indefinitely." By 1933 Admiral Woodward himself recommended to Stimson that the United States should "seek by every means possible, to avoid again becoming involved in a commitment of the nature of the three recent supervisions of Elections in Nicaragua".[115]

Another important reason why Stimson began liquidation of the American ventures in Central America and the Caribbean was that otherwise he could not consistently ask Japan to desist from expansion in Manchuria. The Secretary admitted this himself in later years. In his autobiography he explained that "Particularly after the beginning of the Far Eastern crisis in 1931 [I] was opposed to [intervention by American troops]. . . . It would be used against [me] in the Far East. . . . It would put me in absolutely wrong in China, where Japan has done all of this monstrous work under the guise of protecting her nationals with a landing force."[116]

There is nothing of significance to be added about the means used to carry out the 1930 electoral observation and the 1932 electoral supervision since they were patterned on the 1928 proceedings and agreed upon in advance. But questions did arise as to what would be an acceptable election. As it became apparent that 1932 would witness the last American-conducted election, its importance increased for the Nicaraguan politicians. They began to jockey for position for what promised to be a decisive verdict for years to come. President Moncada proposed a constitutional convention for electoral and other

reforms in lieu of a presidential election.[117] The "in" (Liberal) Party
was badly split and Moncada, like Diaz in 1916 and Martinez in 1924,
was fishing for a coalition of his wing of the party with the Conservatives. He even asked for a constitutional guarantee of minority party
representation in the Congress. In 1930, like Machado of Cuba, he proposed an extension of the presidential term to seven years. Chargé
d'Affaires Willard Beaulac strongly urged that these "reforms" be discouraged because they would complicate the final American withdrawal
and the State Department did refuse to condone any such evasions.

Finally Admiral Woodward decided the question of who should be
the legal candidate of the Liberals by ordering a plebiscite or party
primary. The reunited Liberals then won because this time the presence of Americans could not be interpreted by the voters as a sign of
weakness on the part of the "ins" or of American partiality for the
"outs", as in 1928 since supervision had been voluntarily agreed to in
advance and not as the result of a revolution or threat of revolution.
Sacasa and Chamorro, the two candidates, had agreed privately on the
participation of the defeated party in the Congress, courts, municipal
governments, electoral commission and police.[118]

An American critic of the intervention, Raymond Leslie Buell, challenged the underlying assumption of two party elections and party
compacts thus exemplified by charging that "no system of supervision
is 'fair' which discriminates against third parties and independent
candidates; . . . new groups are necessary if the real views of the Nicaraguan people toward the American occupation and toward internal
problems are to find adequate expression. The participation of third
parties in elections is an established principle in practically every democratic country in the world . . . the very principle of democratic government depends upon the development of a body of independent
voters." [119]

It will be recalled that one of Secretary Hughes' policies to help
establish free elections in Nicaragua so the United States could withdraw its Marines was the formation of a nonpartisan constabulary. The
ironic consequence of this plan to "take the army out of politics" was
that the Commander of the "Guardia", Anastasio Somoza, made himself dictator of Nicaragua soon after the Marines evacuated the country
in 1933 and remained in power either directly or through puppets and
without benefit of anything approaching free elections until his assassination in 1956.[120]

Stimson "burnt the bridges" against any renewed, unilateral American action by announcing in 1931 that the United States could not un-

dertake general protection of American lives and property in countries like Nicaragua disturbed by "brigandage" and by restoring American recognition policy to its pre-1907 criteria which ignored the electoral purity of countries. The 1923 Central American treaty itself, which had spawned so much American electoral participation, was allowed quietly to lapse in 1934 in conformity with President Franklin Roosevelt's "Good Neighbor" policy. For a few years thereafter American Ministers Matthew Hanna and Arthur Bliss Lane continued to interfere in Nicaraguan politics with the apparent approval of Assistant Secretary of State Sumner Welles. Here, as in Cuba, Secretary Cordell Hull's policy of complete noninterference eventually won out. He instructed all of our Ministers in Central America on April 30, 1936 to abstain even from offering advice on any domestic political question.[121]

United States support of free elections in Nicaragua, reluctantly undertaken and, until 1927, half-heartedly carried out, had not efficiently or permanently solved the policy problems which caused it to be adopted. As for promoting democracy as an end in itself, Buell's indictment of the policy in 1931 is sufficient comment: "From the standpoint of Central America, the United States instead of promoting social progress . . . has merely created a feeling of dazed helplessness and a desire to know what the United States will do next. . . . Instead of developing responsibility and independence, a local feeling of irresponsibility . . . thus diminishing the capacity of the country for self government. In Managua, the expression has arisen among house servants: 'Let the Marines do it.' "[122]

IV

MEXICO

Since the Republic of Mexico is older than Cuba and Panama and far stronger in relation to the United States than Nicaragua; so the occasion for an application of the free elections policy could only come with a drastic internal weakening of the Mexican state such as occurred after the overthrow of the forty-five year old dictatorship of Porfirio Diaz in 1910-1911.

Francisco Madero launched the Mexican Revolution against Diaz with the slogan "liberty of suffrage and no reelection." Thus it was in the beginning a primarily political movement of protest against the repeated fraudulent elections by which the old dictator had kept himself in power.[1] So here, as in Central America, it was the Latin Americans who raised the issue of free elections first. Madero's revolt succeeded because of an accumulation of discontent and social unrest and he was unanimously chosen president in October, 1911. Our Ambassador reported that "the elections, while free from the influence of official menace through the police and army, were nevertheless farcical in character and in a very small degree representative of Mexican public opinion."[2]

The Taft Administration was little disposed to quibble over the honesty of elections in a country where the United States had no pressing strategic interests and no treaty right of intervention, so Madero was promptly recognized.

A little more than a year later in February, 1913 Madero was overthrown and treacherously executed in a counterrevolutionary coup led by a nephew of the ex-Dictator Diaz and by one of Madero's own generals, Victoriano Huerta. Indignation was widespread in Mexico, the United States and Europe because, however, frequent the violent changes in executive among the Latin American pseudo-democracies, the rules of the game had usually required that the leaders of the defeated faction should be allowed to escape with their lives into exile. The British Government raised the question of Huerta's criminal culpability in the death of Madero and indicated that it would refrain from recognizing his Provisional Government until a permanent president was elected.[3] The lame duck Taft Administration also cautiously withheld recognition, partly to see if the Mexican people would acquiesce and partly in the hope of extracting a favorable settlement of American claims arising from the revolution and counterrevolution.[4]

The prevailing attitude in the State Department was ably expressed in an undated memorandum of the Department's Solicitor, J. Reuben Clark, to Secretary Knox: "Huerta belongs to the governing class, which represents largely the brains, the intelligence, the education, and above all the governmental experience of Mexico. A government in other hands than those of the governing class must be a wild experiment. . . . An affront to the governing class means to us a loss of influence, prestige, and interest generally, and a corresponding gain in all of these by the European powers . . . in a foreign state having with us a common frontier . . . a danger too obvious to require argument. . . . Brigandage and slaughter have too firm a hold to be eradicated by the mere fact that some one man has been 'elected' President of Mexico. And let's have no illusions on 'elections' in Mexico."[5]

Encouraged by Huerta's inability to obtain foreign recognition, a group of Maderista state governors now started a counter-counterrevolution with the same platform of honest elections on which the late President had ridden to power two years before. "The State Governments" they proclaimed "only desire to repudiate President Huerta . . . [they] will not tolerate the present Provisional Government and their belligerency is a movement to secure a constitutionally elected president . . . they do not believe that President Huerta will permit a constitutionally elected president to succeed him to his present office."[6]

It was this confused situation which Woodrow Wilson faced when he took office in March, 1913. He promptly issued a "Declaration of Policy with Regard to Latin America" which by implication committed his administration to supporting free elections as the criterion for a recognizable givernment: "Cooperation is possible only when supported at every turn by the orderly processes of just government based upon law, not upon arbitrary or irregular force. . . . Just government rests always upon the consent of the governed. . . . We shall lend our influence of every kind to the realization of these principles . . . knowing that disorder, personal intrigues, and defiance of constitutional rights weaken and discredit government. . . . We can have no sympathy with those who seek to seize the power of government to advance their own personal interests or ambition. . . . We shall prefer those who . . . respect the restraints of constitutional provision."[7]

The problem now was how to secure the establishment of a "just government based upon law and the consent of the governed" to replace the arbitrary, unconstitutional regime of the usurper, Huerta.

Wilson gave no indication of how Mexico was to accomplish the return to "orderly processes", but simply continued to withhold recognition from Huerta. Apparently the American President was waiting to see if Huerta would extend his control over all of Mexico and whether he would hold constitutional elections, as he said he would do.[8] On May 1, 1913, Huerta called a presidential election for October 26th.[9]

Soon afterward, spokesmen of several American corporations with large investments in Mexican mining, oil and railroads presented to Wilson through the intercession of his adviser Colonel House the plan of a Judge Delbert J. Haff whereby the immediate recognition of Huerta would be made contingent upon his holding the announced election at some date earlier than October and guaranteeing its fairness. The Constitutionalists, the followers of the murdered Madero, were to suspend hostilities, participate in the election, guarantee its fairness in the territory they occupied, and abide by the results.[10] The plan made a strong impression on Wilson, but on second thought he began to doubt, even if the treacherous Huerta agreed to the proposal, whether the Mexican ruler would carry it out. Once he was recognized as interim president there would be no way of dealing with him, short of armed intervention,[11] if he failed to fulfill his promises.

The same American companies then brought forward a revised plan without the immediate recognition feature.[12] Secretary Bryan commented to the President that "the suggestion they make is a new one, and strikes me very favorably. . . . This seems to me to offer a way out." [13] However, instead of using Judge Haff's proposed settlement which contained no effective guarantee that the election would be fair, Wilson finally informed Huerta on June 14, 1913 that he must provide satisfactory proof of his intentions by holding an early election, free from coercion, by declaring an amnesty and "by observing his original promise not to be a candidate." [14] Bryan displayed the underlying chain of reasoning when he wrote that ". . . We desire to recognize the Government (of Mexico) as soon as we have proof of its acceptability by the people, . . . the only basis upon which stable government is possible. The wishes of the people can be tested by an election fairly held." [15]

So it was that the specific solution of demanding free elections was introduced to the Wilson Administration by private economic interests. Why did they do it? It was alleged at the time that one of the companies, Standard Oil, had backed Madero financially in a rivalry over oil concessions with the British Pearson oil interests which on their part had supported Huerta.[16] The earlier letters of representatives of American companies to President Taft urging him not to intervene against Madero lend some substance to the charge. Already their advice was occasionally phrased in terms of the argument that Madero promised free elections. Judge Haff and his associates may have put forth both of his plans in May, 1913 for the reason they gave: to prevent further loss of life and property, including their own, in Mexico by assuring speedy recognition of a new government which could restore order because it would enjoy the loyal support of all factions. On the other hand, Judge Haff himself was in partnership with an old-line "Liberal" Mexican politician, Calero, who was a candidate for the presidency.[17] At the time of the counter-revolution of February 1913 against Madero, the renegade Huerta had made a pact with General Felix Diaz, the former dictator's nephew, by which it was agreed that Huerta would be provisional president and then support Diaz for the regular term of office.[18] By July, Haff reported to Wilson from Mexico that Huerta was establishing a military dictatorship and would probably impose his own election on the country to the exclusion of Diaz, Calero and other candidates and contrary to the Mexican constitution.[19] Yet Judge Haff had no illusions about the possibility of a fair poll even without Huerta's candidacy: "It ought to be understood by our government," he warned, "that such a thing as an election here in which a president should be chosen who would really represent the will of the majority of the people is impossible." It is possible to conjecture that Haff suggested to Wilson the idea of a guaranteed free election because his favored candidate in the counterrevolutionary camp appeared to be losing out to the militarist, Huerta.[20]

Since nonrecognition alone was apparently not enough to end the destructive civil war in Mexico, Wilson decided in late July, 1913 to send former Governor John Lind of Minnesota on a special mission to Huerta to procure his compliance with the modified Haff plan. This was not a mediatory mission, properly speaking, because his errand was only to Huerta, but Wilson also sent an agent to contact the Constitutionalist leaders. Hence Lind's negotiations may be regarded as at least the preliminaries of mediation.

The terms Lind suggested called for an immediate armistice, security for an early and free election in which all agreed to take part, consent of General Huerta to bind himself not to be a candidate for election as President of the Republic at this election, and agreement of all parties to abide by the results of the election and cooperate in organizing and supporting the new administration.[21] These terms were reinforced with a promise of a loan and a threat to let the Constitutionalists buy arms in the United States. [22] Huerta's Foreign Minister indignantly refused the loan and deftly sidestepped the question of his chief's candidacy by pointing to the ineligibility provisions of the Mexican Constitution.[23]

Wilson's special emissary remained in Mexico for several months to no avail while Huerta played for time and his conservative allies bickered over various possible candidates and coalitions. The holdover Congress with its Maderista majority did what it could to obstruct the government while the factions within the counterrevolutionary camp began to realign along the traditional nineteenth century Mexican party lines of Catholic versus anti-clerical Liberal.[24] In the meantime, the rebel Constitutionalists quite naturally refused to participate in the campaign as long as Huerta remained in office,[25] so the prospect grew of an indecisive result with no candidate achieving a majority. In that case, even if the Catholic candidate had a plurality, the Liberal Congress could reverse the outcome. To forestall this and perpetuate himself in office, Huerta dissolved the Congress, arrested the Liberal opposition and assumed dictatorial powers on October 10th. If the balloting were held at all now, it was clear that he intended to determine the results in a way favorable to himself.[26]

Wilson retorted that he was shocked at Huerta's lawless methods and regarded them as an act of bad faith toward the United States: "It is not only a violation of the constitutional guarantees but it destroys all possibility of a free and fair election. . . . An election held at this time and under conditions as they now exist would have none of the sanctions with which the law surrounds the ballot . . . its results could therefore not be regarded as representing the will of the people. . . . [we] will not recognize as a legitimate government a government established . . . through the empty forms of a mock election." [27]

Now the American President was determined to get rid of Huerta and "reestablish genuine constitutional processes before (i.e., over) the desire for order at any price." [28]

Wilson set about persuading the other powers which had provisionally recognized Huerta in the spring to withdraw their recognition. He suspected the British of backing Huerta for the purely economic reasons mentioned above and grimly told the emissary of the British Foreign Secretary: "I am going to teach the South American Republics to elect good men." [29] Our Ambassador in London, Walter Hines Page, developed the same theme in talking to Sir Edward Grey.

"Suppose you have to intervene, what then?" asked Grey.

"Make 'em vote and live by their decisions," Page responded.

"But suppose they will not so live?"

"We'll go in again and make 'em vote again," said Page.

"And keep this us for 200 years?"

"Yes," said the American Ambassador, "the United States will be here 200 years, and it can continue to shoot men for that little space until they learn to vote and rule themselves." [30]

There had been talk since the summer of 1913 of repeating in Mexico the American experiment in Cuba, of "assisting the people in securing free and fair elections." [31] But the military occupation of Mexico would have been a far larger project and it would have required the cooperation of the Constitutionalists to avoid any semblance of American imperialism. Wilson wanted to guide the Revolution into orderly and democratic channels by obtaining a promise from Venus-tiano Carranza, the rebel leader, that his faction would participate in a new canvass once Huerta were eliminated. [32] Carranza refused to compromise with the old regime in any way and now insisted that national elections could be held only *after* he controlled all of Mexico and had inaugurated economic reforms. [33] Wilson stopped short of recognizing the Constitutionalist chief's "Provisional Government", proclaimed October 17, 1913, but did lift the arms embargo to the latter's advantage.

The American President argued in his annual message to Congress in December, 1913 that an unconstitutional, dictatorial regime like Huerta's could not be lasting, [34] but Huerta proved to be more durable than expected despite the material aid sent to his enemies from north of the border, probably because he was now able to rally nationalist sentiment against foreign intervention. Ultimately, in the spring of 1914, the United States used force in Mexico, not, ironically, in defense of constitutional government and free elections, but on the basis of a traditional case of national honor involving the false arrest of some American sailors at Tampico and the refusal of a Huertista official to salute our flag in reparation. [35] American naval forces occupied Vera Cruz and cut off Huerta from his sources of military supply.

A conference was held in May and June, 1914 at Niagara Falls under the auspices of Argentina, Brazil and Chile to get the United States and Mexico out of this impasse. The mediators proposed a compromise provisional government pledged to amnesty and free elections which the United States would recognize on withdrawal of its forces from Vera Cruz. [36] It was assumed that the Constitutionalists would win the election because of the prestige of their military victory.[37] Bryan rejected the idea of a provisional government made up of "neutrals" and asserted "There can be no such persons in Mexico among men of force and character."[38] The Huertista delegation charged that the United States aimed at the complete triumph of the revolution and argued quite reasonably that "If all the elements of the Provisional Government are to be revolutionary, the liberty of the elections will be a fraud. . . . The Washington Government does not want Mexico to have electoral liberty (for) it is obvious that a free election in a country unused to the exercise of suffrage can only be held under an impartial government."[39]

Carranza also rejected the plan for a Provisional President, so when Huerta resigned on July 14, 1914 the Constitutionalist victory was complete. The revolutionists were thus the beneficiaries of Wilson's policy but they were under no obligation to restore orderly processes of government by holding elections, and as we shall now see, the President himself was probably no longer interested primarily in that objective.

Mexico was a testing ground for Wilson's beliefs about democracy. Before he became President he had posited rigid requirements for the successful practice of government by the consent of the governed: "The degree of popular control must correspond to the stage of a people's development."[40] But he had finished his own electoral campaign of 1912 with an almost mystic faith in "the people." His sympathy for the aspirations of "the submerged 85 percent of the (Mexican) Republic who are now struggling toward liberty"[41] gave him a growing belief in the capacity of all people for self government: "When properly directed, there is no people not fitted for self government." He was sustained in his efforts by the conviction that the world was being swept by a wave of democracy and he felt the pull of duty to foster this trend. So the new chief executive approached the Mexican problem in 1913 as a political one to be solved by holding free elections which would put into power a constitutional government under which their troubles would evaporate.[42]

It is in the light of these views that we must understand Wilson's attitude toward Huerta and his distinction between good and bad revolutions which affords an intriguing parallel to current Soviet doctrine on the same subject. To Wilson, revolution was righteous only when, as with Madero's, it was necessary to establish liberty and self-government; it had no place in a democracy and was deeply wrong when resorted to, as Huerta had, against constitutional government.[43] What a contrast to our midcentury antipathy toward all revolutions!

Americans who had personal experience in Mexico had few illusions about the practicability of meaningful elections in the manner of the United States. We have already quoted Judge Haff to this effect. Others cited the high rate of illiteracy, the existence of masses of uneducated, apathetic and landless Indians in the population, the tradition of corruption, inability to accept defeat peaceably, the lack of political ideals, and the fickleness of the city population.[44] American businessmen in Mexico wrote to Wilson urging recognition of Huerta on the ground that he had complied with the forms of legality and that nothing more could be expected from either Huertistas or Constitutionalists.[45]

Although Wilson's emissary, Governor Lind, a Progressive, initially found the attitude of resident Americans embarrassing—"They have ceased," he charged, "to see things with American eyes, and the disturbing character of [the] elections" [46]—he too soon understood the hopelessness of trying to impose democracy on Mexico by nonrecognition or any other means: "We simply cannot expect elections to be held in the sense they are conducted in the United States. . . . All we can reasonably expect is that homage be decently paid . . . to the forms of democracy . . . and that the laws be observed. . . ." [47] This pessimistic observation did not lead Lind to the conclusion that what Mexico needed was a strong man of the traditional variety, however. Instead he told the President that "The contest now raging in Mexico is political only on the surface; it is essentially economic and social. . . . The agrarian question is a vital factor in the situation." [48]

Since a Huerta dictatorship in the manner of Diaz promised nothing but repression, Lind believed it would not solve this problem. Therefore he urged Wilson to accept a dictatorship for reform in place of an immediate election, once Huerta fell. "When Carranza goes in he will be a dictator for the time being and nothing else. . . . It is only as a dictator that he can accomplish the reforms that are demanded. . . . It seems to me that we should not worry about the [legal] succession." [49] The President gradually came around to this view in 1914 and his interest shifted from political to economic solutions as he came to understand the need for agrarian reform.[50]

Evidence that Wilson now considered reform more important than immediate elections lies in his reaction to the revolt of Pancho Villa. Villa was one of Carranza's henchmen in the Constitutionalist Army. After Huerta's downfall in the summer of 1914, he split with his chief over the spoils just as Huerta and Felix Diaz had in 1913 after they had come to power. Thus, hardly had one civil war ended than another began. Ostensibly, Villa's rebellion was to obtain the immediate elections which Carranza refused.[51] This appeal was calculated to win Wilson's support, but it fell on deaf ears.[52] "The first and most essential step in settling the affairs of Mexico," Wilson wrote Secretary Lansing on August 8, 1915, " is *not* to call general elections. It seems to me necessary that a provisional government essentially revolutionary in character should take action to institute reforms by decree before the full forms of the constitution are resumed." (Emphasis added.) [53]

On October 19, 1915, the United States recognized Carranza's government, thus ending two and a half years of ruptured diplomatic relations without a single popular mandate.[54] The October, 1916 selection of representatives to the Constituent Convention by the people within the territories then controlled by Carranza was the closest the revolution ever came to popular ratification.

Given the conditions in Mexico, elections were an inappropriate method for determining which faction and which rebel chieftain should be president and receive the recognition of the United States. It is to Wilson's credit that he eventually learned this. Whether his policy contributed to or hindered the social revolution which had its formal expression in the Constitution of 1917 is still debated.[55] Probably he could have saved much property and many lives, American as well as Mexican, from destruction in the short run by promptly recognizing Huerta in 1913. In the long run, it is doubtful if Huerta and the old ruling class could have repressed the social unrest of which Madero was only the first manifestation. After all, the cry for free elections began in Mexico not in Washington, D. C. American ideas of democracy had filtered across the northern frontier and influenced the new, small middle class which had grown up under Diaz.[56] American officials only took the idea back from the Mexicans and applied it to the concrete policy problem of restoring an orderly, recognizable, constitutional government there.

It is tempting to speculate whether the Castro revolution in Cuba in 1959 could have been channelled in a direction less dangerous to American security if a more sympathetic understanding of its social and economic goals had been manifested during Castro's first few months in power. E. David Cronon has shown in his study *Josephus Daniels in Mexico*[57] that an American ambassador who is *simpatico,* as Daniels was in the 1930's, can do a lot to mitigate the friction between a revolutionary but non-Communist government like that of Lázaro Cárdenas and the United States. What if some old New Dealer like Henry Wallace had been sent to Cuba as Ambassador in 1959 instead of Philip Bonsal who had a record of association with American companies in Latin America? But then it is inconceivable that men like Eisenhower and Dulles, defenders of the status quo, could have made such a radical gamble as to send such a man.

V

THE DOMINICAN REPUBLIC

American interference in Dominican politics was not the first method applied to the intractable problem of revolutions in that Republic. Our concern originated in the strategic threat to the future Panama Canal posed by their repeated revolutions and the consequent debt delinquency of the Dominican Government which, as in Nicaragua, might precipitate European intervention. In 1904 President Theodore Roosevelt enunciated his "corollary" to the Monroe Doctrine according to which the United States would exercise a kind of preventive intervention whenever it believed that the actions of one of the Caribbean states might provoke such a European intrusion.[1]

The first American action undertaken in fulfillment of the corollary was the negotiation of a customs control convention with the Dominican Republic. Its underlying assumption was that the Dominicans fought their civil wars for control of the revenue of the customs houses and that if these were put under American control the incentive for revolution would be removed and the debts to Europeans could be paid off. The agreement was embodied in a treaty passed by the United States Senate in 1907 and worked well enough that Secretary Knox modelled his draft treaties with Nicaragua and Honduras on it in 1911.[2]

It soon became evident, however, that it was not so much the customs convention as the rule of a strong Dominican executive which preserved order. The assassination of President Caceres (1906-1911) raised the problem of the succession and soon plunged the republic into another series of uprisings and conspiracies which threatened to discredit the American customs receivership. Assistant Secretary Huntington Wilson observed to President Taft with chagrin that "Nearly 90% of the people would be glad to see the revolution succeed. But [it] does not represent the best elements in the country nor are its leaders competent to discharge the functions of Government ... Revolution is not a method for curing evils. ... [Its] success would put a premium on revolution and lead to others. ... Unless this government is prepared to take over management of the Dominican Republic which would produce a hue and cry in Latin America, the solution is difficult."[3]

79

Taft's first reaction to the problem was to send a special Commission composed of William T. S. Doyle, Chief of the Latin American Division of the State Department and Frank McIntyre, Chief of the War Department's Bureau of Insular Affairs in September, 1912. They were directed to effect changes of government personnel and other reforms to restore order pending a new mandate from the people.[4] The rebellious "outs" were clamoring for a fair election, but the Commissioners would placate them only to the extent of forcing the resignation of the unpopular president in favor of an impartial Provisional President, Archbishop Nouel. They accomplished this by threatening to withhold the customs revenues, or if need be, to bring about an American military occupation. Definitive elections were set for May, 1914.

The kindly but ineffective Archbishop lasted only four months as provisional president. In January 1913 he asked for American help in superintending the choice of a regular president at an earlier date but Knox replied that . . . "under the present electoral law it is apparently almost impossible to accomplish much in the direction of free elections, however willing the Government of the United States might be to lend its aid; . . . as a prerequisite to free elections it would seem indispensable to provide some form of previous registration and some form of voting that would prevent fraud." No such reform was possible under the weak provisional government and the country drifted into civil war again while the United States itself was changing administrations.

One of the recommendations of the Doyle-McIntyre Mission had been that we formally declare that we would not recognize any Dominican government attaining power through "armed revolution." This proposal was not immediately put into effect, but when the incoming Wilson Administration found another revolution under way, U. S. Chargé Charles Curtis pressed for, and Secretary Bryan in September 1913 consented to, the announcement of such a threat.[5] Nonrecognition would be a peculiarly effective weapon in this case because it entailed American refusal to pay to the unrecognized government the customs receipts that were the chief source of revenue in the Dominican Republic. Curtis admitted that though this announcement would discourage revolutions, it could not help but encourage dictatorship. The method of nonrecognition had no extended test in Santo Domingo comparable to the Mexican case, however, for the new Minister from Washington promptly adopted a more radical measure to stop the revolution.

Bryan's appointee, James M. Sullivan, arrived in the Republic in the midst of the second civil war in as many years. The threat of non-recognition seemed insufficient by itself so he induced the revolution-aries to consent to an armistice by promising that the United States would guarantee them a free election of delegates to a constitutional convention in the near future. The revolutionists demanded American supervision of the polls, but the Dominican Government objected that this would imply inability on its part to conduct a fair election.[6] In November Sullivan recommended, as a compromise, "a non-interfer-ing scrutiny by open agents appointed by the Department at the prin-cipal towns and polling-places, upon whose joint report the Depart-ment will decide as to the validity of the Constitutional election, the Dominican Government to be informed of our purpose with the assur-ance from us that unless the election of December 15th expresses the will of the people as a whole, the American Government will take full control of the presidential election that follows. . . ."

Bryan made a counterproposal that certain specific conditions be exacted from the Dominican executive: that opposition parties be rep-resented among the judges at each polling place and on the canvass-ing board to which contests should be appealed. But he later accepted Sullivan's suggestion and arranged for three men from the Depart-ment (Hugh S. Gibson, Frederick A. Sterling and Jordan H. Stabler) and thirty agents from Puerto Rico under the American secret police chief there to go and observe the balloting. The Dominican Gov-ernment bitterly opposed the plan and refused to accord official rec-ognition to the observers just as Amador had in Panama.[7] To this President Wilson had Bryan reply ambiguously that the observers came not as a commission, but as individuals to lend "moral support" to the Dominican Government's pledged effort to keep the election free.[8] The observers reported back in December 1913 that there had been a lot of fraud committed by both sides but no governmental intimidation. They cited the victory of 17 out of 24 opposition candi-dates as evidence of the freedom, if not the fairness, of the election. The Mission recommended similar observation of the approaching presidential poll on the ground that it would avoid more radical interference. Minister Sullivan concurred in the request, but a new insurrection interrupted his plans. By that time he was suspected of being partial to the party in power, so the "outs" would not trust American observers under his authority to be objective.

It has been charged that Sullivan suggested the armistice and guarantee of free elections in the fall of 1913 to prevent the imminent downfall by revolution of a government which was favorable to a New York bank to which he was indebted.[9] In refutation it may be pointed out that his method of ending a revolution was no different from Stimson's in Nicaragua in 1927 and that it was a possible interpretation of Secretary Bryan's original instructions to him in September 1913:

"The President directs me to say . . . that the influence of this Government will be exerted for the support of lawful authorities in Santo Domingo, and for the discouragement of any and all insurrectionary methods. You will carry with you a copy of the President's statement of last March [1913] . . . first, that we can have no sympathy with those who seek to seize the power of government to advance their own personal interests . . . and, second, that the test of a republican form of government is to be found in its responsiveness to the will of the people, its just powers being derived from the consent of the governed. . . ."

"We must depend, therefore, upon all the people of Santo Domingo, of whatever party or faction, to join together in securing justice through law and in the election by free and fair ballot of officials whom the people desire."

Sullivan was an ignorant spoilsman in a job beyond his capacities, but the spite with which he was eventually hounded out of office may have had its origin in the rival banking group which he had caused to be displaced in the Dominican Republic, or, it may reflect the wish of the traditional diplomats of the State Department to revenge themselves on an appointee of Bryan's who at least made gestures toward putting into effect the Great Commoner's idealistic, if naive, policy.

The breakdown of Dominican Government in the spring of 1914 led Wilson to take the matter into his own hands. He sent a Commission composed of former New Jersey Governor Franklin Fort and Charles C. Smith to restore order. The plan he handed the Commissioners included provision for a neutral provisional president under whom "At the earliest feasible date . . . elections for a regular President and Congress will be held. . . . The Government of the United States will send representatives of its own choosing to observe the election throughout the republic and it will expect those observers . . . to be accorded the freest opportunities to observe the circumstances and processes of the election."

If the United States Government were satisfied that the proceedings were free and fair it would recognize and support the president and Congress chosen, but "If it should not be satisfied that elections of the right kind have been held . . . another election will be held at which the mistakes observed will be corrected." The observation clause of the plan was incorporated into the agreement of September 8, 1914 reached by the Fort-Smith Commission with the new provisional president. The election was held in October and was closely contested. However, the courts annulled the results in some districts and the losing party withdrew from supplementary balloting which was then held, charging the authorities with large-scale fraud notwithstanding the presence at the polls of American observers.[10] Commissioner Fort reported, to the contrary, that the election was "absolutely free." [11]

The United States fulfilled its part of the bargain by defending the then chosen president, Jiminez, against his enemies for a year and a half until, as we shall see, he resigned, after which American forces occupied the republic and it lost its independence for eight years. Wilson had made the false assumption that all the Dominican politicians wanted was a fair chance to win, when in fact what they wanted was power at any price.

Another familiar method we resorted to in the Dominican Republic was reform of the electoral laws. Bryan and Sullivan were unfamiliar at first with the organizational preconditions of a fair election alluded to by Secretary Knox in his note of the previous January, so they had plunged into the observation of a Dominican election in the Fall of 1913 without assurance that a fair poll was even possible under existing procedures.

In December 1913 the American in charge of the observers resurrected the electoral law reform project in his subsequent report. The elections, he declared, "were held with comparative fairness, taking into consideration an extremely faulty election law. . . . A most general protest is heard on every side against the present election law. . . . It works a great hardship upon the people and practically prevents a full and free expression of their will at the polls by making it very difficult for the majority to get to the polls to vote and by facilitating fraud through repeating. No entirely free elections can be hoped for in Santo Domingo until a census is taken and electoral lists prepared and an entirely new electoral law enacted; . . ."

Consequently, Bryan pushed for amendments to the Dominican constitution and electoral code which would provide for registration of voters, and adequate representation of opposition parties on electoral boards. Despite the failure of the Constitutional Convention to enact these reforms, another American-observed election was held under the old law, as we have seen, in October, 1914 in accordance with the agreement on the Wilson Plan negotiated by the Fort-Smith Commission.

The projected reforms were kicked around as a political football for two more years until the United States occupied the country and took over the government. One may hazard the guess that none of the Dominican politicians really wanted new electoral laws either. Even the "outs" realized that new laws would make their control of the machinery more difficult when they finally got "in".

Just how serious were American officials in demanding free elections in Santo Domingo? Once Sullivan had committed the United States to a guarantee of free elections in order to halt the 1913 revolution, it is manifest from the record that Bryan sincerely intended to carry out that promise and refused to be satisfied with purely pro forma proceedings. Like the American officials in Nicaragua fifteen years later, he whittled away step by step, in response to the protests of the "outs", the advantages normally enjoyed by the party in control of the machinery of government. As in Panama in 1908, this caused the fickle and power-conscious Latin Americans to flock to the standards of the apparent recipients of American favor and produced, despite Bryan's protestations of impartiality, the "out" majority already referred to.

We have seen how in other Latin American states, notably Cuba, the attempts of incumbent presidents to impose their own reelection were a fertile source of revolts. An attempt by Provisional President Bordas of the Dominican Republic to get himself reelected for the regular term had been one of the causes of the September, 1913, revolution which precipitated the first Wilsonian intervention. After the American-observed choosing of delegates in December, 1913, Bordas faced a hostile majority in the Constitutional Convention. But Minister Sullivan now frankly urged Bryan to take sides in the approaching presidential poll: "Bordas is most friendly to our Government and I am disposed to believe is the best possible agency for implanting American ideas of good government in this country. His Government asks me whether the loan can be secured. . . . If this be done it will bear out almost to a certainty his reelection and it will also make the Provisional Government strong enough to deal with Arias . . . who should be eliminated as a bandit."

Bryan balked and insisted on the United States remaining disinterested. He would only go as far as publicly warning the opposition in April 1914 against revolution. When the projected presidential poll was interrupted, as we have noted before, by another uprising, the Secretary, instead of acceding to the Dominican Government's plea for a threat of nonrecognition of the rebels should they win, proposed the resignation of Bordas in favor of another neutral president, despite the failure of this device in 1912 and despite his own rejection of it in Mexico. Perhaps some suspicion of his protegé's motives had entered Bryan's mind. The Phelan Report of 1916 on Sullivan's conduct in the Dominican Republic asserted that because of "the corruption . . . in the Bordas Administration . . . that Government would fall and ought to fall; that upon the basis of the attitude of the Bordas Administration toward free and fair elections it did not deserve support . . ."[12]

Bordas did fall and Bryan probably had the disruptive effects of the Dominican President's ambition for reelection in mind when he got Wilson to add to his mediation plan for the Fort-Smith Commission the next August (1914) the requirement that the new provisional president should not be a candidate himself for the regular term.

Jiminez, the president chosen in the fall of 1914 as a result of the Fort-Smith mission, had no more success than his ephemeral provisional predecessors in controlling the Dominican Congress or the unruly and semi-independent provincial governors. The chief of the latter, General Desiderio Arias, rapidly became the *bete noire* of the State Department. Sullivan had tried to have him stigmatized as a pariah in early 1914. By May, 1916, Minister William Russell advised, after the fall of President Jiminez: "Impossible for any good to come [to] this country by immediate election of President by present Congress because it is probable that Arias or his candidate will be elected. . . . In view of our statements [of the] past few years regarding Arias and also that no more revolutions would be tolerated here, it would seem [that the] final elimination [of] Arias as a political or military factor must now be accomplished. . . . It is my opinion [that] Congress should not be allowed to proceed with [the] election [of a] President. . . ."

Secretary Lansing obliged with the statement that "this Government cannot countenance the election of Arias or any of his friends . . . since the election of any of (them) would result in further revolution and bloodshed."[13] When the Dominican Congress nevertheless designated Francisco Henríquez y Carvajal, a partisan of Arias', as Provisional President, Lansing decided that the "Provisional Government will not be recognized until it shows itself to be favorable to our interpretation of [the 1907] convention . . . and proves itself free from [the] domination of Arias."

Eventually Lansing recommended and President Wilson reluctantly accepted American military occupation to end this impasse. As in Nicaragua the same year, nonrecognition had become a weapon to prevent, not support, free elections when the likely victor was an anti-American revolutionist.

The Marines who occupied the Dominican Republic in 1916 came ostensibly to make free elections possible,[14] but in fact they prevented the selection of another anti-American president and thereafter delayed all elections for eight years. The United States had defined the conditions for democracy ever more strictly until they produced an undesirable winner and the whole policy had to be abandoned temporarily.

The end of the First World War marked the practical disappearance of the strategic threat to American security in the Canal Zone on which the economic, political and military interventions of the United States in the Caribbean area had been directly or indirectly based. Already by March, 1919, the provisional president whom the United States had evicted at the time of its occupation of the Dominican Republic in 1916, pointed out that: "In view of the tremendous magnitude of the issues at stake in the Great War, the United States may reasonably claim justification for their action. . . . However, now that the war has concluded in a victory for the United States . . . all danger . . . in the region of the Caribbean and the Panama Canal has disappeared and such reasons as may have justified the occupation of the country no longer exist. Therefore . . . the United States should now withdraw its military forces and restore the country to the government of its own people."

Other Dominicans, like their Nicaraguan contemporaries, pleaded for American evacuation of their Republic "in conformity with the President's expressed declaration concerning the rights of smaller nations."[15] In the presidential campaign of 1920 the Republicans too made much of Wilson's undemocratic seizure of the Dominican Republic and Haiti[16] and the Republican Congress conducted investigations of American rule there afterwards.[17]

On November 27, 1920, Secretary of State Bainbridge Colby of the lameduck Wilson Administration, wrote Secretary of Navy Josephus Daniels, whose Department was in charge of the occupation: "The increasing agitation among the Dominicans during the last two years for the right of self-government, and the anxiety expressed by the gov-

ernments of other American republics as to our intentions in Santo
Domingo, have caused the Department of State to . . . question whether
the United States might not now well take the first steps in returning
to the Dominicans the Government of their Republic."

The naval and marine officers who administered the country had
austere conceptions of their duty and worked hard to forward the material welfare of their charges,[18] but they regarded the proposal to
restore an elected government as nothing but an encumbrance to their
disinterested labors. The Military Governor of Santo Domingo, Admiral Thomas Snowden, informed the Department of State:

"The question of the election by the people of officers of the Municipal Councils is not a practical matter at the present moment when the
old political parties, a mercenary, grafting, vicious, office-seeking clan
are still awaiting preferment. It is not considered practical just now
for the Military Government to effect its objects with the aid of municipal officers elected by a people who do not yet understand the
proper use of the vote.

"No other form of government can give to these people of the
Dominican Republic what the Military Government is giving them at
this particular epoch in their growth, because it is single-minded in
its devotion to the interests of the Dominican people and works
with an ideal of duty in mind, with no ulterior motives in view." [19]

Hughes, the incoming Republican Secretary of State, overruled the
objections of the military and on June 14, 1921 issued a proclamation
of the conditions under which the United States would withdraw from
the Dominican Republic: "Whereas it is necessary that a duly constituted Government of the Dominican Republic exist before the withdrawal of the United States may become effective, in order that the
functions of government may be resumed by it in an orderly manner. . . ." He then proceeded to outline an elaborate plan of steps by
which such a government would be elected.

At first the occupation forces tried to dictate the procedure whereby
independence was to be restored, as had been done in Cuba. The
relevant steps proposed were:

"1. Appointment by the Military Governor of a Commission of prominent Dominicans to draft a new election law; to this Commission
there should be attached an American Technical Adviser . . . to prepare for the consideration of the Commission a draft of such election
laws. . . .

"4. Convocation of the primary assemblies in accordance with the
provisions of the new election law . . . and the Constitution. These

assemblies shall proceed to elect the electors. . . .

"5. The Electoral College, thus elected . . . shall . . . proceed to elect members of the Senate and Chamber of Deputies. . . .

"7. The Constitutional Convention having been elected in accordance with . . . the Constitution, will proceed to consider the revision of the Constitution. . . .

"11. The Military Governor shall then assemble the Electoral College for the purpose of electing a President in accordance with . . . the new Constitution.

"12. Upon the installation of the President, the Military Governor shall surrender all executive powers assumed by him to the elected executive . . .

The treaty of evacuation was also to protect the economic interests of Americans and improvements built up during the occupation.

Dominican politicians replied to the plan "with a hot blast of protest . . . advising the people not to accept it as this would imply sanction of past wrongs and . . . suggesting that the people refuse to take part in the elections." They were indignant that the Military Governor would not bargain with them for modifications of the plan, but offered it on a "take it or leave it" basis. Also they feared the implication that the American forces would supervise the proposed election to the possible disadvantage of one or another faction.[20] They realized that whoever was left in power when the Americans departed might enjoy a prolonged period of rule. He would have the threat of a new American occupation at his disposal to curb revolutions and no United States guarantee of the freedom of elections beyond the first one to prevent him from staying in power by fraud and force. The Navy Department postponed the balloting and deadlock ensued to the evident satisfaction of the American officers who hoped for a prolonged occupation.[21]

Hughes remained determined to get rid of the political liability of the American occupation. In 1922 he bypassed the military and sent Sumner Welles of the State Department's Division of Latin American Affairs to negotiate a settlement with the Dominican leaders. Welles had little sympathy with military paternalism and doubted that the occupation's material improvements could be lasting when imposed by alien rule and not the result of national effort.[22] He reassured the Dominican politicians that the Department had no desire to have the proposed elections superintended by military officers of the United States but would let a Dominican Provisional Government do it.[23] An Evacuation Convention was therefore signed by four Dominican representatives on July 3, 1922. Welles had a sharp dispute with Admiral Samuel Robison, the current Military Governor, over the evacuation plan but emerged triumphant and forced the latter's replacement.

We have seen that the framing of a new election law was one of the first steps in the various evacuation plans. Strangely enough, the United States had made no move to introduce the long-desired electoral reforms during the first four years of occupation. Possibly the authorities feared that any discussion of political issues would precipitate agitation for independence.

Old line Dominican politicians who had rejected the proposed statutes in 1921 consented to cooperate when permitted to introduce the new law themselves. Once the code was legislated, Hughes had to keep a watchful eye on the Provisional Government lest it "pull the teeth" of the electoral code safeguards with vitiating amendments. One is reminded of the Department's experience with Nicaragua in 1923 and 1928 in this respect. The code, like Dodds' in Nicaragua, was modeled on Crowder's work in Cuba and Minister Russell observed, as others had in the earlier case, that the new electoral law was very complicated and difficult for the Dominicans to understand. It completely revolutionized all previous electoral processes[24] and Commissioner Welles who oversaw its first operation had to admit that it was in the nature of an experiment.

All political parties in the pre-election campaign jockeyed for position and secured technical advantages contrary to the spirit of the law. For instance, two parties, by forming an alliance obtained double the proportion of representatives on the electoral boards that the remaining party had. Welles had the law amended to account for this tactic, but his efforts came to naught, since the losing candidates withdrew when they saw that they had no chance and the final election was uncontested. Nevertheless, he looked back on "the elaboration of a modern electoral code by their own representatives and the holding of free and fair elections by their own Provisional Government in 1924" as far more valuable than the material improvements wrought by the military occupation.

The American Commissioner later wrote a history of the Dominican Republic, significantly entitled *Naboth's Vineyard*, in which he expressed his beliefs about the meaning and necessary conditions for democracy in that country:[25]

• Dominicans had forgotten the theory of democracy from long years of Spanish and Haitian rule. Their leaders had no practical knowl-

edge of orderly procedure in government and no respect for authority
not imposed by force.

• Therefore, the chief menace to orderly, democratic government
was in the utter disregard for the sanctity of the Constitution which
had been amended innumerable times simply for partisan advantage.

• Only the growth of prosperity and education could lead to the
appearance of an electorate able to assure civic consciousness on the
part of the leaders.

• Confidence in the impartiality of the Judiciary as the final arbiters
of electoral disputes was lacking.

• Political parties in our sense had not existed in Santo Domingo.
Their factions were purely personal. It was a continuous struggle
on the part of the "ins" to retain power, and on the part of the "outs"
to return to power. Ephemeral coalitions of factions had broken
down that essential of democracy, a healthy opposition: "The condition is one which cannot be corrected by artificial methods, but . . .
until political parties have been formed, with principles and policies,
personal government is inevitable, and the succession to the Presidency will be dictated by a few politicians, rather than by the great
mass of the plain people, whose interests are the nation itself."

• Finally, a non-political constabulary was necessary. Welles
warned prophetically: "The elements of danger [in this] . . . are ever
present. Should those who compose this force ever become convinced
that their promotion or their well-being depends more upon political
favor than upon their own efficiency and their individual excellence,
the safety of the Republic itself will be jeopardized."

The ironic denouement, in the Dominican Republic as in Nicaragua, of the American plan to "take the army out of politics" in order
to assure free elections was that the Commander of the Constabulary,
Leonidis Trujillo, seized power as dictator in 1930. He remained in
control for thirty-one years with the most brutally authoritarian regime
in Latin America until he was assassinated in 1961.

At the time of Trujillo's coup, in 1930, the State Department displayed a strong aversion to any further involvement in Dominican elections in its instructions to the American Minister: "You are not authorized to suggest any United States participation in or even supervision
of the elections. The last thing we want is to get in a situation where
that would result. . . . The Department desires you to know that it
expects to recognize Trujillo or any other person coming into office
as a result of the coming elections and will maintain the most friendly
relations with him."

VI

HAITI

The case of Haiti closely parallels that of her sister republic on the island of Hispaniola, Santo Domingo. Here too a rapid turnover of governments by revolution exhausted the credit of the state and endangered its independence by threatening to provoke European intervention.[1] Specifically, Secretary Bryan noted German efforts to monopolize Haitian trade and to win influence over its Government.[2]

The first step the United States took in Haiti in January 1914, was to try to obtain a customs control treaty like that obtained earlier from the Dominican Republic. Bryan used the occasion of a Haitian revolution in the fall of 1914 to couple with this proposal the plan of President Wilson for American supervision of elections just put into effect in the Dominican Republic.[3]

The sanction attached to the Wilson plan was of course nonrecognition. Secretary Bryan had accepted the presidencies of two successive revolutionary leaders in May, 1913[4] and February, 1914 as consistent with the President's Statement of March 12, 1913 because they were "duly elected in accordance with the Constitution of Haiti" and were therefore "based upon the consent of the governed", but a third upheaval in eighteen months in November 1914 was too much to brook. This time he tried to make American recognition conditional upon acceptance by the new government of at least the customs control treaty. So rapid were Haitian revolutions though, that he was compelled in December to bow to a *fait accompli* without achieving his goals.

Soon after, in March 1915, the fourth revolt in the two years since President Wilson took office broke out. Bryan now suggested to his chief sending a special Commission to compel the Haitians to submit to American control of their finances and elections.[5] Governor Fort and Charles C. Smith who had performed the identical mission to the Dominican Republic therefore travelled to Haiti. They arrived the day after the triumphant leader of the latest coup had been "regularly and constitutionally elected" and so returned empty-handed.[6]

Subsequently, in May, 1915, Wilson sent Paul Fuller, Jr., to try his hand at negotiating a treaty but with equal ill-success. Fuller recommended that the United States land its marines to obtain a Platt Amendment type of treaty with Haiti.[7]

As early as April Bryan had contemplated a naval demonstration.[8] Bloodshed and a violation of the French Legation in the course of revolution number five gave the United States the excuse in July 1915 it was looking for to intervene and stop the endless cycle of revolutions. As in the Dominican Republic a year later, an occupation ostensibly aimed at protecting democracy actually resulted in its practical extinction for several years. The new Secretary, Lansing, was aware of the inconsistency between the Administration's present action and its past proclamations as he showed in his frank explanation of events to the President on August 13, 1915:

"I confess that this method of negotiation, with our marines policing the Haytien Capital, is high handed. It does not meet my sense of a nation's sovereign rights and is more or less an exercise of force and an invasion of Haytien independence. From a practical standpoint, however, I cannot but feel that it is the only thing to do if we intend to cure the anarchy and disorder which prevails in that Republic. . . . It does not seem to me that the so-called Haytien revolutions are revolutions in fact, but, in reality, represent the struggle of bandits for control of the machinery of government which they utilize solely for the purpose of plunder. None of these so-called 'generals' represent a principle or represent in any way the people of Haiti. . . ."

In preparing for the Fort-Smith mission in February 1915, the perplexed Bryan had directed a questionnaire to the United States Minister in Haiti which reveals the trend of his thoughts about the definition of democracy:

"Was [President] Theodore regularly elected by the Legislature? If so, was he elected for a full term or for the remainder of a term partially expired? If latter how much time remains before the next election?

"When will the Legislature be elected again and what are the qualifications for suffrage? How large a vote is usually polled at the regular elections? . . .

"Was [the Legislature] coerced into the selection of Theodore after his successful insurrection or was he really the choice of the members? . . . Is there a likelihood of their supporting any other successful revolutionists? . . .

"Are there any economic questions involved in the insurrection, or is it purely personal and due to the ambition and popularity of the leaders?"

Minister Arthur Bailly-Blanchard replied ambiguously to the third question: "The Legislature was not coerced into the election of Theodore, who received the entire vote. The proclaiming of a successful revolutionary leader as Chief of the Executive Power is tantamount to his election as President. Upon his entrance in the capital the Chambers are convoked and he is invariably elected. Elections as understood in America do not exist in Haiti. Elections being [sic] simply a continuation of [the] military system under which the country is governed. The population generally takes no part in elections, the voting being done by soldiers acting under instructions. [There are a] few voters who vote many times."

Bryan was disturbed by such a cynical abuse of democracy, but since the Haitian Constitution provided only for indirect election of the President by the Legislature, he had concluded that "there is no way to secure the opinion of the people in regard to any presidential candidate and any successful revolutionist will be able to control the National Assembly." [9] Bailly-Blanchard paid for his realism about Haitian elections by being recalled in March on the charge of having obstructed the Fort-Smith mission.

When Admiral William Caperton landed in July, 1915, he refused to let the overawed Haitian Assembly go through with the farce described above and elect Dr. Bobo, the candidate of the most recent "revolution." Caperton attributed the incessant Haitian uprisings to the professional soldiery, "cacos", who fought for pay and terrorized the civilian, mulatto politicians of the capital. By removing the threat of mercenary violence from the Assembly he arranged the election of a new man, Dartiguenave, who was committed to signing the long-sought American control treaty. [10]

Secretary Lansing's authorization to Caperton for this action on August 9, 1915 shows the change in attitude regarding the significance of elections since Bryan's time: "Allow election of President to take place whenever Haitians wish. United States prefers election of Dartiguenave. . . . I believe that . . . our willingness to have the election of President proceed will have a very salutary effect upon public opinion in Haiti. I do not see why it would not be as easy to control a government with a president as it is to control the Haitian Congress and Administrative officers. . . ."

So it was that the particular circumstances of the occupation permitted the United States to govern Haiti through a puppet president rather than directly by a military governor as in the Dominican Republic.

The American occupation of Haiti proclaimed by Caperton in 1915 lasted for twenty years. Like the shorter occupation of the Dominican Republic, it was characterized by a program of military paternalism compounded here with racial prejudice against the Negroes. This attitude prolonged the period of alien rule because it reinforced the American military rulers' doubts about Haitian capacity for self rule. It was observed of General John H. Russell, High Commissioner to Haiti (1922-1930), that "as a Georgian and a Marine, he represented all that the Haitian elite had found distasteful in the intervention." [11]

The Haitian legislature which Lansing had thought in 1915 would be easy to control obstructed the execution of the American control treaty, so the military governor forced President Dartiguenave to dissolve that body as well as the succeeding legislature which was equally stubborn. Dartiguenave, the military Governor, and Washington officials then drew up a new constitution (Assistant Secretary of the Navy, Franklin D. Roosevelt later claimed to have had a hand in it) and submitted it to a plebiscite of the largely illiterate electorate. The suggestible populace voted for it overwhelmingly which only proved that no substantial body of Haitians was willing to register its opposition to the American occupation openly.[12]

"The whole proceeding," one authority comments, "was farcical, in that the electorate was called upon to pass on a constitution based upon the premise that, for the present at least, the electorate was incapable of selecting representatives capable of passing on such questions." [13]

Although the new constitution was seemingly more democratic in that it reduced the presidential term from seven to four years and provided for popular rather than indirect election of Senators, it contained "transitory articles" which permitted the President to delay the choice of the first legislature as long as he wished and to rule in the meantime through an appointed Council of State.

The State Department condoned the continuation in power every two years of the puppet governments of Presidents Dartiguenave (1915-1922) and Borno (1922-1930). Secretary Hughes did refuse in 1921 to connive at using American influence to secure the election of a pro-American legislature, but his reasons were candidly realistic:

"It is the firm conviction of the Government of the United States that the ends which both Governments desire . . . can only be gained by . . . supporting . . . processes of stable and constitutional government. . . . The foundation upon which such government must rest is

the holding of fair and free elections in which the electorate of Haiti
. . . can participate without coercion of any kind. . . .

". . . If the President of Haiti . . . feels it essential that Legislative
elections be held . . . this Government, while assisting the Haitian
Government to maintain order, will insist that no undue influence be
exerted by the Haitian Executive to control the results of the election.

"[However] *the Department recognizes* the fact *that present conditions* in Haiti would *render it improbable that any truly free elections
could be held, because of the ignorance and illiteracy of the majority
of the voters.* It is *likewise* regretfully forced to the conclusion, that
the results of Legislative *elections, if held without the exertion of
undue influence* by the Haitian Executive, *would probably result in
the election of a National Assembly largely anti-American* in sentiment. . . . [Emphasis added]

"Because of these considerations, the Department has not considered it necessary to advise the President of Haiti to decree the holding
of Legislative elections . . . (and it) would interpose no objection
should the President of Haiti determine to abstain once more from
holding the elections for the National Legislature, and thus permit the
election of his successor to be undertaken by the Council of State. . . ."

Four years later Secretary Kellogg consented to another delay in
elections but admonished President Borno to formulate a plan for
electoral reform under which a legislature might eventually be elected.
These reform proposals were discussed fitfully for two years but
came to nothing.

As the time for the Haitian presidential election of 1930 and the
termination of the treaty of 1915 approached, pressure developed
both among the new Haitian middle class and among American critics
of the occupation policy to hold a legislative election and replace
Borno. Unconvinced that this was a wise course, Commissioner Russell
posed for his superiors in Washington the question "whether . . . the
opinion toward elections in Haiti that has been developed in the
United States . . . is of such importance as to outweigh the logical
conclusion, and to demand the holding of elections regardless of consequences."

Russell suggested four alternatives: (a) "hold elections for the
legislative body and allow it to elect a president in 1930," (b) "have
President Borno decree another two year delay in elections," (c)
"leave the question solely in the hands of the President of Haiti,"
(d) "delay elections again but have the Council of State elect a new
President."

The events of preceding years might have been repeated in 1930. President Borno or some equally cooperative substitute might have been kept in office without benefit even of indirect election until the expiration of the treaty in 1935. But the climate of opinion in Washington favored disengagement from Latin American entanglements for the reasons already discussed in the Nicaraguan case. The opposition group in Haiti tried to force President Hoover's hand by staging riots and a student strike in the Fall of 1929.

Hoover bypassed both the High Commissioner and the State Department and in 1930 he appointed a Commission headed by W. Cameron Forbes of Boston to investigate the situation and devise "sequent steps" for terminating our intervention "even if at the cost of a decrease in efficiency of the Haitian Government." Forbes, like Welles in the Dominican Republic, proved to be no friend of military paternalism despite his experience as Governor General of the Philippines from 1909 to 1913. He charged that General Russell and the Marines had pushed through reforms and policies without explaining them to the Haitians. "Hence they see lots of things being done for them which they don't see the value and object to and only wait for the Marines to leave to undo." [14] The Commissioner had no illusions that a return to elections would end oligarchy in Haiti, but he believed that it was necessary to let the "outs" in to avoid revolution and facilitate American departure. He out-maneuvered the wily Borno by a threat of nonrecognition were the Haitian President to be reelected by his Council of State. Then Forbes forced him to accept a plan whereby a nonpartisan provisional president would be picked for the purpose of holding elections for a legislature which in turn would elect a new President.

One of the principal reforms of the American occupation here as in Santo Domingo and Nicaragua was the creation of a nonpolitical constabulary, the *Garde d'Haiti*. However, this professional police force did not produce a post-occupation dictator as in the other two countries. The President chosen as a result of the Forbes Commission's visit lost no time in exiling the Marine-trained commandant of the *Garde*.[15] President Stenio Vincent himself imposed a quasi-dictatorship on the country when the legisature which had designated him obstructed his policies, but the frequent revolutions of the pre-occupation era were a thing of the past. If the United States had failed to implant democracy in Haiti, it had at least achieved its primary aim by creating stability which lasted until the breakdown of 1957.

COSTA RICA

On January 27, 1917, Federico Tinoco, Minister of War of Costa Rica deposed President Gonzalez Flores. The *coup d'etat* was an egregious challenge to President Wilson's policy pronouncement of March, 1913 regarding non-recognition of revolutionary governments because Costa Rica had been for half a century one of the most stable countries in Latin America with president following president at regular four-year intervals.

Not only did the treason of Tinoco recall unpleasantly that of Wilson's enemy in Mexico, Huerta, but it rapidly developed that there was a tangled web of foreign oil and fruit company rivalries behind recent political events in Costa Rica. A State Department memorandum by Jordan Stabler of the Latin American Division summarized the facts on which Wilson apparently based his policy toward Tinoco:

"From the United Fruit Company's evident desire to inform this Department immediately of Tinoco's *coup d'état* and its insistence that the United States should not intervene, and also in view of the fact that they did not apparently desire to cooperate with the American Minister in sending his cipher message to the Department, and also on account of the connection by marriage between Mr. Keith (of United Fruit) and Tinoco, it would seem that the Fruit Company must at least have known about Tinoco's plot, if it has not aided and abetted him in it."[1]

Stabler then recommended:

"There is no question that Tinoco, aside from the illegality of his action, is absolutely unsuited to be given any recognition by this Government. . . . It is necessary to have in Costa Rica a government which is friendly to the United States, but on the other hand the example which Tinoco has set would have a far reaching baneful effect on the revolutionary parties in the other states of Central America. I feel that a strong policy must be pursued. The President's Latin American policy of 1913 should again be brought clearly to the notice of all Central American governments."

Secretary Lansing portrayed the ousted chief executive, Gonzalez, "as a man of high motives and real patriotism," a "real progressive" who had been overthrown for antagonizing both the foreign companies and

97

the ruling class of the country by his reforms in the taxation and concession laws.[2]   Wilson immediately sympathized with him because of
his own struggles with "the interests" in the United States.   The problem, then, was how to get rid of a revolutionary usurper in order to
discourage future would-be-dictators from "individual unconstitutional
action" in pursuit of their personal ambitions.

The Costa Rican Minister to the United States and other Costa
Ricans urged the American president to follow the precedent of the
Huerta case.   We should withhold recognition until Tinoco held the
elections by which the usurper now proposed to legitimize his coup
and proved his good faith by not being a candidate.   Wilson more than
fulfilled their wishes.   He instructed Lansing to "say to Tinoco that
no government set up by him will be recognized . . . and that no contracts made by any citizen of the United States with such a government
will be recognized by this Government as valid."   Lansing added for
emphasis: "Inform Tinoco that *even if he is elected* he will not be
given recognition.   Free elections were to be the criterion for the
return to recognizable legality.   The taint of revolution could not be
removed merely by following the forms of democracy as permitted by
the 1907 Central American treaty.

Lawyers representing the dictator as well as his American friends
argued that the Huerta analogy was false because there had been no
bloodshed.   They asserted that ex-President Gonzalez' own election
in 1914 was of dubious constitutionality and that he had been
plotting to have himself reelected in 1918.[3]   They arranged to have
Tinoco's rule confirmed by the people and offered to let the Americans
observe the balloting.[4]   Even the services of ex-Secretary Bryan were
enlisted to sway the President, but Wilson replied: "I feel obliged to
retain immovably my position that I will not and cannot recognize a
government which originated in individual unconstitutional action.
This is a test case and I am sure that my yielding in it would break
down the whole morale of our relations, particularly with Central
America. . . . But behind it all, my dear Mr. Bryan, there are contending
business interests in the United States which we ought to be very
careful to disappoint in what is nothing less than an attempt on their
part to use the Government of Costa Rica for their own benefit.[5]

After war broke out with Germany in April, 1917, Lansing sent his
nephew, the later Secretary of State, John Foster Dulles, to investigate
the Costa Rican situation.   Advocates of Tinoco had charged repeatedly that Gonzalez was pro-German and Tinoco pro-Allied, but Stabler
dismissed this factor as "not worthy of consideration."[6]   Dulles now

reiterated this accusation and recommended: "Unquestionably recognition will be the solution of the question most advantageous to the United States in its war with Germany. With recognition we will have in Costa Rica a Government and people with more sincere friendliness to us than any other Central American state. Nonrecognition will, in all probability throw Tinoco into the hands of the Germans and Costa Rica with its strategic position between Panama and Nicaragua will, for a time become a center of German activity."[7]

General Plummer, Commander in the Canal Zone, also recommended recognition of Tinoco for military reasons.[8] Lansing relayed this advice to Wilson and concurred by remarking that "Viewed solely from the standpoint of expediency, it would seem as if the recognition of Tinoco was, under present conditions, probably the better policy . . . I think at the present time the greater issues must alone be considered."

The President's answer to this kind of plea was rigidly idealistic: "I am sorry to find that the letter . . . consists almost entirely of an argument to the effect that the deposed President of Costa Rica was pro-German and anti-American and altogether unworthy. I am not in the least interested in the deposed President and do not see how the argument is apposite in connection with the present questions concerning Costa Rica . . . I have refused to recognize Tinoco in pursuance of a policy with regard to such revolutions which I announced at the very outset of my administration . . . I am following in this matter . . . not a course of policy but a course of principle."[9]

Dulles had warned in his report that nonrecognition was so slow a force that it alone would not discourage revolutions, that it harmed innocent populations, and that if the issue became clearcut between Costa Rica and the United States Tinoco, could secure considerable popular sympathy by appealing to dormant anti-American feeling. He had predicted that it might take more than a year to drive out the usurper. Nevertheless, Wilson at first informed ex-President Gonzalez that while the United States would not recognize Tinoco, it would equally not countenance a fresh personal revolution against him.[10] Reports from the U. S. Chargé d'Affaires in Costa Rica, Stewart Johnson, soon made it apparent that Dulles was correct; "the result desired by [the] Department . . . [is] now dependent on either [an] unduly long further lapse of time or [the] mere chance of [a] successful *coup d' état* unless some military movement is aided from without . . ."

A counter-revolution was not long appearing. Already in December, 1917, Wilson was seriously tempted to support a projected invasion of exiled Costa Ricans from Panama. He admitted that "To have anything at all to do with it is certainly to play with fire and to risk incurring the suspicion of every state in Latin America; and yet, if the man is sincere, what he purposes (always provided his programme does in all good faith include a free and constitutional election) must of necessity claim our sympathy."

Lansing dissuaded Wilson from this rash adventure by arguing that if the President wouldn't follow the course of expediency, at least he should not actively support the reputedly pro-German anti-Tinoco forces. "We are in a peculiarly embarrassing situation in regard to Costa Rica," he warned, "since our settled policy as to nonrecognition of Tinoco, which I feel we ought to continue, runs directly contrary to our interests in prosecuting the war. . . . Only by moral force can a constitutional and duly legalized Government be set up in Costa Rica."

Wilson agreed that Lansing's was the only course honorably open to us, a moral stand in sharp contrast to that taken by the United States in Guatemala in 1954 and in Cuba in 1961, when we actively supported invasions designed to overthrow recognized governments.

Later, in 1918, Johnson suggested in vain that a warship be sent to topple the tyrant in a cable reading: "Situation warrants effort on behalf of democracy against czarism in Costa Rica, more so in view of our fight for same principle in Europe."

In August 1919, two and a half years after his coup, Tinoco came to the end of his resources and resigned in favor of a henchman. Chase, the American Consul at San José, reported that there was likely to be serious trouble in Costa Rica unless an election were held because of the strong public demand for one. Lansing agreed that the United States could not recognize any creature of Tinoco, but that a government had to be formed in accord with the pre-Tinoco Constitution by the depositing of power in the hands of ex-President Gonzalez' "designado" and the holding of free and open elections for president at the earliest possible date.

These requirements were met and the leader of the most recent anti-Tinoco filibustering expedition was elected overwhelmingly, just as Moncada, the successful general in the Nicaraguan revolution of 1927 won the supervised election of 1928. Then, to the surprise and annoyance of his Secretary of State, President Wilson from his sickroom refused to recognize the new President of Costa Rica. He suspected that the United Fruit Company, one of Tinoco's backers, was instrumental in winning the recent election." Only when in 1920 the Costa Rican Congress annulled all of Tinoco's economic concessions would the by now paranoic President concede the purity of the election.

Wilson won his test case, but it was a pyrrhic victory. The three year deadlock undermined confidence in the efficacy of the Central American treaty of 1907 both in Latin America and in the State Department. A Costa Rican, Luis Anderson, one of the leading spirits of the Washington Conference which drafted the treaty, repudiated the Tobar nonrecognition doctrine by 1925. In an obvious allusion to his own country's experience, he called it "lacking in scientific correctness, . . . a remedy [which] may be not only ineffective but in many cases . . . worse than the malady . . . a noble purpose [which] has not accomplished its object . . . of impeding the changes of government that result from revolution. . . ." [12]

During discussion in the State Department about the proper American attitude toward the Leguia revolution in Peru in 1919, an officer of the Latin American Division wrote on a memorandum which urged recognition: "Anything to avoid a second Costa Rica." [13]

Five years later another Departmental officer demurred at a proposal to demand new elections to replace fraudulent ones in Nicaragua with the remark that if the Nicaraguan government refused, [14] "What then? Tinoco got along without our [recognition and] financial aid in Costa Rica."

In Costa Rica, as in Mexico, Wilson had chosen "principle" over "expediency," *i.e.*, national security. This had led him in the latter case to prefer revolutionary reform over stability. In the former case, "principle" had meant refusal to recognize a potentially pro-American president because he had come to power by revolution! The apparent inconsistency dissolves if we remember Wilson's distinction between good and bad revolutions. But why oppose any revolution if not because of its bad effects on American interests? Here we see the danger inherent in making an inflexible "principle" or goal value out of a means or instrumental value.

VIII

HONDURAS

Honduras furnished a test case of the new nonrecognition policy explained in the chapter on Nicaragua even before the Central American treaty of 1907 was signed. Miguel Dávila had displaced President Manuel Bonilla by force earlier in the year 1907. Acting Secretary of State Robert Bacon inquired what steps had been taken to reestablish constitutional government and hold elections for president and congress. He was assured that elections had been called. Thereupon the United States recognized Dávila's provisional government without further ado.[1]

In 1911, four years after the ousting of Bonilla, the ex-president launched a counterrevolution against his successor, Dávila. The State Department sent Thomas Dawson, who had patched up a tenuous coalition in Nicaragua the year before to perform a similar mission in Honduras. Dawson, in effect, named a provisional president and procured a promise "to guarantee absolute liberty to all political parties and to Hondurans in general in the approaching elections." The ineffectiveness of the compact is indicated by the fact that Bonilla was the only candidate.[2]

In 1915 Bonilla's successor, Francisco Bertrand, got around the constitutional prohibition against reelection by resigning in favor of the vice president three months before the balloting. His election also was uncontested. It is a familiar Latin American practice for candidates who expect to lose, usually the "outs," to withdraw and charge fraud in justification of an appeal to arms. In this case however, the Department of State refused to discuss the legality of Bertrand's ruse when a disappointed opponent appealed to the United States not to recognize him. Washington was preoccupied with the neutrality problem in relation to the war in Europe, and so backed "the constituted authorities" in Honduras as in Cuba and Nicaragua the next year.[3]

By 1919, however, the strong stand taken by President Wilson for democracy in Europe had repercussions in Latin America. It became apparent as the quadrennial election approached in Honduras that President Bertrand was determined to impose the unconstitutional succession of his wife's brother-in-law on the country. It was charged that his purpose was to cover up his peculations and perpetuate the jobs of the many relatives whom he had placed in public office. He declared himself dictator and tried to intimidate the opposition, thereby provoking a revolution. Both opposition candidates asked for American aid in the form of a threat of nonrecognition or the sending of troops. Even the Honduran Minister in Washington secretly asked that the United States take steps to assure freedom of elections.[4]

Secretary Lansing laid the problem before President Wilson in these terms: "Should the revolution be successful, a similar situation to that which arose in Costa Rica will be created in Honduras; with the added danger, in this case, of complication in Central American politics, owing to secret treaties negotiated between President Bertrand and Salvador and Mexico. Should the Government of the United States exert its influence to the end that free presidential elections shall be held, the revolution will cease and a legitimate government will come peacefully into power. The question imposed [sic] before the Government of the United States at present, is shall a situation similar to that which prevailed in Costa Rica under General Tinoco be permitted, through non-assistance to the people of Honduras, or shall it not."[5]

This episode is a good illustration of the sequence of policy instruments which the United States had at its disposal for securing free elections, each more coercive than the preceding one. They were:

1. Diplomatic Representations and Protest. As early as March, 1919 the Acting Secretary of State instructed the United States Minister to Honduras "to intimate orally to President Bertrand that this Government expects a fair election in Honduras. . . ."[6] Bertrands's anti-American advisers from Mexico and El Salvador were inciting him to go ahead with his plans on the theory that the United States would not do more than protest.[7]

2. Threat of Nonrecognition. The Department thereupon felt that it was being put to the test. In July, therefore, Minister Jones was directed to warn that the United States was scrutinizing conditions closely because "its future attitude toward those in control of the political destinies of [Honduras would] be guided by their actions."[8] Bertrand replied evasively that Honduras was a republic in name only because of the ignorance of its people, that it must be governed by an "iron hand," and that orderly succession could only be by the officially designated candidate.[9] Whatever his motives may have been, he at least had some notion of the necessary prerequisites of democracy.

3. Good Offices. Soon after Secretary Lansing returned from the Paris Peace Conference to Washington in July 1919, he proposed to President Wilson that the United States offer its good offices to the

factions which were by then on the brink of civil war. He found the
situation analogous to 1911 when the United States invited the disputants to confer aboard an American warship. Such an action, he
thought, might obviate the necessity of proceeding in a more forceful
manner later.[10]

4. Observation of Elections. Since the above proposal met with
no response, Lansing concluded his presentation of the problem to
Wilson, already cited, with a further step: "The Government of the
United States has, in the past, assisted the Republic of Cuba and the
Republic of Panama in maintaining order and assuring free elections.
A similar course would seem highly desirable in the case of Honduras.
In order to avoid a situation similar to that which arose in Costa Rica,
it is necessary for the Government of the United States to assist in
overseeing the elections for president that are to occur in October."

Wilson assented reluctantly, but the move was stillborn because in
the meantime hostilities began between the rival candidates.

5. Threat of Force. In May the Department of State had suggested
to the Navy Department that, since diplomatic representations to
Bertrand were not having much effect, a warship might visit Honduras
for moral effect. In September the Latin American Division of the
Department proposed, and Acting Secretary Phillips transmitted, a
threat of the ultimate sanction, an armed expedition: "President Bertrand has been sent a number of 'toned down' messages in the last four
months none of which have had the slightest effect. I believe, therefore, that a strong message should be sent in the hope that it would be
effective, but with the idea of taking forceful action if the message
alone does not accomplish the desired result. . . . I have included a
line in the cable regarding the destruction of lives and property in
Honduras so that we may have protection to American interests as
additional justification for our action."[11]

This menace on top of the revolt of his enemies was enough to force
Bertrand's resignation (September 8, 1919).

It proved to be easier to get rid of President Bertrand than to get
his victorious enemies to permit a genuinely free ballot. The United
States did secure the succession of an impartial provisional president,
the second *designado*, but it could not prevent a split between the two
factions which had helped oust Bertrand. General Rafael López
Gutiérrez, the candidate who had led the revolution, took advantage
of his military superiority to assure his victory at the polls. The
adherents of Dr. Membreño, his erstwhile ally, complained bitterly to
the State Department and asked for a postponement of the election

until López' forces were demobilized. Phillips hinted at nonrecognition, reasserted American impartiality, and tried to effect a reconciliation, but in vain. As the commander of the U. S. S. *Baltimore* reported from the scene, "As a matter of fact, neither wants a free, fair election. The Gutierristas want me to make . . . sure [*sic*] the election of Gutiérrez. Should it be necessary to call for intervention, as seemed true in the day of Bertrand, they crave intervention. If his election is sure, intervention is a crime and a man suggesting it is a traitor to his country. So also with the Membreñistas. . . ." [12]

Rather than prolong the crisis, Lansing bowed to the *fait accompli* and recognized the victor.

It can hardly be said that the United States improved the quality of democracy in Honduras and it certainly did not prevent civil war but only speeded its termination. One unintended by-product of American intervention was to enable Germans whose properties had been expropriated during the World War to recover them, for the Germans financed the successful revolution just as the United Fruit Company was reported to have financed Bertrand's unsuccessful bid for continued power. [13]

The interest of the United States in preventing revolutions that were sure to attend imposed successions like that of 1919 in Honduras was enhanced as we have seen by the new, more specific nonrecognition clauses of the Central American Treaty of 1923. [14] The first case to arise under the new treaty, as under the old, was in Honduras. Four years after the crisis of 1919 the political situation of that year was repeated even to the detail that it was a president's brother-in-law who was chosen as successor. But this time the "outs" of 1919 were "in" and López Gutiérrez showed every intention of perpetrating fraudulent elections of the very kind he had ostensibly revolted against before. This blatant inconsistency undoubtedly helped to alienate the State Department's sympathies from him just as Emiliano Chamorro's *volte face* on American supervisions of elections did in Nicaragua later.

Dana G. Munro, American authority on Central America whose activities in Nicaragua we have recounted earlier was at that time Assistant Chief of the Division of Latin American Affairs. He pointed out the significance of the problem in a Division Memorandum of February 19, 1923: "Either [imposed] election of Lagos or a successful revolution would create a situation very embarrassing to the Department. The recently signed General Treaty of Peace and Amity . . . is not legally binding on the United States, but it can't disregard the principles established by the treaties without undoing the work of the recent conference. The existence of an unrecognized government in

Honduras would be a grave danger to the peace of all Central America. External interference as before 1907 might cause international wars in Central America. This danger is by no means an imaginary one. . . . I believe that there would be a fair chance of preventing a dangerous situation from arising if the United States Government exerted its influence to persuade President López Gutiérrez to permit a free election. . . . It is of course not certain that even the holding of a free election would eliminate the danger of revolution, but it would greatly diminish this danger and it would give the United States some ground on which to base its policy if disturbances should afterwards occur." [15]

Again a sequence of methods was employed. They were:

1. Diplomatic Representation and Protest. In accordance with Munro's advice Secretary Hughes dispatched the usual diplomatic note expressing interest in the maintenance of constitutional government in Honduras, regret should a candidate be imposed or a revolution break out, and confidence that President López who came into office as the result of a popular movement which aimed to vindicate the principle of electoral liberty proposed to uphold this principle in the forthcoming election.[16] The note, like others of its kind. was ignored.

2. Coalition Government. It will be recalled that Munro had urged a policy of "establishing an administration which fairly represents the best elements in the community . . by an agreement between the party leaders" in his influential study, *The Five Republics of Central America* published in 1918. It is not surprising therefore to find him advocating the same solution in Honduras.[17] The Secretary again took his advice and expressed "hope that a way may be found to avoid . . . disturbances *either* by agreement between the various factions upon one compromise candidate *or* by holding a free election." [18]

Neither Munro's Division Chief, Francis White, nor U. S. Minister to Honduras, Franklin Morales, agreed with the former alternative which amounted to a by-passing of free elections. Both expressed themselves in favor of having the two traditional Honduran parties each unite on a single candidate "to educate the people of Honduras in the elementary principles of democratic republican government." [19] This arrangement would forestall a three-cornered race in which no candidate might obtain a majority. In the end, both approaches to the problem came to nothing since the rival candidates could not agree upon compromises, either intra-party or inter-party.

3. Threat of Nonrecognition. By June, 1923, the political impasse had created so much uncertainty that American efforts to rehabilitate Honduran finances were jeopardized. Therefore Hughes took a more

threatening step by announcing on June 30, 1923 that: "The attitude of the Government of the United States with respect to the recognition of new Governments in the five Central American Republics whose representatives signed at Washington on February 7, 1923 a General Treaty of Peace and Amity, to which the United States was not a party, but with the provision of which it is in the most hearty accord, will be consonant with [its] provisions."

The Honduran candidates discounted this pronouncement as a bluff. Evidently it impressed President López sufficiently, however, to induce him to keep the voting that fall free enough so that Carías Andino, the opposition candidate, received a plurality of the votes. The various factions of the government party shared the rest. This result threw the election into the Congress, where a deadlock soon developed.

The United States then faced a new kind of problem for the solution of which its own experience offered little guidance. Fortunately our two party system had afforded clearcut electoral decisions on most occasions and had allowed the outcome to be decided in Congress only once, in 1824. The danger was that President López would contrive a coalition of factions in the Honduran congress to deprive Carías of his plurality victory and thereby incite the cheated candidate to revolt. A similar problem arose in Peru in 1962.

Hughes had at first interpreted the 1923 treaty to mean that its provisions applied only in the case of a coup d'etat or revolt by the opposition,[20] but by December he reversed himself and threatened ". . . that the Government of the United States would find it fully as difficult to recognize an administration placed in office by oppressive measures on the part of the existing authorities as to recognize an administration coming into power by any other unconstitutional procedure . . . "

When President López took advantage of the Congressional impasse to proclaim himself dictator on the expiration of his term, Hughes withdrew United States recognition from him.

4. Force: Military Occupation. The long delayed revolution burst forth in the Winter of 1924. This time the United States dispatched warships to both coasts of Honduras and sent a column of marines to the capital for the protection of foreign lives and property in the chaos which accompanied the departure of the losing government forces. The State Department was then in a better position to insist upon a compromise solution than it had been in 1919. Military intervention alone did not succeed in imposing agreement on the warring factions. No sooner had one coalition of generals won the upper hand than it split apart over the question of which general should be presi-

dent just as in 1919. Each faction then bid for the support of the defeated government leaders.

5. Mediatory Mission. The situation seemed to require another mediatory mission like Dawson's in 1911. In April 1924, Hughes prevailed upon President Coolidge to appoint Sumner Welles, the successful negotiator of the evacuation of our forces from the Dominican Republic, to be his personal representative for mediation of the Honduras civil war.[21] The Secretary of State suggested to Welles that an appropriate solution would be "either the election of a constitutional President by the existing Congress or the establishment of a provisional government of such a character as to give assurance that new elections could be held under conditions of freedom and fairness."[22]

While Welles was carrying on negotiations between the parties, the rebels completed their victory in the civil war and lost interest in compromise. It was only the presence of United States naval forces which enabled Welles to exact a face-saving agreement from them, the "Pact of Amapala." The pact provided for a neutral provisional president who was to convoke elections for a constituent assembly and then guarantee the free choice of a constitutional president for the next term. The crucial arrangement was for a coalition cabinet like that of 1919 to make the "guarantee" effective, but it was not carried out.

The chiefs of the revolution continued to jockey among themselves for the presidency. Hughes finally succeeded in forcing their withdrawal from candidacy by a threat of nonrecognition under the 1923 treaty,[23] but inevitably the vote merely ratified the victory of the revolutionists.

As in Cuba and Nicaragua, the Department of State by this time was becoming wary of the ceaseless attempts of Honduran politicians to win American endorsement or intervention on their behalf. The next Secretary of State, Frank Kellogg, commended Chargé d'Affairs, Lawrence Dennis, in 1925 for telling the Honduran Government that its problems should be solved by native statesmanship, not by American arms: "The Department feels that no lasting improvement can be attained in Central America as long as all parties look to Washington for the last word. Unless there is responsibility among the people themselves for the conduct of their Government and a desire among the people themselves for improved conditions, any efforts on the part of this Government would appear to be illusory. . . . The center of Honduran political activities is in Honduras and not in Washington and . . . regeneration must come from within."

The Department's long standing concern lest political instability in

Central America provoke European intervention was not the only American interest operating in these Honduran electoral disputes. Behind the rivalries of Honduran politicians and generals stood foreign economic interests which hoped to gain from the victory of one or another faction. As we have seen in the 1919 episode, the chief of these interests were the American fruit companies which had bought up confiscated German property in the First World War, lost it again after the revolution of López Guitiérrez and proposed to regain it in 1923.

Representatives of the Cuyamel Fruit Company and the Standard Fruit & Steamship Company bombarded the State Department with partisan appeals in which they skillfully adopted the language of free elections, for instance: ". . . the defenders of [the capital] represent practically no popular element but merely the ambitions of a few professional politicians desiring to perpetuate themselves in office, whereas the following of Generals Carías, Ferrera, Tosta and Martínez Funes [the rebels], represent the will of practically the entire people. . . . The Revolution disrupts [our] work all [we] want is the organization of a stable government." [24]

Commissioner Welles was not deceived by this kind of talk and reported indignantly: "[I believe] that the disasters which have lately overwhelmed the Republic of Honduras can in large measure be attributed to the direct intervention of certain important American interests located in that Republic. . . . It was difficult for the members of the Liberal Party . . . to understand that the policy of the Government of the United States was one of complete impartiality between Conservative and Liberal parties . . . when the forces of the revolution were paid and armed with American money and American arms and ammunition given by American business interests and when the property of these same interests was protected against the forces of the Liberal party by the warships . . . of the United States Government." [25]

Thus it cannot be said that the United States was unwittingly pushed into intervening in Honduran elections on behalf of private economic interests. Contrary to the assertions of economic determinists, it went in despite such interests. Inevitably though, its intervention had unintended favorable effects on the position of those interests, effects which were probably much more lasting than any slight gains to Honduran democracy which may have resulted.

The polls of 1928 and 1932 were relatively free as proven by the fact that the party out of power won in both cases. [26] Then just as in Nicaragua, the Dominican Republic, Haiti, and Cuba, a dictator emerged in the 1930's as the chief legatee of the United States' free election policy. He held power for sixteen years by repeatedly prolonging his term of office. He was none other than General Carías Andino, the candidate of 1923 and the leader of the revolution of 1924 whose slogan was "free elections."

IX

EASTERN EUROPE

For a decade after the inauguration of the Good Neighbor Policy toward Latin America in 1933 the interest of the United States in free elections abroad was dormant. In fact, the State Department leaned so far over backwards in treating Latin American dictators like Batista, Somoza and Trujillo to state visits in Washington and military aid that liberals of both continents, forgetful of their own earlier demands for nonintervention, accused us of maintaining these tyrants in power.[1] A whole structure of pan-American treaties was built up which made it increasingly difficult for the United States ever legally to resume any of the methods we have discussed for the promotion of democracy in the hemisphere: diplomatic interference, nonrecognition, military intervention, all were prohibited.[2]

Thus it was that our next involvement with free elections came during World War II in an entirely different quarter of the globe, Eastern Europe, where the United States had practically no prior experience and therefore has not applied its hard-earned lessons from experience in Latin America. The dispute in Eastern Europe has differed in two vital respects from the Latin American cases: it has been part of a "cold war" contest between the United States and another Great Power, Russia, and it has taken place in an area where, far from enjoying the military predominance we have had in the Western Hemisphere, we have been at a distinct disadvantage in power. The similarities which, on the other hand, make the comparison fruitful and provide continuity are firstly that in much of Eastern Europe the conditions for democracy are almost as lacking as in Latin America, and secondly that the demand for free elections came as much from indigenous political leaders as from Americans.

The causes of a Great Power rivalry like the cold war between the United States and the Soviet Union since World War II are many. There is a natural tendency for victorious allies to fall out over the division of the spoils. The Allies who finally defeated Napoleon almost went to war among themselves during the Congress of Vienna over the Polish-Saxon question. Without the common foe to unite them, minor irritations are magnified out of all proportion as the policy-makers and opinion-leaders on both sides become engrossed in the day-to-day struggle with the new rival. Autocratic Czarist Russia loomed almost as implacably and dangerously to liberal Britons throughout the nineteenth century as Communist Russia does to us today. The feud gathers a momentum of its own over the years until the participants lose all detachment and forget the original causes of dispute or else the causes are simplified into unquestioned formulae suitable only for propaganda purposes. Scholarly objectivity becomes difficult then even in a democracy. Yet, as Professor Morgenthau has warned us,[3] if diplomacy is to be revived as an alternative to war, we must develop the ability "to look at the political scene from the point of view of other nations" as well as our own.

The most persistent and publicized of the Western demands in the cold war has been for "free and fair elections" in Eastern Europe. How did this particular goal become a bone of contention, a symbol of the growing ideological and power contest between the rival superpowers?

The origins of the cold war are imbedded in the war aims of the preceding world conflict. Herbert Feis has reminded us that the three Great Powers allied against Germany and Italy in the second world war, Great Britain, the United States, and the Soviet Union, had only one war aim they shared: the defeat of Nazi Germany.[4] For Great Britain, the first to join combat with Hitler, it was a war of sheer survival. Winston Churchill made this clear when he promptly extended offers of help to his old enemies, the Russian Communists, immediately after the German attack on Russia in June 1941. A single-minded concentration on winning the war to the neglect of postwar political considerations is usually attributed only to the Americans. Churchill is applauded for his foresight in advocating landings on the "soft underbelly" of Europe to preclude Soviet occupation. Yet he is said to have replied to reproaches about aiding the Yugoslav Communist Partisans instead of the Chetniks in 1943. ". . . the less you and I worry about the form of government they set up, the better. That is for them to decide. What interests us is which of them is doing the most harm to the Germans?"[5] Insofar as Churchill could afford independent war aims despite Britain's being militarily the weakest of the three, he pursued traditional balance-of-power goals: the restoration of the nineteenth-century European state system, the preservation of the British colonial empire, and the safeguarding of the established social and economic order.

Beyond these narrowly national and class interests which could hardly be expected to inspire Americans, Churchill was the past master at articulating the universal values of democracy. It was on this level that he reached agreement with the leaders of the United States. President Franklin Roosevelt and Secretary of State Cordell Hull were both deeply suspicious of Churchill's Tory predilections for monarchy, empire, and traditional diplomacy, but they could share with him at least the democratic slogans, if not the optimistic expectations, of the Wilsonian and Lloyd George liberals of the first world war. Thus it was easy for them to draw up together the provisions of the Atlantic Charter in 1941 even before the United States formally entered the war. Among these principles are to be found two expressions of national self-determination, that touchstone of the liberal program in the international sphere:

"Second. They desire to see no territorial changes that do not accord with the freely expressed wishes of the peoples concerned;

"Third. They respect the right of all peoples to choose the form of government under which they will live; and they wish to see sovereign rights and self-government restored to those who have been forcibly deprived of them. . . ." [6]

Free elections or plebiscites were implicit in both principles.

Could the Soviet Union subscribe to this common denominator of war aims and thus convert the United Nations from an expediential military alliance into a more enduring association upon which to build a permanent peace organization after the war? The first British approaches to Stalin in 1941 revealed that the Communist dictator at the very nadir of his fortunes was interested most in securing British and American acceptance of his territorial aggrandizements of 1939 to 1941: the Baltic States, Finnish Karelia, Eastern Poland, and Rumanian Bessarabia.[7] He also wanted recognition of Russia's special interests in Rumania and Finland proper. In return, he was quite prepared to concede British postwar military domination of Western Europe including bases in France, Belgium, the Netherlands, Norway, and Denmark. Acquisition of the former group of Eastern European countries was the fruit of his collaboration with Hitler under the Molotov-Ribbentrop Pact. To condone their seizure would therefore have been a hard pill for the British to swallow even had there been no Atlantic Charter. But Southeastern Europe was the area over which the Soviet dictator had quarreled with Hitler in 1940, thus bringing upon his country the German invasion. He would hardly settle for less than a sphere of influence there from Britain, a more distant and weaker partner.

In addition, Stalin too could argue in terms of the language and procedures of national self-determination that the Russians had conducted plebiscites in these areas before annexing them.[8] Britain was willing to overlook the fraudulent character of these totalitarian elections for fear that continued insistence on the point would drive Russia into a separate peace with Germany as had happened in 1918 and 1939.[9] Roosevelt continued until the Teheran Conference in 1943 to press for new plebiscites, which were a favorite panacea of his, to be held in the Baltic States and Eastern Poland.[10] In any event, the Soviet emissary signed the Declaration of the United Nations which incorporated the principles of the Atlantic Charter on January 1, 1942, but with the vague yet significant reservation that the practical application of these principles would necessarily adapt themselves to the circumstances, needs, and historic peculiarities of the particular countries.[11]

One encouraging aspect of these early inter-Allied negotiations was precisely that Soviet demands were so entirely in the realm of traditional national security goals—border changes, bases, and spheres of influence. Roosevelt and his advisers got the impression that Stalin was working for Russia rather than for world communism.[12] The dissolution of the Comintern and the signing of the Czech-Soviet treaty reinforced this belief. The latter agreement pledged the Russians not to interfere in the domestic affairs of Czechoslovakia when the Red Army liberated the country.[13]

Hull, however, was opposed to playing the game by the old balance-of-power rules. In 1942 he succeeded in preventing a secret protocol from being added to the Anglo-Soviet Treaty of Alliance which would have fixed Russia's western frontiers at a time when she had minimal bargaining power. Hull relied instead upon the principles of the Atlantic Charter to circumscribe Stalin's territorial ambitions. Further, he tried to forestall any unilateral determination of the form of government in reconquered states by occupying armies. At both the Quebec and Moscow conferences in 1943 he negotiated for a "Declaration of Four Nations on General Security." Point six promised that after the termination of hostilities "they will not employ their military forces within the territories of other states except for the purpose envisaged in this declaration and after joint consultation."[14] Hull's motive was to avoid the danger that bickering over secret treaties would disrupt the common war effort or come back to haunt the peacemakers after the war as happened in 1919. It is open to question whether an earlier and more precise definition of Allied war aims in Eastern Europe would have had any effect on Soviet behavior once the Red Army flooded over the area, but at least it might have clarified the issues between the Allies and prevented some illusions from developing in the West about the likely nature of the postwar settlement. Many writers on the subject have argued with hindsight that the United States should have doled out its Lend-Lease aid to Russia in the latter part of the war only on the condition that the Soviets abided by the Moscow Declaration.

As it happened, the first enemy or enemy-occupied countries to be invaded by the United Nations were not on the Soviet front. Instead, French North Africa and Italy were the first to crumble before Allied assaults in 1942-43. The American and British governments and their commanders in the field handled the armistice negotiations and organized military government in these areas to suit themselves. These unilateral actions must have confirmed to the Russians what their Marxist-Leninist ideology would already have led them to expect: the army which reached and occupied a country first would dictate its form of government.[15]

True, the Western Allies made ringing declarations that the French and Italian people should decide for themselves who would govern them. Free elections were talked about for the first time as the criterion of democracy. In practice, however, deals were made with enemy authorities to facilitate surrender, with Admiral Darlan in North Africa and with General Badoglio in Italy, which gave promise of more conservative versions of "democracy" than could ever be acceptable to the Soviets in their own neighborhood.[16] Free elections were ultimately held in both France and Italy and Communists sat in their coalition cabinets until 1947, but they proved to be no more effective in the Soviet cause than the democratic members of coalition cabinets in Eastern Europe were to be in ours. Especially indicative was Churchill's defense of the Italian and later the Greek monarchies as barriers against communism. Clearly the likelihood of social conflict if not of international war between communism and democracy was already in Churchill's mind in 1943. He wanted to draw the line between the two systems, which he was to dub the "Iron Curtain" in 1946, as far east as possible. The line could in fact have been drawn about a hundred miles further east in 1945, thereby including Berlin, Prague, and Vienna on our side. This would have saved us from our present difficult position in the first city, obviated years of tedious negotiation over the Austrian treaty and possibly kept at least the Czech part of Czechoslovakia free; all at the cost, however, of a weakened moral position in the cold war because we then could not have been sure but that the conflict was our fault for not having honored our agreements with the Soviets.

In Italy, Soviet liaison personnel were tardily informed of Western political plans and then all too frequently presented with accomplished facts. Stalin asked for the formation of an Allied Military-Political Control Commission to consider negotiations with Germany's allies as they surrendered. At the Moscow Conference of Foreign Ministers, a month after the Italian surrender, Molotov won agreement on seven urgent political measures for the extinction of fascism in Italy and the creation of an all-party cabinet. But here, as in France and Belgium the next year and as in Japan in 1945, the circumstances of liberation decided from the beginning which conception of democracy, Western or Soviet, would win out. Fortunately for us, free elections in none of these countries have produced a Communist majority.

The Soviet government later maintained with some plausibility that the organization of Allied control in Italy was a good model for use in countries liberated by the Red Army.[17] They ruthlessly exploited their military advantage to impose Communist rule on Germany's other allies, Rumania, Bulgaria, and Hungary, before the eyes of the helpless Western members of the Allied Control Commissions. I do not mean to imply by this comparison that the two forms of government are equally good or that the Soviets would not have communized their sphere of occupation whatever we did in ours. I wish only to point out how our actions must have looked from the Soviet point of view.

Poland was the test case for the Soviet interpretation of the principles of the Atlantic Charter and the United Nations Declaration. This was both because it was the country in whose defense Great Britain finally went to war with Germany and because it was the first Allied state which Russian troops entered in pursuit of the retreating Germans. When Roosevelt had asked British Foreign Minister Eden in March 1943 if he thought that the Soviets were determined to dominate Europe by force after the war, the latter was still able to reply in the negative. He did add, though, that while the Soviet Government would not insist on having a Communist government in Poland, it would demand a friendly one.[18] Both the British and Americans acknowledged the legitimacy of this aspiration. As Stalin repeatedly pointed out, Poland had been the corridor through which Germany attacked Russia twice in thirty years. Any Russian government, Communist or not, would be determined that the Polish government must be friendly to it and not just a neutral playing her two great neighbors off against each other.   Czar Alexander I would have understood and approved Stalin's demands in this area.

Several acts of the Polish government-in-exile were apparently regarded by Stalin as proof positive of its "unfriendliness": its dogged refusal to negotiate over changes in Poland's eastern frontier, its insistence on retaining the authoritarian constitution of the prewar Polish regime, and its public demand that the International Red Cross investigate the Katyn massacre of captive Polish officers.   By contrast, Finnish conservatives like Paasikivi were flexible enough to win the Soviet dictator's confidence despite their country's wartime alliance with Germany.   Stalin broke diplomatic relations with the London Poles in April 1943 and set about creating a Communist-dominated substitute, the later Lublin government, to enter Poland in the wake of the Red Army.   The controversy over which of these governments, London or Lublin, or what combination of them should rule Poland took up much of the time of the Big Three meetings at Teheran and Yalta.   The Western Allies began to think of free elections as the proper test to decide which claim to represent the true will of the Polish people was valid.

This argument with Communist Russia was a new kind of debate for the Western democracies.   In their fight with Nazi Germany, Fascist Italy and Imperial Japan, the issue was clear-cut because the respective ideologies were diametrically opposed.   Now they had to meet an opponent who used the same language of democracy, self-determination, and anti-imperialism, but with an entirely different meaning. As Churchill commented: "Far more than Poland was involved.   This was the test case between us and the Russians of the meaning of such terms as democracy, sovereignty, independence, representative government, and free and unfettered elections." [19]

The fundamental incompatibility between the Soviet goal of a friendly Poland and the Western objective of a Polish government representative of the popular majority was long obscured by the adamant position of the government in exile on the Polish boundary issue.   The British were especially vulnerable to Soviet arguments in this matter because the Curzon line of 1919 which Stalin now demanded for Russia was a British decision as to the eastern border of the undeniably Polish ethnic area.   For the Poles to reject it even when offered compensation in the west at Germany's expense lent substance to Stalin's accusations of unfriendliness or at least indicated an utter lack of realism on the part of the exiled Polish leaders.   There was, after all, some cogency to the analogy the Russian dictator drew when he wrote to President

Truman in April 1945: "The question of Poland has the same meaning for the security of the Soviet Union as the question of Belgium and Greece for the security of Great Britain. . . . I do not know whether there has been established in Greece a really representative government, and whether the government of Belgium is really democratic. The Soviet Union was not consulted when these governments were being established there. The Soviet Union did not lay claim to interference in these affairs . . ." [20]

Stalin might have added that the United States has jealously maintained a more loosely controlled yet nonetheless real sphere of influence in Latin America under the Monroe Doctrine for many years. Purely from the point of view of national security, there is something to be said for the analogy between recent American indignation at Soviet encouragement of Castro's anti-American policy in Cuba and Stalin's attitude toward American efforts to install a freely elected and thereby anti-Russian regime in Poland.

Roosevelt occasionally showed some awareness of the contradiction between free elections and a pro-Soviet Polish government. He told Eden in 1943 that "while there might be a liberal government in Poland at the time of the Peace Conference, they might well be thrown out within a year." [21] Churchill, too, advised the London Poles after the Teheran Conference to accept political dependence on the Soviets as though they had been defeated in war. [22]

The Polish exiled politicians and their friends in the Polish underground took up the cry for free elections with fervor just as Latin American politicians, when out of power, have demanded that the United States intervene in their countries to compel the parties in power to assure a free ballot. They were apparently confident that the ancient hatreds of the Poles for the Russians would win for them in any really fair electoral contest, so their speeches and proclamations of war aims early and consistently emphasized free elections as the criterion for that democracy to which all of the United Nations were publicly pledged. [23] For some of the Polish leaders like Mikolajczyk, the appeal was probably genuine. For others, their records under the prewar Pilsudski dictatorship speak for themselves.

Did Stalin ever entertain the hope that a majority of Polish voters would freely choose a party or combination of parties which he could trust to remain friendly to him after the Red Army departed from Polish soil? Nothing in his previous record or in the Leninist ideology could lead us to believe that he would take such a chance. Yet some writers do assert that both the Russians and the native Communists were surprised and disappointed by the extent of their defeat in the free elections held in Austria and in Hungary in the fall of 1945.[24] These setbacks may simply have confirmed the opinion Stalin had given at Potsdam that "any freely elected government in these countries will be an anti-Soviet government, and we cannot allow that."[25]

The United States, as we have seen, had long experience with trying to foster free elections in the poorly prepared countries of Central America and the Caribbean during the first third of the century. This should have warned the American leaders of the difficulties in carrying out that policy. But such is the discontinuity of democratic foreign policy-making that almost no one raised any objection when the demand for free elections was written into the Yalta Declaration on Liberated Europe in February 1945:

"The establishment of order in Europe . . . must be achieved by processes which will enable the liberated peoples . . . to create democratic institutions of their own choice. This is a principle of the Atlantic Charter—the right of all peoples to choose the form of government under which they will live. . . . To foster the conditions in which the liberated peoples may exercise these rights, the three Governments will jointly assist the people in any European liberated state or former Axis satellite State . . . to form interim governmental authorities broadly representative of all democratic elements in the population and pledged to the earliest possible establishment through free elections of governments responsive to the will of the people and to facilitate where necessary the holding of such elections."[26]

An agreement on Poland spelled out the conditions for "free and unfettered elections" even more explicitly.

Anthony Eden voiced some qualms to Secretary of State Stettinius, saying privately that it was asking rather a lot of the U.S.S.R. to get assurances of really free elections in Poland.[27] The only cautionary note on the American side was from Secretary of War Henry Stimson who was not at Yalta but who warned President Truman shortly after he came into office in April 1945, that "we have to understand that outside the United States, with the exception of Great Britain, there are few countries that understand free elections; that the party in power always runs the elections, as I well know from my experience in Nicaragua [in 1927]."[28] Stimson, as President Hoover's Secretary of State, had begun the withdrawal of the United States from its electoral intervention in Latin America in the early 1930's and the Roosevelt Administration had completed the task under the "Good Neighbor" policy. Now the free elections policy was being revived in a different but equally inappropriate part of the world. True, the electoral difficulties in Latin America stemmed almost entirely from domestic political conditions whereas those in Eastern Europe were only partly internal and largely the result of external pressures from the Soviet Union; but many of the problems are similar.

In the early years of the cold war which rapidly developed after Yalta, the United States and its allies have attempted to use several of the same methods to secure free elections in Eastern Europe which we had employed with scant success in Central America and the Caribbean a generation earlier. Among these were nonrecognition, the creation of coalition governments, diplomatic protests, and election observation and supervision.

At Yalta, Roosevelt and Churchill sought to obtain "effective guarantees" for the Declaration on Liberated Europe quoted above. The State Department had proposed to the President that Polish elections be supervised by an Emergency High Commission for Liberated Europe.[29] At the Conference, "observation" by the Allied ambassadors in Poland was substituted for the proposed "supervision." Then Stalin hypocritically rejected even this modified form with the argument that it would be offensive to Polish sovereignty. Later at Potsdam, Secretary of State James Byrnes repeated the offer for joint observation of elections and extended it to Italy, Greece, Hungary, Rumania and Bulgaria. The drawback of observing elections, as the United States had discovered in Panama, Nicaragua, Haiti, Santo Domingo, and Cuba, was the problem of what to do next if fraud or force were observed. Only if the government controlling the elections faced further and more effective sanctions would mere unfavorable publicity deter it from winning the election by unfair means. Observation logically points to supervision and both British and American leaders were for the most part reluctant to take on the major responsibilities the latter entailed.

The democratic leaders therefore concentrated on creating a genuine coalition out of the Lublin and London groups to govern Poland during the interim before elections could be held. Precedents for this arrangement existed in liberated Allied states like France and Yugoslavia as well as in conquered enemy countries like Italy and Rumania. None of the Western negotiators at Yalta or during the following spring seem to have appreciated the vital significance of the allocation of certain posts in a coalition cabinet, especially the Ministry of the Interior with its control of the police. A numerically tiny Communist party in possession of some key posts and supported by Soviet occupation authorities could negate democratic cabinet and electoral majorities, as was soon demonstrated in Hungary. Coalition governments make free elections possible in only two situations: (1) where there is a broad constitutional consensus and therefore confidence among the parties that the loser will have a fair chance to win in the next election; or (2) where both sides apparently believe that they will win, as in the Turkish election of 1950 or in Cuba in 1908.[30] Coalitions have seldom worked in Latin America unless accompanied by United States supervision of a scries of elections.

The British and Americans did ask for and receive Stalin's assurances that the Polish elections would take place within a month or two of the conference, and that Mikolajczyk's Peasant party could participate without hindrance.[31] The matter of timing was of great importance because the longer an election was delayed, the better a police regime could "prepare" the way for victory. The Polish election in question was not finally held until January 1947.

Given their weak military and therefore poor bargaining position in Eastern Europe in these last months of the world war and the first months of the cold war, the Western powers could do even less to promote free elections there than Soviet Russia could do to bring about successful Communist revolutions in France and Italy. It should be recalled that the American leaders believed in early 1945 that Soviet military aid would be vital in the final conquest of Japan. After the war, it was simply not politically possible for the governments of the democracies to maintain large enough military forces in Europe to back up their diplomatic protests even if they had been able to persuade their people suddenly to regard the recent Soviet ally as the new chief enemy.[32]

Already before Yalta, the Polish government-in-exile had urged the United States and Great Britain not to recognize the Russian-sponsored Lublin government until really free elections took place in the homeland.[33] Churchill tried at the Conference to use the threat of nonrecognition as a bargaining tactic to gain concessions on this matter from Stalin but was apparently undercut by Roosevelt's impatience to reach an agreement.[34] Throughout the spring of 1945, recognition was indeed withheld in a vain effort to compel the Polish Communists to fulfill the Yalta Declaration. In July this last bargaining point was surrendered in return for a useless acknowledgement by the now reconstituted Lublin regime of its obligations to provide the necessary conditions for meaningful elections.[35]

The United States also denied recognition for many months to the

increasingly Communist-dominated regimes of defeated Bulgaria and
Rumania to compel them to preserve freedom of the press, of speech
and of assembly, to release political prisoners, to give the opposition a
fair chance to campaign and to end the police terror.[36] Nonrecognition carried with it a threat to refuse to sign a peace treaty with the
defeated Axis allies and to deny them seats in the United Nations.
Occasionally temporary concessions were wrested from Communist
rulers by this means. In August 1945, for instance, the Bulgarian government postponed elections which would have been patently unfree.[37]
That fall, Secretary Byrnes sent Mark Ethridge, a newspaper pub-
lisher, to investigate conditions in Bulgaria and Rumania.[38] The mission was reminiscent of many special missions United States Presidents and Secretaries of State had sent to Latin America in the early
days of the century to straighten out electoral imbroglios. With the
Soviets in occupation, it had no effect.

In November of the same year, however, the Soviet occupation authorities permitted a relatively free election in Hungary as we have
seen. The Smallholders' Party won an absolute majority of 57 per
cent of the vote. In the next year and a half, the Soviet army of occupation was instrumental in subverting the coalition cabinet in which
the Smallholders had most of the seats. Evidently diplomatic recognition had some value even to Communist rulers but once granted it
was no longer available as a sanction. We eventually broke off diplomatic relations with Bulgaria but in no case did we withdraw recognition of a Communist government and recognize a non-Communist
government-in-exile. The outcome therefore in all cases where the
Russian armies were in sole occupation of a country was the same:
totalitarian dictatorship. The United States could topple a Huerta
from power in Mexico, a Tinoco in Costa Rica, or a Chamorro in
Nicaragua with little more than a refusal to recognize them, but this
method was bound to be no more effective in bringing demoracy
to Soviet-controlled Eastern Europe than in undoing the Russian and
Chinese revolutions as long as the United States was unwilling or
unable to take more drastic measures.

Another technique open to the United States was the promise of or
suspension of loans to governments which were not permitting free
elections. It had little effect on the Communist government of Poland
in 1946. With the Marshall Plan, we bent over backwards not to set
political conditions on our economic aid and still the Soviets required
their satellites to refuse it for fear of their being weaned away.

Least effective of all the methods used to secure free elections in both

Latin America and Eastern Europe were the repeated diplomatic protests the United States made on the basis of the Yalta Declaration and later of the peace treaties with Bulgaria, Rumania, and Hungary. Reading the long record of protests and idle threats, one cannot help but feel that Byrnes was more interested in building up a good legal and propaganda case for the United States in the cold war than in actually reversing the Communist *faits accomplis.*

What if the Soviets had consented to a joint supervision of elections in their sphere? The experience of Greece illustrates the difficulties of a truly impartial observation or supervision of elections where many of the prerequisites for a peaceful alternation in power are lacking.

In Greece as in Poland and earlier in Latin America, the demand for free elections came initially from within. The first issue to be decided in the Greek case was whether the exiled King should be allowed to return after the war. All parties agreed on a plebiscite on this question but the conditions under which it should be conducted were the object of bitter dispute. A coalition government made up of representatives of both the Greek government-in-exile and the Communist-dominated guerrilla forces was formed in 1944 which reminds us of the coalition cabinets in the Soviet-occupied states, but with the proportions of Left and Right members reversed. After the British landed in Athens and established the new government in power, controversy arose over the disarmament of the guerrillas. The Left withdrew from the coalition and in December 1944 attempted a coup d'état but failed to overcome the better armed British units. The civil war was terminated by an agreement which stipulated that regular elections and a plebiscite should be held within the year. In the meantime the erstwhile rebels were to surrender their weapons and the Communist party was to emerge as a legal political organization.

Neither side lived up to its pledges. Both sides spread terror in the areas they controlled to intimidate the other's voters.[39] The possession of the machinery of government and the presence of British troops gave the Right almost as decisive an advantage as Russian occupation gave the Left in Poland and elsewhere in the Balkans. The Left then demanded postponement of the elections until faulty electoral registers could be corrected and captive rebels amnestied. The parties of the Right and the British both rebuffed this dilatory maneuver.

Consistent with their position on Poland at Yalta and Potsdam, the Western Powers volunteered their services in Greece as election observers.[40] The U.S.S.R with equal consistency refused to participate. It would have been a bad precedent for them. A mission of some

1,200 Americans, British, and French actually watched at the polling booths in March 1946 and reported that the election proceedings on the whole were free and fair. In a narrow technical sense they probably were. Even this could not be said of the Communist-controlled elections in Poland in January 1947.

The Greek elections did not take place in a vacuum. Quite aside from the possibility of fraud and terror before the observers arrived or after they left, the voters were inevitably influenced by the cold war alignments of the parties. No matter how impartial the British troops and the Allied observers tried to be, citizens of a country which had known much violence and little democracy in the immediately preceding years were naturally inclined to play safe and jump on the bandwagon of the winning side. Americans should have known this from their experience of observing and then supervising elections in Cuba, Panama, and Nicaragua a generation earlier. There, too, the American role in the election had itself become the principal campaign issue; so however technically free of fraud and overt force the polling was, free elections settled nothing.

The Leftist opposition in Greece boycotted the election and prepared for revolution just as the side which expects to lose often does in Latin America. The Allied mission estimated that this abstention reduced the vote by about 15 percent.[41] Five months later, the plebiscite on the monarchy was held under similar conditions but with only informal outside observers. The King won.

In subsequent years, Greek politics have oscillated between extreme Right and Left of Center. So far the United States has been spared the embarrassment of a Communist electoral victory. We would probably not tolerate that drastic a shift any more than the Russians would tolerate the fall of a pro-Soviet regime in Hungary in 1956. When faced with the possibility of a Communist victory in the Italian elections of 1948, we influenced the outcome by a promise to return Trieste to Italy and by a campaign of letters from Italian-Americans to their friends and relatives in the mother country.[42]

The American position in the cold war has continued to be based in part on charges of Soviet violations of the free elections pledge in the Yalta Declaration.[43] For a while in 1952-53 it even appeared that the Republican Party would scrap the ineffective Democratic policy of nonrecognition and protests in favor of a more active policy of "liberation" or "rollback." By that time, however, the U.S.S.R. had atomic weapons; and once in power the Republicans quickly retreated to the former policy except for an increase in propaganda activity.

It is my contention that this is an ill-advised position to defend. Of the countries of Eastern Europe now under Communist domination, only Czechoslovakia had an unblemished record of democracy in the interwar period.[44] All the rest—the Baltic States, Poland, Hungary, Rumania, Bulgaria, Yugoslavia, and Albania—were dictatorships of varying degrees of repressiveness for at least part of those twenty years, not to mention long centuries of Turkish, Russian, and Austrian tyranny before their brief reappearances as sovereign states. The prerequisites for free elections and representative democracy—literacy, economic development, and social stability [45]—were absent in some and only partly fulfilled in others. It seems fair to ask how long democracy would have lasted even if the Red Army had not been present. The record of fallen democracies on our side of the Iron Curtain during the cold war, especially in Asia, points to a pessimistic answer.

It is worth noting that in two of the three countries in the region which most closely approximated the necessary conditions for democracy (Finland and Austria), the Soviets did not use force to prevent free elections. True, the Red Army did not occupy all of either country, but then why did the Soviet rulers not communize what they did control as in Eastern Germany? The answer lies hidden in Soviet archives. One can at least note the presence of strong Social Democratic parties in both Finland and Austria which refused to throw their lot in with the Communists. A recent study of Finnish-Soviet relations concludes that the most important consideration in the Soviet decision not to seize Finland in 1948 was probably its geographical location away from the main line of Soviet defenses in Central Europe. But this had not exempted Finland from Soviet attack in 1939. The author also notes that "Finland's political climate was less favorable from the Russian point of view than Czechoslovakia's" and the unfavorable "reaction in the West to the coup in Prague was a contributing factor." [46]

It is just possible that Stalin intended the third East European democracy, Czechoslovakia, to be a showpiece for the possibility of coexistence, of reconciling Western-style democracy with a pro-Soviet foreign policy. His successors withdrew from Austria in 1954 on a similar gamble, the neutralization of democratic Austria. Whatever Stalin's long-run intentions, for three years, 1945-48, Czechoslovakia was what President Benes hoped it would be, a kind of bridge between East and West. Then it fell victim to the cold war. In the atmosphere of the Iranian dispute, the Truman Doctrine, the Marshall Plan, the exclusion of the Communist Parties from the coalition cabinets in France and Italy and of mutual recriminations in the United Nations, the possibility of a serious diminution in Communist electoral strength which loomed in the next Czech election was apparently intolerable to Stalin.[47]   He pulled the levers of power to topple Benes' government.

Before we castigate the Russian dictator too severely for this act, let us ask ourselves what we would have done if the Communists had won the tightly contested election in Italy two months later in 1948 despite our aforementioned intervention?   The British left no question about what they would do when they ejected the Communist-front government of Cheddi Jagan in Guiana in 1953.[48]   The United States may have given its answer less openly when it tacitly supported the anti-Communist revolution in Guatemala in 1954,[49] and condoned the indefinite postponement of all-Vietnamese elections since 1956. Even Nehru of India invoked constitutional emergency powers to remove the freely elected Communist government in the state of Kerala.

We have been prone to assume as President Roosevent did in 1943 that "no nation in the world that is free to make a choice is going to set itself up under a [totalitarian] form of government. . . ."[50] But what if they do? Then we would face the same dilemma the Soviet rulers, from their point of view, faced in Poland: should people be allowed, as Justice Holmes said, to go to Hell in their own way, or should we assume that we know what is better for them and us and act accordingly? Which is more important to us—our security or their freedom of choice?

To hang on to the paper claims of Yalta and Potsdam for free elections may give us a sense of self-righteous virtue and a small propaganda gain; but by encouraging resistance to Communist rule which we are not prepared to aid militarily it may also contribute to the loss of many innocent lives as it did in Hungary in 1956.[51]

Our legal claims in the area should not be given up without a suitable *quid pro quo*. Otherwise, it might properly be objected that we were engaging in "appeasement" since Communist parties would remain in the West as centers of espionage and subversion even if they had little chance of winning power by election in Western Europe. The nature of the guarantees we ought to demand of the Soviets for relinquishing our claims is one of the most difficult and least studied of problems facing our diplomacy.[52] Under present power conditions it would seem that a measure of national freedom, if not free elections, can come to Eastern Europe only through some form of mutual "disengagement" such as George Kennan has proposed.[53] This would have to take into account Russia's legitimate security interests in the area.[54] Alternatively, the best that can be hoped for is a spheres-of-influence agreement like the Anglo-Soviet understanding of 1944 which the Russians astonishingly honored in the case of Greece during the critical days in the fall and winter of 1944-45.[55] The former course would amount to a new emphasis on national self-determination as America's goal in the cold war. Free elections would then be the criterion for national sovereignty only where, as in Germany, the conditions for them may exist. The aid we have given to "national communist" governments in Yugoslavia and Poland may show that we are quietly coming around to this position despite our continued propaganda campaign for free elections.

FREE ELECTIONS SINCE WORLD WAR II

Eastern Europe is not the only area in which the United States has become involved with other countries' domestic politics and elections since the Second World War. The various interventions can be categorized into four different kinds.[1] The first I have just dealt with: countries occupied by the Red Army or controlled by the Soviet Union or Red China through Communist governments. Besides Eastern Europe these include East Germany, North Korea, North Vietnam, Mongolia, and of course the centers of Communist power in China and Russia. Some would add Guatemala until 1954 and Cuba since 1959. As I concluded in the previous chapter, the prospects for free elections in these states are poor, especially when a satellite is contiguous to the Soviet Union or Communist China and within their respective spheres of vital interest. The only hope for a return to democracy is as part of a diplomatic bargain providing for mutual disengagement or exchange of territories.

The second category is the opposite of the first: situations of prolonged military occupation by the United States and her allies such as Western Germany and Austria, Italy, Japan and South Korea.[2] Here as in Cuba (1898-1902 and 1906-1908), the Dominican Republic (1916-1922) and Haiti (1915-1930) the problem was to create governments in whose hands we could leave the countries when the occupation ended, governments which would, hopefully, be both stable and democratic and therefore favorable or at least neutral toward us in the Cold War. With respect to our former enemies: Germany, Austria, Italy and Japan, the restoration of democracy was an explicit war aim in World War II. Its accomplishment was facilitated not only by our near-complete control but also by the presence in a relatively high degree of the prerequisites of democracy including some previous history of constitutional government and free elections.[3] Without going into the merits of specific occupation policies like denazification, demilitarization, decartelization and reeducation or the longrun prospects of stable democracy in the former Axis states, I think it can be generally agreed that in the shortrun our experiments there have enjoyed enough success to remove them from the agenda of free elections problems. Free elections have remained our adamant precondition for the reunification of East and West Germany. If some commentators would argue for the modification of this requirement, it is not out of any doubt about the technical feasibility or meaningfulness of all-German elections, but from a recognition that reunification and free elections are irreconcilable from the Soviet point of view without, at the very least, a guarantee of German neutrality like Austria's since 1954. In Central as in Eastern Europe, we are touching upon an area of legitimate Russian security interests.

In Korea, and, we might add, Viet Nam although the latter has not been formally occupied by American troops, we find different conditions from Germany's: the fairness, freedom and significance of re-unifying elections would be in some doubt. Since the communist Viet Minh would have a good chance of victory in all-Vietnamese elections, it is we who have raised obstacles to their being held under the Geneva agreements of 1954. Instead, we sustained the Ngo Dinh Diem regime in South Viet Nam both economically and militarily until 1963 even though its elections hardly reached the standard of purity we have set elsewhere.[4]

In South Korea we assisted in an election inspected by the United Nations in 1948.[5] Then for twelve years we defended the increasingly dictatorial government of Syngman Rhee. When Korean students rioted against Rhee's rigged elections in 1960, Secretary of State Christian Herter reprimanded the South Korean president and thereby significantly contributed to his downfall.[6] Presumably so drastic a move came only after years of secret and unavailing diplomatic representations. For a year the democratic but corrupt and inefficient Chang government held sway until in May, 1961 a military coup took place. Initially the U. S. Embassy and the American commander of United Nations Forces in South Korea tried to support Chang's "freely elected and constitutionally established government as the only recognized government of the Republic of Korea,"[7] but we quickly gave way for fear that Chang would gradually lose the country to the North Korean communists.

The third category of postwar interventions consists of our own former colonies and those of our allies. The Philippine Republic and the Commonwealth of Puerto Rico are the major examples of our successfully transmitting democratic institutions,[8] but it should be remembered that the process took place gradually over a long period of occupation. After the Second World War, The Philippines showed signs of going the way of Central America and of becoming, as one of her own presidents said, "just another banana republic." The first post-independence election was quite "dirty." In 1953, however, Philippine democracy, possibly with some covert assistance from American army officers and intelligence agents, survived the crucial experience of a peaceful electoral transfer of power from the "ins" to the "outs." [9] Young Filipino professional men organized the National Movement for Free Elections primarily to police the polls against fraud and violence. The incumbent Liberals feared that they would lose in a clean election, for their Nationalist opponent, Ramon Magsaysay, was widely known to be favored by Americans because of his success in wiping out the pro-communist "Huk" rebellion. When one of the "out" party leaders, Senator Laurel, made a direct appeal for American intervention to assure an honest election, the Liberals tried to save themselves by charging foreign interference. In this way they hoped to arouse Filipino nationalism on their own behalf, but the accusations boomeranged and actually aided the Nationalist candidate.

Washington officials and Admiral Raymond Spruance, the U. S. Ambassador, took great pains to maintain their neutrality between the two candidates, but they made it clear to the Philippine government that the conduct of the election was of vital concern to us. The Liberal Foreign Secretary replied bitterly that even a manifestation of "concern" about the free expression of the Filipino people's will from a foreign official was by itself an indication of doubt that there would be a free election and was thereby an indictment of the party in power to the aid and comfort of the opposition. As in Latin America, the impartiality of the United States was not believed and therefore in effect was impossible. When officers of the Joint U. S. Military Aid Group went out to observe the elections just to make sure that arms given by us to the Philippine Republic were not being misused to thwart the free will of the voters, the people took this as a sign of American favor to the "outs." However, the outcome of the episode was more fortunate than in Latin America, for the Philippines now seem to have achieved a broad political consensus and a functioning two party system.

We have been reluctant to interfere in the proceedings whereby our European allies have divested themselves of their colonial empires since World War II. Usually fairly elaborate plebiscites and elections have marked an important stage in the process and the British in particular have accumulated a storehouse of experience from which the Western hemisphere might well learn.[10] The United States has participated only indirectly through its membership on the United Nations Trusteeship Council which has concerned itself with elections in Togoland,[11] the Cameroons and Somaliland although we have, of course, been deeply embroiled in the affairs of the Congo since 1960.

Fourthly, we have probably exerted influence either indirectly or surreptitiously on elections even within some of the countries allied to us in the cold war. For instance, the transition of Turkey from a one party dictatorship to a two party democracy in 1946-50 may have been facilitated by distribution of a U. S. Information Agency pamphlet entitled "A Government Founded by the People."[12] The association of Turkish officers with Americans and Western Europeans in N.A.T.O. may have helped influence them to overthrow the Menderes government in 1960 when it showed signs of subverting Turkish democracy.

Evidence of diplomatic, military or Central Intelligence Agency interference in our allies' elections is of course extremely difficult to obtain this soon after the events. Recently Justice Douglas charged the C.I.A. with interceding in foreign elections with money.[13] Where a strong, non-Communist alternative to the ruling party exists as in Turkey, the United States can indulge the luxury of pressing quietly for free elections. Where the alternative does not exist as in Taiwan, we clearly have to give priority to our security interests even at the cost of a propaganda loss and limit ourselves to working for the creation of those conditions in which a democratic multi-party competition is feasible. The danger is that incumbents often try to picture their opponents to us as Communist and anti-American; the truth of these charges is hard to verify.

For reasons mentioned at the beginning of chapter Nine, the United States has been especially reluctant to get entangled again in Latin American election controversies. For instance in 1959 William B. Macomber, Jr., Assistant Secretary of State, replied to a letter of Senator Jacob Javits (Republican, New York) regarding charges that the United States was supporting dictatorial regimes in Latin America. He stated that the principles of continuity of diplomatic relations and of nonintervention embedded in the Charter of the Organization of American States inhibits the United States from taking action to promote democracy in the hemisphere. He quoted a press release of President Eisenhower of August 14, 1958 that while "the United States support of representative democracy must of course be within the principle of nonintervention, there are however ways in which the United States can and does support and promote democracy without violating this principle, for example, by aiding in the maintenance of peace and security, by helping create the economic and social conditions under

which democratic processes can be strengthened, as well as by continuing ourselves to follow democratic traditions." [14]

Although the full diplomatic records are, of course, not available for
the recent period, it seems safe to say that the United States has in
fact rigorously abstained from interfering in the domestic politics of
her southern neighbors since the 1930s except where nonintervention
would have meant losing a country by default to an extracontinental
totalitarianism. The exception accounts for our four major lapses from
nonintervention since the Good Neighbor Policy went into effect in
1933: Argentina (1945), Guatemala (1954), Cuba (1961) and the Dominican Republic (1961).

In the first case, it was Nazi infiltration that we feared. The danger
was real but the mistake was to continue our opposition to the military
regime in Argentina after the fall of Nazism in Europe. Secretary Hull
believed that the Argentine government of General Edelmiro Farrell
which had refused to break diplomatic relations with Germany and
Japan was unrepresentative of the majority opinion in Argentina. Hull
therefore refused to recognize him for over a year in 1944-45. The
Secretary thus tacitly adopted the Uruguayan "Guani formula" which
provided for collective nonrecognition of revolutionary governments
that did not cooperate for hemispheric defense against the Axis during
the war. The new doctrine was somewhat different from President
Wilson's doctrine of legitimacy since a government did not have to be
democratic to be recognized. It is reminiscent of the Tobar Doctrine
in the Central American treaties of 1907 and 1923 in that it was Latin
American in origin though it did happen to suit Hull's purposes.
Bolivia's revolutionary regime supported by the Argentines, also went
unrecognized from December 1943 until June 1944 on these premises.
Later in 1945, Uruguayan Foreign Minister Rodriguez Larreta even
proposed that collective security measures provided for in the Act of
Chapultepec be used against any totalitarian American regime which
was violating the basic rights of its citizens. Naturally his proposal
was received unfavorably by the other Latin American governments,
many of which were themselves authoritarian dictatorships. [15]

After the war, our Ambassador to Argentina, Spruille Braden, stated
that the United States wished to see democratic governments in every
country in the world but had recognized Farrell finally only by force
of circumstances namely, to win Latin American acceptance of the
United Nations Charter. As Assistant Secretary of State for American
Republics Affairs after August 1945, Braden launched a blatant interference in the Argentine electoral campaign of February 1946. He

tried to defeat Col. Juan D. Peron, the Nationalist candidate, by publishing a "Blue Book" on the pro-Nazi activities of the Argentine officers' clique and its candidate. The effort miscarried. Peron was able to pose as the martyr of Yankee imperialism and won the sympathy of a solid majority of the people in an honest election.

The State Department also underestimated the popular appeal of Perons domestic program in labor and public welfare. The democratic Argentine people seemed to have disproved a cherished axiom of United States political thinking—that a people will choose democracy and repudiate totalitarianism if given a free choice.[16] Peron's victory set off a series of military coups in Latin America against democratically elected governments, most notably in Peru and Venezuela in 1948. The State Department, having burned its fingers on Peron, restricted itself to a circular note expressing concern with the overthrow of popularly elected governments. In practice, it recognized the new military dictators promptly and extended military aid to them on the mistaken assumption that they would aid us in the Cold War.

Action in the second and third cases of United States intervention was aimed at Communist infiltration of Latin American governments. The Monroe Doctrine had stated that "any attempt on the part (of Europe) to extend their system to any portion of the hemisphere is dangerous to our peace and security." We have tried not very convincingly to reconcile our support of invasions of Guatemala in 1954 and Cuba in 1961 by exiles with our obligation under the charter of the Organization of American States not to intervene. At Caracas in 1954, Secretary Dulles secured an O.A.S. resolution which specifically condemns "the control of the political institutions of any American state by the international Communist movement . . . as a threat to the sovereignty and political independence of the American States . . ."[17] The resolution doesn't account for the possibility that a majority of the people in a Latin American country which has suffered from authoritarian military dictatorship may approve of a quite radical revolutionary regime which can then secure aid only from Communist Russia and China. In that case we are faced with the same embarrassing choice between free elections and national security which we tried to force on the Soviets in Poland after World War II. Perhaps fortunately for us, Castro of Cuba has not tried to demonstrate the popularity of his government by staging an election.

The burden of my story so far has been largely negative: the United States has tried to promote democracy in regions or under circumstances in which the chances of success have been slim. The policy implication has been that we should not attempt the impossible. But another theme has been that free elections are only a means to the goal of national security. In Latin America, at least, the free elections method became inappropriate when the threat of European intervention which it was originally designed to prevent dissolved after the First World War. Now in the 1960's the danger has reappeared in the even more insidious form of Soviet-inspired communist subversion. Once again governmental instability and revolutions pose a threat to our security. A policy of strict nonintervention may mean sitting back helplessly while still another country slips irrevocably behind the iron curtain. Insofar as the discontent which makes communist subversion possible is caused by repressive governments unresponsive to the demands of popular majorities, we are forced to take an interest in the domestic politics of our allies. Clearly we must keep democratic free elections as means and as end carefully separated. Other things being equal, we have a preference for the spread of democracy to as wide an area as possible, but not at the cost of national security interests. Where a free election would produce a communist victory as it probably would in Viet Nam, the price of consistency may be too high, unless it were counterbalanced by a simultaneous electoral victory for parties favorable to us elsewhere, as for instance in a reunited Korea or Germany.

In Latin America there are signs, as we have already seen, that our resolve to keep hands off is again weakening under the pressures just described. From the first days of the Castro regime in Cuba influential Americans like the columnist David Lawrence and presidential adviser Adolf A. Berle, Jr. were demanding that elections be held on the island. Lawrence wanted them as a precondition to recognition,[18] Berle as a prerequisite of economic aid.[19] Castro, like the Mexican revolutionists of half a century before who had also come to power on a platform of free elections and then disavowed them in favor of drastic social reform, may well have had a substantial majority of Cubans behind him in January 1959. He claimed that he did not wish to be diverted from the struggle for redistribution of wealth and economic development by sterile electoral quarrels over patronage which had characterized all previous Cuban elections. I have suggested earlier, in comparing Cuba to Mexico, that if we had accepted Castro's preference at the beginning and extended sympathetic aid we might have avoided the present sharp threat to our national security to which his antagonism has led. At least we could hardly be worse off than by following the course we have.

The Johnson Administration has shown by its espousal of the Alliance for Progress and the Peace Corps that it recognizes better than its predecessors the need to build up the economic and social bases of democracy in Latin America before insisting on the precise practice of democratic forms. But what if properly elected legislatures refuse to pass necessary laws for land and tax reform as in Brazil or if American-armed military leaders frustrate the popular will as in Peru in 1962? In the latter case, the military intervened to prevent the Peruvian Congress from electing Raul Haya de la Torre of the Apra Party president. U. S. Ambassador James Loeb apparently tried to prevent the breakdown of democratic procedures and when he failed, President Kennedy withheld recognition for a month lest a rash of military coups spread over the continent as in 1948.[20] The usual Latin American reaction against our mild interference soon set in. Little appears to have been accomplished although the junta did fulfill its promise to stage new elections in 1963. On the other hand, a dangerous precedent for renewing the old, futile policy of nonrecognition in Latin America has been established.

A more encouraging development for a short while was the tumultuous transition of the Dominican Republic after Trujillo's assassination in 1961 from one of the most repressive dictatorships in the hemisphere to a democracy.[21] Even before the tyrant's death, Senator George Smathers of Florida had proposed to him that the O.A.S. supervise Dominican elections from which the Trujillo family would be excluded in order to assure the fairness of the polls.[22] In June, 1960, the Venezuelan government charged Trujillo with complicity in an attempt to assassinate its president, Romulo Betancourt. While many Latin American states would not condone collective action to overthrow a dictator merely because he was an oppressor of his own people, intervention by him in the internal affairs of another American state aroused their indignation. A meeting of O.A.S. Foreign Ministers was therefore held in August. Secretary Herter proposed that an international commission supervise elections in the Dominican Republic with a threat of economic sanctions to compel agreement. The other states still shied away from setting a precedent for the O.A.S. participating in elections since any one of them might be the next to be supervised, but they did insist on the suspension of diplomatic relations with the Dominican Republic and an arms embargo until Trujillo should mend his ways.[23] After the dictator's demise, an O.A.S. observation commission was dispatched to the Republic to assure proper preparations for the scheduled December 1962 balloting. The Commission was aided at a crucial juncture by the opportune arrival of a U. S. warship which prevented a countercoup by other members of the Trujillo family. We have poured economic aid in to bolster the provisional government and keep Castro's admirers from seizing power too. As usual, the Dominicans refused to believe in the impartiality of American aid, but the election was the fairest in many years. There could be, of course, no guarantee that the strategic island republic would not backslide to civil war and dictatorship at some future date—which it did in the fall of 1963. It takes more than one robin to make a spring.

What clearly commends the technique of using an international organization like the O.A.S. to promote free elections is that it can pool the knowledge of many members, much of which may be far more pertinent to local conditions than our experience is, and it can also spread the blame which accrues to all external interference, especially in case of failure. In general, it would seem adviseable for the United States to work through the O.A.S. or the United Nations when strategic motives oblige us to take part in other countries' elections.

XI

CONCLUSIONS

The United States has not deliberately embarked upon a policy of promoting democracy in other countries. It has supported free elections as an answer to certain concrete policy problems which accompanied its rise to world power. The chief of these has been how to prevent or halt revolutions. In practically every case related in this study, political stability was the direct or indirect goal of American electoral intervention. Even where the immediate problem has been the liquidation of American military occupation or the decision whether to recognize a new regime, the desire to foster stable government has been at its root. In situations of the former type, the United States has wished to leave the occupied state in a condition most conducive to peaceful acquiescence by the populace to their new government with a view to preventing a repetition of the disturbances which had caused American concern in the first place. In situations of the latter type in which the question was whether to recognize a new regime, the issue has arisen because nonrecognition was adopted previously as a technique for discouraging revolutions. The only exceptions to the anti-revolutionary goal of the United States policy have been the few cases such as Panama in 1903, Nicaragua in 1909, Guatemala in 1954, Hungary in 1956, Cuba in 1961 and South Vietnam in 1963 in which the immediate aim has been rather to validate uprisings which have been deemed favorable to our security.

Why this obsessive concern with the political stability of our neighbors? Primarily, it is because conditions of unrest and civil war may provoke or legally excuse intrusion by foreign powers hostile to us. Ever since the Monroe Doctrine, the United States has publicly proclaimed such interference in the Western hemisphere to be a threat to its security. Since 1898 we have been strong enough to combat it. With the Truman Doctrine we have extended our sphere of influence to large parts of the Eastern hemisphere.

Why promote political stability by supporting free elections? Why not simply strengthen the military dictatorships which have ruled many of the states in question? It could be argued against the latter course that even the best entrenched dictators must die or fall from power eventually and the disorders usually attendant upon the transfer of rule where force has been used to maintain a regime are liable to be explosively violent.[1] What American policy makers have argued has been that the best way to stop revolutions led by the members of the parties out of power is to ensure that the elections already provided for in their constitutions should be free of fraud and violence. Americans tend to believe that the real cause of their neighbors' frequent revolutions is the indignation of the losers in elections over being coerced or cheated out of victory. That is what the representatives of "out" parties who troop to Washington to protest against the tyranny of the "ins" tell American officials. That is what rebels tell American mediators. There has been nothing in the recent historical experience or ideology of the United States to contradict this assumption. Secretary Root was a lone dissenter when he challenged the cherished American doctrine that government derives its just powers from the consent of the governed.[2] The United States is itself the product of a successful revolution, so it can not consistently aid in suppressing uprisings against tyranny elsewhere. We have reasoned that the only way both to prevent revolutions and to determine whether they are justified if they do break out, is to guarantee free elections.

We have seen in several case histories—Panama (1903), Cuba (1906, 1917), Nicaragua (1909, 1927), Mexico (1913), the Dominican Republic (1913), Costa Rica (1917), Honduras (1919, 1923)—that various economic interests, both American and foreign, have tried to influence United States policy towards these countries in ways favorable to themselves by pleading in terms of the presence or absence of free elections. With the possible exception of Secretary Philander Knox, American policy makers, both Democratic and Republican, have doggedly resisted all attempts to get them to use the power of the United States for private economic gain beyond the protection of foreign lives and property permissible under international law. The free elections policy unavoidably has had unintended consequences, both beneficial and detrimental, for private businessmen, but these have not been the cause of official policy. When the United States has acted to protect the lives and property of foreign businessmen in Latin America by stopping revolutions with promises of free elections, it has done so to preclude intervention by their own governments. President Wilson in his policies toward Mexico and Costa Rica bent over backwards not to let commercial considerations sway official policy. Since World War II, administrations of both political parties have insisted only on adequate compensation for the extensive nationalizations of American-owned private property. After all, the specific policy of supporting democratic political institutions does not lend itself as well to private economic exploitation as outright annexation or military occupation.

A word should be said about the immediate goals of policy makers in promoting democracy. In the day-to-day operations of foreign policy, the ultimate ends in a chain of reasoning such as we find invoked to justify support of free elections are seldom mentioned by the subordinate officials who bear the brunt of the work. Instead, the "desk man" in the Latin American Division or the diplomat in the field has invoked various intermediate or secondary goals—for instance, popular acquiescence to governments, compliance with treaties, or free elections, as an end in themselves—to justify the application of specific measures like nonrecognition, observation or diplomatic protest. In other words, 'instrumental values" have tended to become "goal values." This tendency to obscure the original purpose of the policy has inhibited reassessment of its effectiveness and led to its persistence after the initial justification has ceased to be valid. Now that our security is menaced again in the Caribbean, the policy has been revived in that area.

Just as the decision to support free elections has been only one link in a chain of reasoning which reaches back in most cases to considerations of military safety, so has the propagation of democratic processes in turn required a choice of methods. Nine of these are distinguishable in our case studies:

1. Establishing a treaty right of intervention;
2. Diplomatic representations and protests;
3. Nonrecognition of new governments;
4. Mediation by special missions;
5. Observation of elections;
6. Electoral law reform;
7. Supervision of elections;
8. Threat and use of military force;
9. Elections by the fiat of the United States.

Not all of them have been used in any one case, let alone in any one episode; nor have they necessarily been applied in any fixed sequence. For analytical purposes, I have ranked them in order of their coerciveness, from the least to the most. There has been a natural tendency, in fast, to apply them in this order. The State Department, particularly, has preferred the less coercive methods and proceeded toward more forceful means only if the first steps have proved to be ineffective and further action unavoidable. This was most clearly illustrated in the Honduran episode of 1919.

The exceptions to this usual progression have been due to special circumstances in a situation, such as the greater power and more distant location of a country vis-a-vis the United States,[3] the personal preferences of the dominant American statesmen of the moment (E.g., Taft vs. Root, Kellogg vs. Stimson) and the amount of learning from experience which has taken place. The most considerable exceptions to the sequence have been those episodes in which the problem has been how to liquidate an American military occupation as in Cuba in 1902 and 1908, in the Dominican Republic in 1922 and in Germany after 1945. There the power of the United States has already been supreme and military personnel with a professional preference for the most direct and coercive techniques have been either in control of the situation or on the scene to implement the decision. With these qualifications in mind, let us examine the typical sequence of means and the effectiveness of each.

1. *The Treaty Right of Intervention.* The existence or absence of a treaty right of intervention or a treaty prohibiting intervention is an important element in determining what more, if anything, the United States will do in support of free elections. American foreign policy makers have mostly been lawyers who from the habits of legal training and practice have naturally thought and acted in terms of legal norms and forms in their conduct of foreign relations. George Kennan has deplored the effects that this "legalistic-moralistic" approach to international problems has had on our foreign policy.[4] Policy makers like Root (Cuba), Taft (Panama), Knox (Nicaragua), and Bryan (Nicaragua, Dominican Republic, Haiti) have striven to obtain legal sanction for American interference.

The treaties themselves have not made intervention obligatory upon the United States in any circumstances, nor have most of them required explicitly that it should take the form of guaranteeing democratic procedures, but the existence and form of a treaty can facilitate support of free elections and indicate the means likely to be employed. Thus the Cuban (1902) and Panamanian (1903) treaties encouraged the prompt adoption of strong measures; the Central American treaties (1907, 1923) provided only for nonrecognition and therefore help account for the hesitancy of the State Department to proceed to more coercive techniques in Costa Rica, Honduras and Nicaragua. Electoral intervention in the Dominican Republic had to be based on a strained interpretation of the Customs Control Treaty of 1907. Once the good word of the United States has been engaged in an agreement or treaty, even if only by implication, Americans have felt morally responsible for carrying out the letter of the law and for insisting that other signatories do likewise. They have done so with a rigor born of a Calvinist and capitalist belief in the sacredness of contracts and reinforced by the dictum of international law that *pacta sunt servanda*.

2. *Diplomatic Representations and Protest.* The weakest form of action which the State Department has taken to support free elections on the basis of the treaty rights of the United States has been the traditional diplomatic protest. Sometimes it has been delivered as a preliminary to or in accompaniment of stronger methods; more often it has been the favored device of cautious diplomats to avoid such steps. Excellent examples of the ambiguity of these diplomatically phrased warnings are the notes which Secretary Colby dispatched simultaneously to the Cuban and Nicaraguan governments in 1920. In a sense, diplomatic protests against election fraud have really been intended as substitutes for real activity and approached nonintervention because they have tempted the parties in control of the electoral machinery to try to call the bluff of the United States and present it with a *fait accompli* as happened in the Cuban and Nicaraguan episode in 1920 and in Eastern Europe in the 1940's.

However, these mild protests have served as a not very effective brake on the worst electoral corruption and coercion because established regimes have never been sure of unqualified American backing against revolutionaries after the Cuban civil war of 1906. So they have been wont to give their controlled elections some greater semblance of legality when the State Department protested than their nineteenth century predecessors did, lest the unpredictable Yankees seize upon domestic disorders as an excuse for "impartial intervention." Syngman Rhee learned this to his sorrow in 1960.

Furthermore, the seemingly harmless protest can contain an implied threat of nonrecognition, of withdrawal of financial support or even of military invasion and forced supervision of the election. Sometimes these steps have in fact been explicitly threatened in the protest. Another, less drastic method of increasing the sanction of a protest has been to publish it, after first threatening to do so, for example, in Nicaragua in 1920. Whatever their form, diplomatic representations and public pronouncements, if not joined to threats of stronger action, have been the least effective policy instruments for bringing about free elections.[5]

3. *Nonrecognition.* We have seen in the Central American cases and again in connection with the Guani Doctrine in the Second World War, that the idea of using the act of recognizing new governments

as an instrument of policy to promote stability and democracy in foreign states probably originated among idealistic Latin American jurists.
We adhered reluctantly to the practices prescribed by the Central
American treaties of 1907 and 1923 in the hope that they would discourage revolutions.

Gradually what has begun purely as a policy tool has become,
through habit and precedent, practically an end in itself and has been
enforced by us with greater vigor than by the originators of the treaties.
Soon the United States was threatening or applying nonrecognition to
countries like Panama (1908), Mexico (1913-1915), the Dominican Republic (1912, 1913, 1916) and Haiti (1914, 1915) which had not signed
a treaty legalizing this deviation from the usual requirements of international law. We have actually withheld recognition from new governments in Latin America, pending free elections, as in the following
cases:

State	Cause	Dates
Nicaragua	12- 1-1909— 1- 1-1911	Revolution (U. S. supported)
Mexico	2-18-1913—10-19-1915	Coup d'etat
Peru	7-29-1913— 2-12-1914	Preventive coup d'etat
Dominican Republic	4- 7-1916—occupied,	
	11-29-1916	U. S. disliked President-elect
Costa Rica	1-27-1917— 8- 3-1920	Coup d'etat
Bolivia	7-12-1920— 2- 4-1921	Coup d'etat
Mexico	5-22-1920— 9- 3-1923	Revolution
Honduras	2- 1-1924— 1-22-1925	Coup d'etat and counterrevolution
Nicaragua	1-16-1926—11-17-1926	Coup d'etat and counterrevolution
Ecuador	7-10-1925— 8-13-1928	Coup d'etat
El Salvador	12- 3-1931— 1-26-1934	Coup d'etat
Bolivia	6-30-1930— 9-17-1930	Coup d'etat
Peru	8-22-1930— 9-17-1930,	
	3- 1-1931— 3- 5-1931	Successive coups d'etat
Argentina	9- 7-1930— 9-17-1930	Coup d'etat
Brazil	10- 3-1930—11- 8-1930	Revolution
Chile	6- 4-1932—10-21-1932	Successive coups d'etat

More recent cases like Bolivia (1943-44), Argentina (1944-45), Nicaragua (1947), Venezuela (1948-49), Panama (1949), and Peru (1962)
have been less clearly connected with any promises of free elections.
Outside of the Western hemisphere there have been the prolonged
nonrecognition of Communist regimes in Russia (1917-1934), China
(1949 to the present), and more briefly Poland, Rumania and Bulgaria
(1945). The Wilson Administration cited the lack of elections as one
reason for refusing to accept the Bolshevik regime in Russia,[6] but
Secretary Hughes shifted the grounds to the Communists' unwilling-

ness to discharge Russia's international obligations.[7]   Violation of the Yalta pledge of free elections played a big role in the Polish case in 1945 as we have seen.

The one element which all these cases have had in common was that they all followed revolutions or *coups d'etat*.   On no occasion have we actually withdrawn recognition from a regularly constituted and unopposed government simply because it failed to hold free and fair elections.   Even in Nicaragua in 1909, Knox handed Zelaya's Minister his passports only after the American-backed revolution had started. This fact has greatly vitiated pre-election threats of nonrecognition made to governments which were preparing to win by fraud or violence.   They have often regarded and treated the threat as mere bluff.

In none of the cases of nonrecognition pending free elections in South America, as distinguished from Central America, have more coercive means been brought to bear if this method failed.   Either the criteria for recognition have been changed, or we have overlooked electoral irregularities and accepted the mere form of a popular mandate.   Even in the strategic Central American region where stringent treaty requirements for recognition were in force, the United States occasionally recognized revolutionary governments after patently unfree elections for instance, in Guatemala in 1922.

Only in Nicaragua, Mexico, the Dominican Republic and Honduras did our government follow up its nonrecognition with more active policies.

How effective has nonrecognition been in obtaining free elections where it has been used for that purpose?   Threats of nonrecognition have usually been sufficient to eliminate the unconstitutional candidacies of incumbent presidents for reelection as in the Dominican Republic in 1914 and in Nicaragua in 1916, 1920 and 1924.   President Wilson drove the usurper Tinoco from power in Costa Rica solely by not recognizing him.   But in no case, except possibly in Honduras in 1924, has such a threat succeeded in halting the myriad minor acts which cumulatively make up an unfree or unfair election unless the threat has been accompanied by stronger sanctions.   In Eastern Europe nonrecognition was utterly ineffective in the face of Soviet military might.

Such influence as we have been able to exert in favor of democracy by means of nonrecognition is attributable to several special circumstances: (1) the disproportionate power of the United States in relation to the unrecognized state; (2) the propensity of European and

Latin American countries to follow our lead with regard to recognition in areas of special interest to us; (3) the effect of nonrecognition on foreign credit and ability to buy arms; and (4) the refusal of the United States to pay customs receivership receipts to an unrecognized government. As recently as 1960 the shortage of arms and credit played a part in the downfall of the Trujillo regime in the Dominican Republic.

Despite all these weighty considerations, Latin American revolutionists have repeatedly braved American displeasure. The picture of David standing up to Goliath has been as apt to rally nationalistic sentiment behind the unrecognized president as it has to encourage disaffection among his people. On the whole, nonrecognition, while one of the cheapest arrows in our quiver, has been also tended to be one of the least accurate.

4. *Mediation by Special Missions.* Nonrecognition, like diplomatic protest, is an essentially passive means of inducing other countries to hold free elections. The least coercive measures of a positive nature that can be taken are the traditional diplomatic procedures of good offices, conciliation and mediation. They may take the form of conciliation between opposing factions by the resident American diplomatic representative. In Central America our favorite tactic was to offer the neutral facilities of a United States warship for inter-party or inter-state conferences. Since this conciliation has been directed primarily toward restoring or preserving peace, the outcome has not been necessarily favorable to free election, though the conferees in Central American examples were likely to turn to that solution because of the requirements of the 1907 and 1923 treaties.

American presidents and secretaries of state have sent a number of "troubleshooting" missions to investigate critical situations where they have felt that we have had special interests and special obligations to keep the peace. The practice has continued since the Second World War. Because of the personal prestige of these emissaries they are given greater discretion to recommend and even decide solutions to disputes than are the regular diplomatic representatives. The judicial aura of mediation has tended to make special commissioners act impartially toward the parties to such a dispute and recommend solutions favorable to the holding of free elections.

Some idea of the number and variety of these special missions is afforded by listing them.

Country	Year	Commissioners	Purpose
Philippines	1899	Schurman et al.	Study political situation
Philippines	1900	Taft et al.	Restore civil government
Panama	1904	Taft	Settle treaty controversy
Cuba	1906	Taft, Bacon	Settle civil war over disputed election
Panama	1908	Taft	Settle election dispute
Nicaragua	1909	Adm. Kimball	Report on civil war
Nicaragua	1910	Dawson	Obtain agreement on succession and finances
Honduras	1911	Dawson	Settle civil war over election
Santo Domingo	1912	Doyle, McIntyre	Prevent revolution by reforming government
Philippines	1913	Prof. H. Ford	Investigate capacity for self government
Mexico	1913	Gov. Lind	Obtain agreement on conditions for recognition
Mexico	1914	Justice Lamar et al.	Resolve U. S.-Mexican dispute on Vera Cruz
Mexico	1914	Fuller	Mediate civil war among Constitutionalists
Santo Domingo	1914	Gov. Fort, Smith	Mediate civil war with election plan
Haiti	1915	Gov. Fort, Smith	Mediate civil war with election plan
Haiti	1915	Fuller	Negotiate customs control
Costa Rica	1917	J. F. Dulles	Investigate conditions for recognition
Cuba	1919	Gen. Crowder	Reform electoral law and supervise registration
Cuba	1920-3	Gen. Crowder	Settle electoral dispute
Nicaragua	1920	Maj. Miller	Supervise registration
Philippines	1921	Wood, Forbes	Restore American control
Nicaragua	1922	Prof. Dodds	Reform electoral law
Santo Domingo	1922-4	S. Welles	Prepare American evacuation including elections
Honduras	1924	S. Welles	Mediate civil war caused by electoral dispute
Nicaragua	1924	Prof. Dodds	Supervise registration
Tacna-Arica	1926	Gen. Pershing	Arrange for plebiscite
Nicaragua	1927	Stimson	Mediate civil war caused by electoral dispute
Nicaragua	1928	Col. McCoy	Supervise election
Haiti	1930	Forbes et al.	Restore legislative elections
Guatemala	1930	E. C. Wilson	Obtain agreement on recognition
El Salvador	1931	J. Caffery	Obtain agreement on recognition
Cuba	1933	S. Welles	Mediate civil war

Many of these missions have started out with more coercive methods, such as electoral law reform, observation or supervision, already decided upon. They were not therefore examples of mediation, properly speaking. The mediatory mission, as well as good offices in general, has often produced a written agreement which has been the basis for the subsequent application by the United States of the other methods and has served in lieu of formal treaties which would have to run the gauntlet of the United States Senate. Sometimes a simple promise by a government to "guarantee" free elections, or to carry out specific action to that end has been all that was sought and obtained.

In other cases mediation has produced an intra- or inter-party compact. The State Department has often insisted on the honoring of these domestic agreements with as much vigor as if they were solemn, formal treaties. Whenever Americans have sponsored intraparty compacts on behalf of the party in power without acting to assure the honesty of the actual balloting, they have in effect helped to prevent rather than promote free elections. Likewise, a coalition of all major parties for a single slate or for a division of offices afterward is an alternative to free elections rather than a means of achieving them. The coalition device was widely resorted to in postwar Europe. In Eastern Europe the Soviets insisted on single slate elections in their satellites, notably Poland. In Austria the predominant Social Democrats and Peoples' Party evolved a permanent coalition to present a united front to the occupation authorities and to exclude the extreme Right and Left. A system of prearranged party rotation in office terminated the Colombian civil war in 1957. But it is not clear that the United States had a hand in the last two arrangements. It did play a major part in setting up a coalition government in Laos to end a civil war in which the side favorable to us was losing.

Even where mediation has produced a promise by all parties in a present or threatening civil war to abide by the results of an election, the pledge is foredoomed to violation unless the weaker party has some concrete guarantee of a fair chance, such as American observation or supervision. As a minimum to be effective a promise to accept the test of "ballots, not bullets" requires the creation of a provisional coalition government with equal distribution of the key positions of power in the cabinet: army, police, justice, and a neutral president to hold the balance.

5. *Observation of Elections.* We have seen in the cases of Panama (1908), the Dominican Republic (1913), Nicaragua (1924), and Greece (1946) that the United States undertook to observe elections

because parties out of power threatened revolution if we did not act in some way to guarantee their fairness. We were unwilling to allow foreign parties to decide for themselves about the correctness of the results where revolution might entail American military intervention. Thus, American policy makers have faced an ugly dilemma of either helping the "in" party to suppress what in American ideology appears to be a justified rebellion by the "outs" against tyranny, or of stepping in to act as an impartial ballot judge. Because of this quandary, election observation is the logical consequence of non-recognition and mediation, else how can we be certain that the conditions for recognition have been properly met or the terms of a mediated settlement fulfilled?

Election observation has proved to be ineffective if not accompanied by an explicit threat to penalize observed fraud. The threat could be one of nonrecognition or of annulment of the unsatisfactory balloting and the holding of a new vote under direct American supervision. Otherwise, the "ins" would be tempted to practice fraud and violence anyway, again in the hope that the United States could be made to accept a *fait accompli*. If that prospect appeared likely, we would lose the confidence of the "outs". If they then withdrew, the observation of an uncontested election would be meaningless. On the other hand, parties in power have opposed foreign observation because it implied American lack of confidence in their rule. The "outs" might exploit this as proof that the observers favored them. This deleterious effect of observation on the chances of "in" candidates has been accentuated if the observers are in military uniform as may have been the case in the Philippines in 1953.

Observation of the Greek election in 1946 and the Korean election in 1948 did not induce the acquiescence of the "outs", especially the Communists, to the victor's rule, but it did give Americans a better conscience about supporting the established governments when civil war broke out.

6. *Electoral Law Reform.* American observers in the Dominican Republic and Nicaragua and American mediators in Cuba concluded that the fraud they detected had its origin in deficient election laws; so the reform of electoral codes has been the next logical step after observation.

Americans have not been alone in this proclivity to be legalistic. Central American delegates to both of the Washington Conferences, 1907 and 1923, introduced articles relating to electoral reform. The latter Conference adopted El Salvador's proposal of a complicated

"Convention Relating to the Preparation of Projects of Electoral Legislation." [3]

The elaborate codes drawn up by Colonel Crowder for Cuba (1907, 1919), Professor Dodds for Nicaragua (1922), and Sumner Welles for the Dominican Republic (1922) were not suited to the conditions of Latin America because they were based on the experience and laws of the United States. In practice, they were amended into innocuity and interpreted by the parties in power to favor themselves.

Sometimes promises of electoral law reform have been a way for both the State Department and Latin American parties in power to evade the present issue of freedom of elections. The "outs" have not been deceived for long by this tactic and have soon presented the United States anew with the choice between revolution and a fair poll. Therefore, electoral law reform has tended to lead to direct American supervision.

7. *Supervision of Elections.* Supervision has been the penultimate step in American support of free elections. Military occupation and the dictation of election procedure are, of course, more coercive, but they only add weight to the authority of the supervisors without changing the kind of task those officials have to perform. The reasoning which has led the United States from reforming a country's electoral code to supervision of its elections was well exemplified by General Crowder's remark about Cuba, "It makes no difference what the laws are, unless we administer them, (they) will do no good."

Because supervision involves an apparent infringement of a country's most cherished rights of sovereignty, the State Department has resisted the adoption of this technique. In any case, it does not have the proper machinery for conducting this kind of activity. Its diplomats are experts in negotiation and representation, not in governing other countries. Besides, they have been increasingly aware of the ill effects that any form of intervention, no matter how impartial and well meant, has had on United States relations with the rest of Latin America. Perforce, the Department had to turn for help to the military, particularly to the United States Marines. The career diplomats in fact have been successful in avoiding supervision in all cases but those in which we were already deeply involved militarily: Cuba, 1908; Panama, 1912, 1918; Haiti, 1917, 1918; Nicaragua, 1928, 1930, 1932.

The Department most often has evaded the unwanted responsibility by accepting as final the refusal of the recognized executive of a country to request American supervision—for example, Honduras 1919, Cuba 1920, Nicaragua 1916, 1924. Only where the party in power has been in imminent danger of losing control to a successful revolt of the opposition party, or when the key power positions have been so equally divided between the parties that the outcome was in doubt, would the incumbent executive request American supervision as a desperate last resort. This act has usually been taken as a sign of weakness by the voters and resulted in victory for the "outs" unless, as in Nicaragua in 1930 and 1932, American supervision has been in fulfillment of a commitment antedating the previous election.

8. *The Threat and Use of Military Force.* Diplomatic protests, non-recognition, mediation, observation, electoral reform and supervision often have had the tacit or open sanction of American military and naval force behind them. The point in the sequence at which compulsion has been exerted has differed from one spisode to another. In Cuba (1898) and Panama (1903) it accompanied the births of the two republics. In the second Cuban intervention (1906) it preceded electoral reform and supervision. In Mexico (1914, 1916) it precipitated the fall of one dictator but had no effect on the fortunes of another. In Nicaragua invasion followed nonrecognition in both 1909 and 1927 and was a prelude to mediation and supervision in the latter instance. In Haiti (1915) and the Dominican Republic (1916) the marines landed after unsuccessful applications of most of the other methods, but they brought not supervision of elections but the suppression of all voting for fifteen and eight years respectively. On the other hand, an American march to the Honduran capital in 1924 ended a revolution and led to a reasonably free, if meaningless election.

Military action for free elections has taken many forms from the "hovering" of a warship off the coast of a Central American or Caribbean country for "moral effect" during a revolution or election, through the establishment of "neutral zones" during civil wars, to full-fledged military expeditions and occupation. A timely naval demonstration prevented the Trujillos from returning to the Dominican Republic as recently as 1961.

On the whole, military force is an unsuitable method for promoting free elections because it flagrantly violates the principle of self-government, because it is necessarily conducted by military men more accustomed to authoritarian organization than to democracy, and because the total power enjoyed by the occupying state over the occupied is a constant temptation for paternalism and annexation. Yet in retrospect, the United States did its best job of implanting democracy in the country it occupied longest, the Philippines, and Great Britain left India after two hundred years the most stable democracy on continental Asia. Perhaps occupation is effective only over an extended period which gives time for the bases of democracy to be established.

9. *Elections by the Fiat of the United States.* The most direct and compelling means of enforcing free elections has been simply to order or legislate them during an American occupation. This was the procedure followed in effect in both Cuban occupations. The United States also tried to dictate the procedure for elections during the occupation of Haiti and the evacuation of the Dominican Republic. American occupation authorities exerted a powerful influence in the framing of postwar constitutions for Germany, and especially Japan.

The successful dictation of the installation of democratic procedures is possible even in the short run only where a new state is being organized or where there is substantial agreement on the part of all indigenous factions because their own constitution has collapsed. Otherwise, even if temporary obedience can be exacted, the likelihood is that the work of the occupation will be sabotaged or amended or revoked as soon as the Americans depart.

How have Americans defined free elections? What conditions have they thought were necessary and what kind of elections have they been ready to accept as "free and fair"? American policy makers have approached the problem with varying degrees of sophistication. Most of them have started with little practical knowledge of the operation of democratic institutions outside their own country. Throughout each of the periods with which we are dealing an individual process of learning has taken place. By and large, the greater the amount of personal experience with foreign elections, the greater has been the skepticism a man felt about the practicability of making them "free" in the West European and North American sense. Unfortunately, however, this painfully acquired wisdom has not accumulated. Many of the key decisions have been made not by the career officers of the State Department but by presidents, secretaries, assistant secretaries and other relatively inexperienced policy makers in the top posts in Washington. Therefore, the policy has tended to go through cycles of experiment, learning and rejection. The overlapping of individuals makes it difficult to trace any general cycles, but it might at least be suggested that they have coincided to some extent with major changes of party in the White House.

Some of the examples of the operation of this cyclical pattern have been: (1) Taft's change of attitude between his Panamanian and Cuban missions of 1904-1908 in which he demonstrated deep concern for free balloting, and his indifference once he became president; (2)

Wilson's reversal on Mexico between 1913 and 1915; and (3) Stimson's reappraisal of the Nicaraguan problem between 1927 and 1932, not to mention his fruitless warning to Truman in 1945 about the poor chances of democracy in Eastern Europe. The Kennedy Administration's active role in Dominican affairs and its nonrecognition of Peru in 1962 appeared to mark the beginning of another such cycle.

We have observed three different reactions to the growing realization that there are essential prerequisites for democracy some of which were unfulfilled in various foreign republics. One was to pursue the will-of-the-wisp through the series of ever more coercive methods described above. Some of the complex legal and political problems this group has had to wrestle with in deciding what constitutes a "free election" have been:

(1) Does an election have to be contested to be free?

(2) Does it show partisan bias for the United States to help the factions of one party to agree on a candidate?

(3) Can indirect elections be considered democratic?

(4) Does the candidacy for reelection of an incumbent president or his relative make a fair election impossible?

(5) Does the postponement of an election by the extension of the presidential term constitute a violation of free elections?

(6) Is an election free which excludes anti-United States candidates?

(7) Is an election free which excludes third parties?

A second course has been to rely on paternalism to create by economic development and education the prerequisites for democracy. The third path has been to follow Secretary Root in his restrictive interpretations of the Platt Amendment, the Hay-Bunau-Varilla Treaty and the Central American convention of 1907. This entailed, the reader will recall, accepting without further inquiry the word of de facto governments that elections they had staged to legitimize themselves were "free and fair", but it also meant intervention on behalf of the party in power when revolutions against it posed a real danger to foreign lives and property.

Secretary Stimson purposely reverted to Root's policy when he announced in 1930 that the United States was returning to the pre-1907 criteria for recognition.[9] In matter of fact, we have settled for something less than the ideal of free and fair elections in most episodes in which our forces were not in actual occupation of a country. Various palliatives and promises for future improvement have been offered the losers to stave off their revolts. Some Departmental officials seem to have believed that by "settling for half a loaf" improvement would take place after economic development and educational progress have had time to effect politics.

*   *   *

The policy of supporting free elections evidently has not been very effective in achieving the goals of American policy makers for which it has been adopted. I have concluded above that the original and ultimate aim of the policy in most cases has been to preserve the security of the United States by promoting stability and discouraging revolution in certain strategically important areas. Americans have pursued this particular policy for that goal because they have mistakenly assumed, that fraudulent and coerced elections are the cause of revolutions in countries which already have democratic constitutions.

The policy has succeeded in creating stability only where our military and naval power has been exerted as in Cuba (1906-08), Panama (1903-31), Nicaragua (1912-25, and 1927-33), and the Philippines (1898-1946) or where the policy has had the unintended, ironical and self-contradictory result of paving the way for a strong dictatorship as in Nicaragua, Cuba, the Dominican Republic and Haiti after 1933 and South Korea and South Vietnam more recently.

Clearly there is something irrational about a policy which succeeds in its ultimate purpose, stability, only by failing in its ostensible immediate purpose—free elections. The reason for this lies in the nature of the politics of Latin America and other underdeveloped areas which make successful support of democracy as an end in itself impossible no matter how comprehensive the means employed. In order to understand this, it is necessary to take a brief look at these characteristics and the impact of American electoral intervention on them:[10]

• *Imitation of the U. S. Constitution.* All of the Latin American republics and some Asian ones have borrowed the presidential system from the United States in the course of the nineteenth and twentieth centuries. The superficial identity of institutions has meant that the burden of proof has lain on anyone who has proposed radically different forms of government even if the proposed forms would be more consistent with the actual conditions and practices there. Hence also the American prescription of legal reform for the faulty operation of the foreign copies when they haven't seemed to work. Because colonial revolutionists imitated our Constitution voluntarily they themselves have been at first ready to ask for and defend American intervention in an effort to make the borrowed institutions function properly. Only later when these idealists began to count the costs of "bringing in King Stork" have they resigned themselves to other solutions such as "guided democracy."

• *Fluidity of Factional Coalitions.* Although the two major parties in most Latin American countries early in the century, Conservative and Liberal, were composed of different elements of the population and were divided by bitter partisan antagonism, Americans have been shocked to find no "real" issues debated in Latin American elections. Perhaps they had not observed their own election campaigns realistically! Since there seemed to be no deep convictions about principles behind party differences, Americans have finally concluded that the so-called parties must be only factions or cliques fighting for revenge and the spoils of office.

With nothing but personal ambitions represented in party rivalry, there should logically be as many factions as leaders, but the existence of the indivisible American-type executive necessitates the coalescence of the inimical factions into two ill-defined alliances at election time. Once "in", an alliance promptly splits up again into its component parts over the division of the spoils because there are never enough jobs to go around in an underdeveloped country. The pressure for government jobs is due to the lack of equally prestigious and remunerative alternative occupations in business and industry.[1] In such a situation, the stakes at issue in an election are high: persecution, discrimination, confiscation, imprisonment or exile all too often await the losers. Because of this, the "ins" can not afford to let the "outs" win an election and the "outs" cannot accept defeat without an appeal to arms.

The consequence of these characteristics is a constant shifting of political alignments which has frustrated all American attempts to discover by free elections a stable majority which could enjoy the allegiance, or at least the acquiescence, of enough of the population to prevent successful revolutions until the next balloting. The "out" parties, especially in Cuba, Panama and Nicaragua, have claimed to represent an overwhelming majority of the people in their countries. The fact that there are always more dissatisfied jobseekers than satisfied jobholders has lent their claims some authenticity. The evidence they have offered that they enjoyed the confidence of a suppressed majority has been convincing enough at the time to bother American consciences and bring about supervised registrations and elections to determine the "real" size of the major parties.

• *The Problem of Reelection.* In discussing the Central American treaties of 1907 and 1923 we have seen that Latin American preoccupation with the reelection of executives has gone far beyond our concern with it. The problem of the peaceful and periodic transfer of power in a presidential government has been aggravated by the nepotism and discrimination characteristic of their Latin culture and premodern economies. One observer of Latin American practices concluded from this that "the principle of rotation in office . . . has become one of the fundamental political traditions . . . and . . . (its failure) one of the underlying [causes] . . . of most revolutions in Central America. . . . A series of Executives may be dictators in form, but the very fact that they are changed periodically results in the introduction of new elements into the Government." [12] From these facts has arisen the strict constitutional and treaty prohibitions against reelection which we have cited. It might be noted that it was the attempt of President Chamoun of Lebanon to change the constitution so that he might be eligible for reelection which precipitated the Lebanese civil war of 1958 in which the United States had to intervene.

From the late 1920s on, Latin American presidents turned from reelection to extension of their terms of office by constitutional amendment. Thus they could stave off the whole problem of elections until a more propitious time. Our State Department protested against this practice in the Dominican Republic (1927) Haiti (1927, 1930), Cuba (1927) and Nicaragua (1930), but with little effect except in the last case. "Continuismo" has more recently appeared in Asia and Africa.

• *The Use of Force in Politics.* The result of nepotism, mutual distrust and animosity, the drive for spoils and the absence of the essential conditions for democracy in the population has been the use of force and fraud in elections by all parties, though the advantage, of course, has lain with the party which has controlled the electoral machinery. There has been utter lack of confidence that if a party's enemies should win office by election, the latter would thereafter respect the rules of the game and give the "outs" a fair chance of winning the next time. This has produced a vicious circle of government-controlled elections and revolt by the losers. Members of each party have come to believe that any means are justified to save their country, and themselves, from their opponent's rule. In a situation like this, where violence is ever near the surface, the army is naturally very powerful and independent of civilian control. [13]

• *The Bandwagon Effect.* The ordinary voter or small office holder in a political system in which "winner takes all and for keeps" has found the penalties of being on the losing side so high and the rewards of joining the prospective "ins" so important that he can not afford to take a position in accordance with any philosophic principles which he might imagine he finds in one party more than the other. He has had to estimate as late as possible in the campaign which side would win and then jump on the bandwagon.[14] The consequence of this phenomenon is that very slight rumors or strained inferences from the words and actions of military and foreign power holders have been enough to precipitate an avalanche of votes for the favored side.

• *Uncontested Elections.* Revolution thus has appeared to be the cheaper alternative to the leaders of the prospective losing side in an election since they can not expect a fair chance to win. At the very least they may abstain from voting, as a protest, to prevent the winners from claiming their allegiance on the ground of a legitimate victory. Such an uncontested election has usually been the signal for a rebellion.

The appearance of the United States on a political scene with the gap just described between formal rules of government and actual practice has produced a policy dilemma. The "ins" have used American guarantees of independence and stability to forestall revolts against their imposed elections. The "outs" have then appealed to the United States against such a tacit support of tyranny. They have asked that we either guarantee free elections or allow revolutions against fraudulent elections. If American intervention has not been forthcoming, the "outs" would start a revolution to force the hand of the North Americans. The losing side in a civil war, be it "in" or "out", has appealed for American aid because they felt, "rather the Americans than our opponents."

Because the American reaction to the above appeals has been unpredictable from time to time and from place to place, other consequences have followed. The United States has been eased into the position of naming candidates and presidents and vetoing others despite its repeated and earnest protestations of impartiality between candidates and parties. Each party has wanted a candidate who would meet with American approval, so the "center of political activity" of these countries has shifted to Washington. The position of Minister to the United States has become of almost equal importance to that of President in these circumstances.

The irritating uncertainty and loss of sovereignty implied by these results has led foreign politicians increasingly to lobby in the United States Congress and to propagandize through the American and their own press with a view to forcing us to give up our electoral interventions. Critics abroad have pointed to the inconsistency between American words and deeds, to the contradiction between present American opposition to revolution and our own revolutionary origin. They have pointed to examples of dishonesty in Uncle Sam's own backyard. With each change of party control in Washington, they have hoped for a reversal of policy. On occasion they may even have helped the "out" party in the United States with campaign material as in the 1920 election.

As foreign populations have experienced American intervention and occupation, inevitably friction has arisen and produced popular resentment. American racial prejudice has antagonized some and affronts to sensitive national honor and patriotism have alienated others. Therefore, Americans who have found no "real" political issues in the politics of some underdeveloped countries have been blind to the obvious paramount issue wherever American military, political and diplomatic intervention are felt: the extent and duration of that interference itself. Political leaders may be obsequious toward the United States in public but they have their own ways of standing up to us. If they believe that their opponents have the final endorsement of Washington, they can turn to stirring up the latent xenophobia of the populace as a last resort.

When open opposition to the United States has been impossible, those leaders who have solicited American help in elections have often tried to conceal their requests or to blame their domestic foes for the necessity of this affront to national honor and sovereignty. There has been a lot of maneuvering to get us to accept the onus of demanding publicly what they have themselves asked for in private. This has run counter to the State Department's determination to avoid criticism by acting only when foreign executives request our intervention. The fact that American interference itself has become the main political issue also accounts for the seeming ingratitude of its beneficiaries. Once a party is in power, it attacks all forms of American participation in their electoral processes even if the "ins" owe their success to foreign supervision of the previous election. If they did not play the ingrate in this way, they would be smeared as American puppets.

The policy dilemma, the bandwagon effect, and the exploitation of American intervention as a political issue all point to one conclusion: that impartial support of free elections is impossible. Since the impartiality of the supervising power is presumably a condition of any support of a really "free" ballot, we are driven to the further conclusion that the support of free elections as an end in itself is self defeating in countries where genuine democracy has not already existed.

No matter how disinterested the American policy makers in Washington and their representatives in the field, every American word and action is bound to be misinterpreted as favorable to one side or the other in an election or civil war, given the political milieu unfolded above. Impartiality is inconceivable to people who have never known it from their own governments. In short, a technically "free and fair" election can never play the role assigned it by democratic theory—a real test of party strength, as long as American participation influences the minds and ballots of the voters.

REFERENCES

FOREWORD

1. *New York Times,* July 27, 1960.
2. This belief was exemplified by President Roosevelt in a speech in 1943 in which he said: "No nation in all the world that is free to make a choice is going to set itself up under the Fascist form of government, or the Nazi . . . or the Japanese war lord form." Robert E. Sherwood, *Roosevelt and Hopkins,* New York: Harper, 1948, p. 702.
3. Hans J. Morgenthau, *In Defense of the National Interest,* New York: Knopf, 1951.
4. Albert K. Weinberg, *Manifest Destiny,* Baltimore: Johns Hopkins University Press, 1935, p. 102.

CHAPTER I

1. Samuel F. Bemis, *The Latin American Policy of The United States,* New York: Harcourt, Brace & Co., 1943, p. 123.
2. Charles E. Chapman, *A History of the Cuban Republic,* New York: Macmillan, 1927, pp. 131, 149.
3. *Ibid.,* p. 91.
4. Richard W. Leopold, *Elihu Root and the Conservative Tradition,* Boston: Little Brown, 1954, p. 29; for Roosevelt, Message of the President to Congress on Establishment of Diplomatic Representation in Cuba, *Papers Relating to the Foreign Relations of the United States* (Hereinafter cited as "Foreign Relations") 1902, p. 321.
5. Garel A. Grunder, and William E. Livezey, *The Philippines and the United States,* Norman: The University of Oklahoma Press, 1951, pp. 29, 72.
6. Chapman, *op. cit.,* pp. 132, 149; Hermann Hagedorn, *Leonard Wood,* 2 vols,. New York: Harper, 1931, p. 302.
7. Philip C. Jessup, *Elihu Root,* 2 vols., New York: Dodd, Mead, 1938, p. 538.
8. Hagedorn, *op. cit.,* p. 261.
9. Elihu Root, *The Military and Colonial Policy of the United States;* addresses, edited by Robert Bacon and James Brown Scott, Cambridge: Harvard University Press, 1916, p. 286.
10. Hagedorn, *op. cit.,* July 3, 1899, p. 218.
11. Wood to Root, February 16, 1900, June 3, 1900, Root Papers.
12. Root, *op. cit.,* p. 172.
13. Jessup, *op. cit.,* pp. 288, 304, 306; for other references: Hagedorn, *op. cit.,* p. 347; Wood to Root, Feb. 16, 1900, Root Papers; Root, *op. cit.,* p. 163.
14. Root to Dana, January 16, 1900, cited in Jessup, *op. cit.,* p. 305; Root, *op. cit.,* p. 193.
15. Jessup, *op. cit.,* p. 304.   16. Root, *op. cit.,* p. 172.
17. Root, *op. cit.,* p. 167 re Puerto Rico.
18. Wood to Root, June 3, 1900, Root Papers.

19. Wood to Root, February 8, 1900, Root Papers.

20. Chapman, *op. cit.*, p. 131; Wood to Root, April 12, 1900, Root Papers.

21. Grunder & Livezey, *op. cit.*, p. 98.　　　22. Hagedorn, *op. cit.*, p. 267.

23. Wood to Root, February 16, 1900, Root Papers.

24. Wood to Root, August 6, 1900, Root Papers.

25. Russell H. Fitzgibbon, *Cuba and the United States*, 1900-1935, Menasha, Wis.: Banta, 1935, p. 86.

26. Hagedorn, *op. cit.*, p. 278.　　　27. *Foreign Relations 1902*, p. 321.

28. Samuel F. Bemis, *The Latin American Policy of the United States*, New York: Harcourt, Brace, 1943, p. 408, citing Jessup, *op. cit.*, I, p. 317.

29. Ludwell L. Montague, *Haiti and the United States, 1714-1938*, Durham, N. C.: Duke University Press, 1940, p. 266. Chapman, *op. cit.*, p. 217.

30. Leland H. Jenks, *Our Cuban Colony*, New York: Vanguard, 1928, p. 73.

31. Taft wrote to Knox years later that Root's chilliness to his administration could be explained by the humiliation Root had suffered in South America when the Cuban intervention took place in the middle of his good will tour. Taft to Knox, December 18, 1913, Knox Papers; Cf., Taft to Root, September 15, 1906, Taft Papers

32. Chapman, *op. cit.*, p. 216; also see: Henry F. Pringle, *The Life and Times of William Howard Taft*, 2 vols., New York: Farrar, 1939, p. 305.

33. Taft to Roosevelt, September 21, 1906, Taft Papers.

34. James Brown Scott, *Robert Bacon, Life and Letters*, Garden City: Doubleday, Page, 1923, p. 118; Taft to Roosevelt, September 16, 21, 22, 1906 re Bacon's opposition; Jessup, *op. cit.*, p. 531 quotes Root to General James H. Wilson, October 24, 1906 in which he admits intervention was necessary once the Cuban government had collapsed.

35. William F. Sands, *Our Jungle Diplomacy*, Chapel Hill: University of North Carolina Press, 1944, pp. 4-6.

36. Taft to Roosevelt, September 16, 1906, Taft Papers.

37. Taft to Roosevelt, September 20, 1906, Taft Papers.

38. Epitome of Events Attendant upon Establishment of the Provisional Government in Cuba, Enclosed by Minister Edwin V. Morgan in his October 13, 1906 to Secretary of State, *Foreign Relations 1906*, Part I, p. 490.

39. Proclamation of Taft as Provisional Governor, September 29, 1906, *Foreign Relations 1906*, Part I, p. 491; Taft to Roosevelt, September 27, 1906, Taft Papers.

40. Taft to Col. Wiley, October 7, 1906, Taft Papers.

41. Chargé Sleeper to Secretary of State, September 1, 1906, *Foreign Relations 1906*, I, p. 465; Chapman, *op. cit.*, p. 198.

42. David A. Lockmiller, *Magoon in Cuba: A History of the Second Intervention, 1906-1909*, Chapel Hill: The University of North Carolina Press, 1938, p. 146.

43. Provisional Governor Magoon to Taft, October 20, 1906, Taft Papers.

44. Jenks, *op. cit.*, p. 100; Also Lockmiller, *op. cit.*, pp. 150-153.

45. Chapman, *op. cit.*, p. 232, and Taft to Roosevelt, October 3, 1906, Taft Papers; Lockmiller, *op. cit.*, p. 71 attributes the appointment to Root.

46. Chapman, *op. cit.*, p. 232.　　　47. Sands, *op. cit.*, pp. 62, 63.

48. Magoon to Taft, November 29, 1906, Taft Papers.

49. Taft to Magoon, November 22, 1906, Taft Papers.

50. Lockmiller, *op. cit.*, pp. 181-183.

51. Taft to Laffan, October 7, 1906, Taft Papers; Taft to Charles Taft, October 9, 1906, *Ibid.*

52. Roosevelt to President-elect Gomez, November 16, 1908, *Foreign Relations 1908*, p. 251.

53. Taft to Roosevelt, September 22, 1906; Chapman, *op. cit.*, p. 213.

54. Taft to Roosevelt, October 3, 1906, Taft Papers.

55. Lockmiller, *op. cit.*, p. 183.

56. Taft to Roosevelt, September 22, 1906. Taft Papers; Taft to Charles Taft, October 9, 1906, *Ibid.*

57. Consul Steinhart, Havana, to Secretary of State, September 12, 1906, *Foreign Relations 1906*, Part I, p. 476.

58. Chapman, *op. cit.*, p. 314.

59. The accounts of the elections of 1916 and 1920 are drawn largely from *Foreign Relations 1917, 1919* and *1920.*

60. Lansing to Tumulty, May 4, 1916, Wilson Papers.

61. Chapman, *op. cit.*, p. 368.

62. H. C. Laikin of the Cuba Company, 49 Wall St., to Polk, February 28, 1917, Polk Papers.

63. Polk Diary, February 28, 1919, Polk Papers.

64. Gonzales to Polk, February 4, 1919, Polk Papers.

65. Ambassador Gonzales to Polk, personal, June 17, 1919, Polk Papers.

66. Chapman, *op. cit.*, p. 406.

67. Chapman, *op. cit.*, p. 447 says Cubans charged Crowder was "muzzled" for political reasons.

68. Memorandum of interview with Cuban Chargé, Dr. Padro y Almeida, August 21, 1923, Hughes Papers.

69. Stokeley Morgan to Secretary of State, Memorandum of Division of Latin American Affairs, April 11, 1927, Archives. Russell Fitzgibbon says this was the first case of "Continuismo in the Caribbean area. See Asher N. Christensen, ed., *The Evolution of Latin American Government*, New York: Holt, 1951, p. 431.

70. Secretary Hull to the Appointed Ambassador in Cuba (Welles), May 1, 1933, *Foreign Relations 1933*, V, p. 283.

71. Bryce Wood, *The Making of the Good Neighbor Policy*, New York: Columbia University Press, 1961, pp. 85, 91, 97.

72. E. D. Cronon, "Interpreting the New Good Neighbor Policy: The Cuban Crisis of 1933", *Hispanic American Historical Review*, XXXIX (November 1959), 531-567 contrasts the policies of Josephus Daniels in Mexico and Welles in Cuba to the advantage of the former. Also see Robert Freeman Smith, "The United States and Latin American Revolutions", *Journal of Inter American Studies*, IV, 1 (January 1962), 89-104.

73. Bemis, *The Latin American Policy of the United States*, p. 281.

CHAPTER II

1. Bemis, *The Latin American Policy of the United States*, pp. 149-150. But see also R. A. Friedlander, "A Reassessment of Roosevelt's Role in the Panamanian Revolution of 1903," *Western Political Quarterly*, June, 1961.

2. *Foreign Relations 1903*, November 13, 1903, p. 246.

3. December 11, 1903, Jessup, *op. cit.*, p. 406.

4. January 6, 1904, *Foreign Relations 1903*, p. 344ff.

5. Jessup, *op. cit.*, p. 407.

6. *Foreign Relations 1904*, p. 546.   7. *Ibid.*, p. 578.

8. William D. McCain, *The United States and the Republic of Panama*, Durham, N.C.: Duke University Press, 1937, p. 48; Minister Squiers to Secretary Root, November 23, 1906, Archives.

9. Taft to Roosevelt, December 19, 1904, Taft Papers.

10. Remarks of Secretary of War Taft at a banquet, December 1, 1904 enclosed in Barrett to Hay, December 6, 1904, *Foreign Relations 1904*, p. 634.

11. Taft to Roosevelt, December 19, 1904, Taft Papers.

12. Minister Magoon to Secretary of State, November 10, 1905, *Foreign Relations 1905*, pp. 716-717.

13. Magoon to Taft, November 10, 1905, Taft Papers.

14. Memorandum of Secretary of State Root to Secretary of War Taft, February 21, 1906, enclosed in Secretary of State to Chargé Sands, February 26, 1906, *Foreign Relations 1906*, Part II, p. 1204.

15. McCain, *op. cit.*, p. 68.

16. December 4, 1905, *Foreign Relations 1905*, p. 720.

17. McCain, *op. cit.*, p. 65.   18. Sands, *op. cit.*, p. 64.

19. Magoon to Taft, July 10, 1906, Taft Papers.

20. Minister Squiers to Secretary Root, November 22, 1906, Archives. Since the U.S. Archives are so admirably catalogued, I will not burden the reader with the file numbers of individual despatches in my citations.

21. Chargé Sands to Secretary Root, October 12, 1906, Archives.

22. *Foreign Relations 1906*, Part 2, p. 1196.

23. Squiers to Root, December 9, 1907, Archives.

24. Squiers to Root, April 22, 1908, Archives.

25. Squiers to Root, December 13, 1906, Archives.

26. Taft to Roosevelt, May 16, 1908, Taft Papers.

27. Taft to Roosevelt, May 9, 1908, May 16, 1908, Taft Papers.

28. Roosevelt to Taft, May 11, 1908, Taft Papers.

29. Taft to President Amador, May 12, 1908, enclosed in Minister Squiers to Secretary of State Root, May 12, 1908, Archives.

30. President Amador memorandum to Hon. J. C. S. Blackburn, enclosed in Minister Squiers to Secretary of State, May 12, 1908, Archives; also Jessup, *op. cit.*, p. 525-526.

31. Minister Squiers to Secretary of State, May 19, 1908, Archives.

32. Obaldia to Secretary of State, June 17, 1908, Archives; Minister Squiers to Secretary of State, May 29, 1908, Archives.

33. Minister Squiers to Secretary of State, July 4, 1908, Archives.

34. Minister Squiers to Secretary Root, July 4, 1908, Archives; Arthur H. Dean's *William Nelson Cromwell 1854-1948*, New York: Ad Press Ltd., 1957, has a chapter defending Cromwell's activities in Panama, but says nothing about the elections.

35. Minister Squiers to Root, May 19, 1909, Archives.

36. Chargé Andrews reported by 1911 that: ". . . advancing radical anti-American views . . . (is) one of the simplest routes to influence with the masses in Panama." Chargé Andrews to Secretary of State, May 17, 1911, Taft Papers.

37. G. T. W.(eitzel), Memorandum Concerning Election of the President of Panama, August 11, 1910, Taft Papers.

38. Chargé Marsh to Secretary of State, August 15, 17, 1910, Taft Papers.

39. Chargé Marsh to Secretary of State, August 26, 1910, Taft Papers.

40. Chargé Marsh to Secretary of State, September 2, 9, 12, 1910, Taft Papers.

41. Acting Secretary Wilson to Chargé Marsh, September 1, 1910, Taft Papers.

42. President Mendoza to President Taft, September 3, 1910, Taft Papers.

43. Chargé Marsh to Secretary of State, September 10, 1910, Taft Papers.

44. Taft to Acting Secretary Wilson, September 12, 1910, Taft Papers.

45. The account of the 1912 election is drawn from *Foreign Relations 1912*, pp. 1133-1163.

46. McCain, *op. cit.*, p. 72.

47. F. H. Huntington Wilson, *Memoirs of an Ex-Diplomat*, Boston: Bruce Humpries, 1945, p. 256.

48. McCain, *op. cit.*, p. 73.

49. Lansing to Wilson, July 3, 1916, Wilson Papers.

50. McCain, *op. cit.*, pp. 74, 75.

51. Dr. Porras to the Secretary of State, December 28, 1927, *Foreign Relations 1927*, III, p. 494.

52. Secretary Stimson to Minister Davis, January 15, 1931, *Foreign Relations 1931*, II, p. 903; McCain, *op. cit.*, pp. 90, 248.

53. J. Lloyd Mecham, *The United States and Inter-American Security, 1889-1960*, Austin: University of Texas Press, 1961, p. 292.

54. Secretary Root to Taft, February 21, 1906, *Foreign Relations 1906*, Part II, p. 1205.

55. *E.g.*, Magoon to Taft, July 10, 1906, Taft Papers.

CHAPTER III

1. Bemis, *The Latin American Policy of The United States*, p. 159ff.

2. James Brown Scott, "The Central American Peace Conference of 1907", *American Journal of International Law*, Vol. 2, 1908, p. 133; William I. Buchanan, *The Central American Peace Conference, Held at Washington, D. C., 1907*, Washington: U. S. Government Printing Office, 1908.

3. William S. Robertson, *Hispanic American Relations with the United States*, New York: Carnegie Endowment for International Peace, 1923, p. 129.

4. *Foreign Relations 1907*, Part II, pp. 693, 696.

5. Lawrence Dennis, "Revolution, Recognition and Intervention", *Foreign Affairs*, Vol. 9, p. 205, quotes Secretary of State Seward as having said after the American Civil War: " 'Revolutions ought not to be accepted until the people have adopted them by organic law with the solemnities which would seem sufficient to guarantee their stability and permanency.' "

6. Robertson, *op. cit.*, p. 133.

7. Jessup, *op. cit.*, p. 511; Huntington Wilson, *op. cit.*, p. 172, says that Doyle ran the conference.

8. George T. Weitzel, *American Policy in Nicaragua*, Washington, 1916, reprinted in United States, 64th Cong., 1st Sess., Sen. Doc. No. 334, "Memorandum on convention . . . relative to an interoceanic canal and a naval station . . . signed . . ." February 8, 1913, pp. 9, 15, 16.

9. John G. Coolidge, *Random Letters From Many Countries*, Boston: Marshall Jones, 1924, p. 387.

10. Unsigned, undated memorandum (1909?) enclosed in "Suggestions for speeches by the Secretary . . . made in the Division of Latin American Affairs" for Knox's Latin American trip, Feb. 3-April 23, 1912, Knox Papers; also see: George T. Weitzel, *Nicaragua and the Bryan-Chamorro Treaty,* (printed speech), 1927, p. 3: "Protection to be effective must come before, not after, the lives and property are destroyed."; and George T. Weitzel, "The United States and Central America: Policy of Clay and Knox," *The Annals of the American Academy of Political and Social Science,* July, 1927, Vol. CXXXII, p. 121.

11. Knox to Taft, Sept. 28 (?) 1909, Knox Papers.

12. Taft to Knox, Dec. 22, 1909, Taft Papers.

13. Salvador Castrillo to Secretary of State, April 6, 1909; F. K. Hill, USN, report, June 8, 1909; Salvador Castrillo to Chargé Gregory, May 28, 1909; Commander Benson, USN, report, June 21, 1909; Drew Linard, US Consul in Bluefields, Nicaragua, July 5, 1909, Archives.

14. Salvador Castrillo to Stimson, October 19, 1927, Stimson Papers.

15. J. Butler Wright to Polk, December 18, 1915, Polk Papers.

16. Samuel F. Bemis, *A Diplomatic History of the United States,* New York: Henry Holt, 1949.

17. Knox to the Nicaraguan Chargé, December 1, 1909, *Foreign Relations 1909,* p. 455.

18. Harold N. Denny, *Dollars for Bullets,* New York: Dial Press, 1929, pp. 84, 85.

19. Weitzel, *American Policy in Nicaragua,* p. 13; William T. S. Doyle, "Memorandum Regarding the Eligibility of Doctor Jose Madriz to be Provisional President of Nicaragua," Division of Latin American Affairs, December 20, 1909, Knox Papers.

20. The new government installed with American aid abolished monopolies granted by the Zelaya regime which had discriminated against foreigners. Charges were made in later years that Secretary Knox had a personal financial stake in certain mining concessions in Nicaragua which Zelaya was threatening with competition. If so, it would be the only known case where a high U. S. official used the policy of free elections to promote his own economic interests. Since Knox advocated a policy of promoting American trade and investment abroad, the same conclusion can be reached without positing a personal benefit. See: United States, 69th Cong., 2d Sess., "Hearings before the Subcommittee on Foreign Relations of the United States Senate . . . pursuant to S. Con. Res. 15, Relative to Engaging the Responsibility of the Government in Financial Relations between its Citizens and Sovereign Foreign Governments." January 25, 26, 27, February 16, 1927 for the testimony of Toribio Tijerino and Thomas Moffat, ex-United States Consul in Bluefields, Nicaragua 1909 and Acting Special Agent in Charge near the Government of Nicaragua, on duty with the Mixed Claims Commission, Nicaragua 1910-1911; Wilfrid Hardy Callcott, *The Caribbean Policy of the United States, 1910-1920,* Baltimore: Johns Hopkins University Press, 1942, p. 279, cites the polemic of Rafael de Nogales y Mendez, *The Looting of Nicaragua,* New York: McBride, 1928, p. 7 citing Horace Blanco-Fombona, *Crimines des Imperialismo Norteamericano,* Mexico: Ediciones Churubusco, 1927, pp. 7-8.

21. Castrillo to Secretary of State, Sept. 12, 1910, *Foreign Relations 1910,* p. 762.

22. Copy enclosed in Secretary Knox's instructions to Minister Northcott, Jan. 20, 1911, *Foreign Relations 1911*, pp. 652-653.

23. Roscoe R. Hill, "Nicaragua", Chapter XVI of *The Caribbean Area,* edited by A. Curtis Wilgus, Washington, D. C.: The George Washington University Press, 1934, p. 298.

24. Minister Dawson to Secretary of State, Oct. 28, 1910, *Foreign Relations 1910*, p. 765.

25. Denny, *op. cit.*, p. 94, Consul Moffatt to Secretary of State, November 28, 1910. *Foreign Relations 1910*, p. 767: ". . . elections were held . . . no disorder occurred . . . hundreds of Liberals voted for the Conservative deputies . . . this assembly will elect Estrada unanimously."

26. Weitzel, *American Policy in Nicaragua*, p. 13.

27. The account cited is drawn from *Foreign Relations 1911 and 1912.*

28. Weitzel, *American Policy in Nicaragua*, p. 21.

29. Dana G. Munro, *The Five Republics of Central America, Their Political and Economic Development and Their Relations with The United States,* New York: Oxford University Press, 1918, p. 245.

30. Weitzel, *American Policy in Nicaragua*, p. 8. This was not from any naivete on Weitzel's part. He regarded the thirty-five years of peace (1858-1893) when a Conservative oligarchy rotated the presidency among themselves as the ideal for Nicaragua.

31. Selig Adler, "Bryan and Wilsonian Caribbean Penetrations, *Hispanic American Historical Review,* Vol. XX (May, 1940), *passim.*

32. Bryan to Wilson, June 16, 1913, Wilson Papers.

33. Bryan to Wilson, June 12, 1914, Wilson Papers.

34. Arthur S. Link, *Woodrow Wilson and the Progressive Era, 1910-1917,* New York: Harper, 1954, p. 96.

35. Chargé Gunther to Secretary of State, December 21, 1911, *Foreign Relations 1911*, pp. 670-671.

36. Bryan to Wilson, July 31, 1913, Wilson Papers.

37. *Congressional Record,* 63d Cong., 2d Sess., Vol. 51, Part 12, p. 11614, July 6, 1914.

38. Anna I. Powell, "Relations between the U. S. and Nicaragua," *Hispanic American Historical Review,* Vol. VIII, p. 59 citing *Congressional Record,* January 13, 1927, p. 1574. Root's speech was made on January 7, 1915.

39. Bryan to Wilson, January 23, 1914, Bryan Papers.

40. Bryan to Wilson, January 15, 1914, Wilson Papers.

41. Bryan to Wilson, January 22, 1915, Bryan Papers.

42. Bryan to Wilson, January 23, 1914, Bryan Papers.

43. Bryan to Wilson, January 22, 1915, Bryan Papers.

44. Weitzel "Nicaragua and the Bryan-Chamorro Treaty", *op. cit.*, p. 11.

45. Wright to Secretary from Division of Latin American Affairs, January 14, 1916, Archives.

46. Chargé Wicker to Secretary, January 31, 1916, *Archives.*

47. Unsigned telegram from Nicaragua, February 10, 1916, Archives.

48 Memorandum of conversation between Mr. Wright and Mr. Clark, April 22, 1916, Archives.

49. J. B. Wright, Division of Latin American Affairs, Memorandum on Nicaragua, February 28, 1916, Archives.

50. Minister Jefferson to Secretary of State, April 27, 1916, Archives.

51. Minister Jefferson to Secretary of State, September 21, 1916, April 27, 1916, Archives; Denny, *op. cit.*, p. 177.

52. *E.g.*, Chargé Wicker to Secretary of State, December 15, 1915; Wright Memorandum, February 28, 1916; Minister Jefferson to Secretary of State, April 27, 1916, Archives.

53. Minister Jefferson to Secretary of State, September 17, 21, 1916, Archives.

54. Minister Jefferson to Secretary of State, September 26, 1916, Archives.

55. Secretary Lansing to Minister Jefferson, August 25, 1916, Archives.

56. Minister Jefferson to Secretary of State, June 15, 1920, *Foreign Relations 1920*, Vol. III, p. 295.

57. Department of State, *Biographic Register*. Munro became Assistant Chief of Division in 1923 and Chief of Division in 1930.

58. Dana G. Munro, *The Five Republics of Central America*, p. 30. The quotations are from pages 308, 310 and 259.

59. See Testimony of Juan Leets in: U. S. Congress, Senate, *Nicaraguan Affairs*, Hearing before the Committee on Foreign Relations, U. S. Senate, 62nd Cong., 2nd Sess., 1912, Washington: U. S. Government Printing Office, 1913, p. 9.

60. George B. Davis, Judge Advocate General, War Department, Memorandum, January 3, 1910, Archives.

61. Davis to Tumulty, January 21, 1921, Wilson Papers.

62. The Judge Advocate General, War Department (Crowder) to the Chief of the Division of Latin American Affairs, Department of State (Rowe), April 14, 1920, *Foreign Relations 1920*, III, 293. The record of the 1920 election is to be found in *Foreign Relations 1920*, III, pp. 293-311.

63. Denny, *op. cit.*, p. 181.

64. Roscoe R. Hill, "American Marines in Nicaragua, 1912-1925" in *Hispanic American Essays*, A. Curtis Wilgus, ed., Chapel Hill: University of North Carolina Press, 1942, p. 356.

65. Secretary Hughes to Chargé Thurston, October 8, 1923, *Foreign Relations, 1923*, Vol. II, p. 608.

66. Memorandum by the Secretary of State of a Conversation with the Nicaraguan Minister (Chamorro), September 28, 1923, *Foreign Relations 1923*, Vol. II, p. 606.

67. Wilfred H. Callcott, *op. cit.*, pp. 452-453.

68. Hill, *op. cit.*, p. 294; Secretary of State to Minister Ramer, January 18, 1923 (footnote), *Foreign Relations 1923*, II, 605.

69. Secretary Hughes to Chargé Thurston, June 5, 1924, *Foreign Relations 1924*, II, p. 508.

70. Weitzel, "Nicaragua and the Bryan-Chamorro Treaty" *op. cit.*, p. 5.

71. Munro, *The Five Republics of Central America*, p. 310.

72. Harold W. Dodds, "The United States and Nicaragua," *Annals of the American Academy of Political and Social Science*, CXXXII, July 1927, p. 136.

73. Unsigned letter to Senator Borah, February 13, 1926, C. P. Anderson Papers.

74. Dodds to Munro, May 21, 1924, Archives.

75. Chargé Thurston to Secretary of State, August 12, 1924, Archives; Munro to Acting Secretary Grew, August 14, 1924, Archives.

76. Hill, in *The Caribbean Area*, p. 296; Denny, *op. cit.*, p. 196.

77. Chandler P. Anderson Diary, December 17, 1924, Anderson Papers.

78. Anderson Diary, February 16, July 7, 1924, January 17, 1925, C. P. Anderson Papers.

79. H. K. Thompson to Anderson, July 9, 1924, C. P. Anderson Papers; Diary, July 16, 1924.

80. Memorandum, Division of Latin American Affairs, Munro to White, March 3, 1924 re Castrillo memorandum, Archives; Memorandum of interview with Nicaraguan Chargé and Senor Tijerino, Nicaraguan Consul General in New York with Francis White, Munro and Hughes, May 3, 1924, Hughes Papers.

81. Memorandum of October 12, 1922 attached to Hughes to Harding, October 21, 1922, Hughes Papers.

82. Isaac J. Cox, *Nicaragua and the United States, 1909-1927*, Boston: World Peace Foundation, 1927, p. 745.

83. *Conference on Central American Affairs, Washington, December 4, 1922-February 7, 1923*, Washington: U. S. Government Printing Office, p. 287.

84. Radio address on "Latin American Relations", January 20, 1925, cited in Memorandum on "Latin-American Intervention and the Monroe Doctrine" (1933-34), Hughes Papers.

85. Memorandum on "Latin American Conference: 1. The Central American Conference of 1922-23", (1933-34), Hughes Papers.

86. Enclosed in Chargé Smith to Secretary of State, November 4, 1922, Archives; also: Cox, *op. cit.*, p. 770 cites an editorial of the same import from the Diario del Comercio, February 14, 1923.

87. Memorandum on "Latin American Conference", *op. cit.*

88. Chandler P. Anderson, "The Central American Policy of Non-Recognition", *American Journal of International Law*, January 1925, p. 166.

89. Except when otherwise noted, the account of the events of 1925-32 is drawn from the volumes of *Foreign Relations* for those years.

90. "Biographical data relating to President Diaz", first part of a memorandum initialed S(tokeley) W. M(organ), January 11, 1927, Stimson papers. Anderson Diary, April 7, 1927: "I told (Stimson) that as amazing as it might seem, Secretary Kellogg had himself told me that he had never read this treaty until long after he had refused to recognize Chamorro on account of it."

91. C. P. Anderson Diary, October 6, 1926, Anderson Papers.

92. Lewis S. Gannett, "Our Policy and Responsibility in Nicaragua," *Censensus*, Vol. XII, No. 4, June, 1928, Stimson Papers.

93. Chandler P. Anderson Diary, December 2, 1924, C. P. Anderson Papers; Harold N. Denny, *op. cit.*, pp. 239, 243, 254. Rivalry with Mexico played an important part in the 1909 intervention in Nicaragua too, as is revealed by the Knox papers.

94. Unsigned telegram dated January 2, 1927 from Bluefields, Nicaragua; Memorandum from Douglas H. Allen, January 11, 1927, C. P. Anderson Papers.

95. Stimson Diary, March 31, 1927, Stimson Papers.

96. Memorandum for Hon'able Henry L. Stimson, Re: Nicaragua, April 8, 1927, from D. H. Allen, Stimson Papers; Stimson Diary: March 31, April 6, 7, 9, 1927, Stimson Papers.

97. Stimson to A. C. Taylor of Thomas Nelson & Sons, December 2, 1927, Stimson Papers.

98. Stimson Diary, April 5, 1927, Stimson Papers.

99. Stimson Diary, April 30, 1927, Stimson Papers.

100. Secretary Kellogg to Stimson, May 4, 1927, Stimson Papers.

101. McCoy to Stimson, July 13, 1927, Stimson Papers.

102. Executive Memorandum No. 14, September 7, 1928, American Electoral Mission in Nicaragua, H. W. Isbell, ed., McCoy Papers.

103. Munro to Secretary Kellogg, September 14, 1927, Stimson Papers.

104. Francis White to Stimson, November 2, December 6, 1927, Stimson Papers.

105. Anderson Diary, November 1, 1926, C. P. Anderson Papers.

106. Francis White to Stimson, August 23, 1927, Stimson Papers.

107. English text of Stimson's speech at Leon, Nicaragua, April 28, 1927, Stimson Diary.

108. Secretary Kellogg to Minister Eberhardt, May 18, 1928, *Foreign Relations 1928*, III, p. 491. Professor Dodds explained that the ephemeral third parties of Central American politics were created for bargaining purpose or by a major party to lure the voters of the other major party. Harold W. Dodds, "American Supervision of Nicaragua Election", *Foreign Affairs*, Vol. 7 (1928), p. 494.

109. American Electoral Mission in Nicaragua, Summary of Events and Policies from the Stimson Agreements to Date, Revised up to September 1, 1928, McCoy Papers.

110. "Memorandum of conference with Mr. Root, July 6, 1927 Re Nicaragua", Stimson Papers.

111. Francis White to McCoy, November 18, 1928, McCoy Papers.

112. Stimson to Secretary of State, April 20, 1927, *Foreign Relations 1927*, Vol. III, p. 323; Stimson Diary, April 30, 1927, Stimson Papers; Henry L. Stimson, *American Policy in Nicaragua*, New York: Scribner, 1927, p. 61.

113. Bryce Wood, *The Making of the Good Neighbor Policy*, New York; Columbia University Press, 1961, p. 35. Also J. O. Baylen, "Sandino: Patriot or Bandit?" *Hispanic American Historical Review*, XXXI (August 1951), 394-419.

114. Dana G. Munro, "The Establishment of Peace in Nicaragua," *Foreign Affairs*, Vol. XI, 1933, p. 701.

115. Wood, *op. cit.*, p. 25.

116. Henry L. Stimson and McGeorge Bundy, *On Active Service in Peace and War*, New York: Harper, 1948, p. 182.

117. Munro, "The Establishment of Peace in Nicaragua", p. 701.

118. Munro, "The Establishment of Peace in Nicaragua," p. 702.

119. Raymond L. Buell, "American Supervision of Elections in Nicaragua", Foreign Policy Association, *Information Service*, Vol. VI, No. 21, December 24, 1930, p. 395.

120. *Foreign Relations 1935*, Vol. IV, pp. 842-887 for Somoza's rise to power.

121. Wood, *op. cit.*, pp. 147-148.

122 Raymond L. Buell, "The United States and Central American Revolutions." *Foreign Policy Association, Report*, Vol. VII, No. 10, July 22, 1931, p. 203.

CHAPTER IV

1. Howard F. Cline, *The United States and Mexico*, Cambridge: Harvard University Press, 1953, pp. 118-120.

2. Ambassador Henry Lane Wilson to Secretary of State, October 18, 1911, *Foreign Relations 1911*, p. 519.

3. Ambassador Wilson to Secretary of State, February 25, 1913, *Foreign Relations 1913*, p. 738.

4. Secretary Knox to Ambassador Wilson, February 21, 1913, Taft Papers; Link, *op. cit.*, p. 108, quotes Chandler P. Anderson's diary to the effect that Knox said he would have recognized Huerta if he and Taft had realized that President Wilson wouldn't.

5. "Suggestive Points on the Mexican Situation", n.d., initialed J.(oshua) R.(euben) C.(lark), Knox Papers.

6. Constitutional Governor Maitorena of Sonora to Secretary of State, March 7, 1913, *Foreign Relations 1913*, p. 759; the Plan of Guadalupe is in *Foreign Relations 1914*, p. 590.

7. March 11, 1913, *Foreign Relations 1913*, p. 7.

8. Link, *op. cit.*, p. 111.

9. Ambassador H. L. Wilson to Secretary of State, May 1, 1913, *Foreign Relations 1913*, p. 798.

10. Ray Stannard Baker, *Woodrow Wilson: Life and Letters*, Garden City: Doubleday, Doran, 1913, Vol. IV, pp. 245-249; Link, *op. cit.*, pp. 111-112, citing "Mexican Settlement", MSS drafted by Wilson ca. May 8-10, 1913, Wilson Papers.

11. Baker, *op. cit.*, IV, p. 248.

12. J. Kruttschnitt, Chairman of Southern Pacific Railroad to Bryan, May 26, 1913; E. Brush and S. W. Eccles to Bryan, May 26, 1913, Wilson Papers.

13. Bryan to Wilson, May 27, 1913, Wilson to Bryan May 28, 1913, *Ibid.*

14. Cline, *op. cit.*, p. 144.

15. Bryan to Wilson, July 19, 1913, Wilson Papers.

16. U. S. Attorney General Wickersham to Taft, May 8, 1911, Taft Papers; James E. Clark to Wilson, March 3, 1913, Wilson Papers; London Daily News clipping, ca. November 1, 1913, Wilson Papers.

17. Riley W. Allen, Williamsport, Pa., to Wilson August 9, 1913, Wilson Papers enclosing S. W. Rider of U. S. and Mexican Trust Co., to Allen.

18. Ambassador Wilson to Secretary Knox, February 19, 1913, *Foreign Relations 1913*, p. 722.

19. D. J. Haff to Cleveland H. Dodge, July 22, 1913, Wilson Papers.

20. By September, 1913, Chargé O'Shaughnessy reported to Bryan that political passions between liberals and clericals were high over the issue of educational policy.

21. Drafts dated July 30, August 4, 1913, Wilson Papers.

22. Link, *op. cit.*, p. 114.

23. Chargé O'Shaughnessy to Secretary of State, September 22, 1913, *Foreign Relations 1913*, p. 834.

24. Bryan to Wilson, September 25, 1913, Bryan Papers.

25. Hale to Wilson, September 28, 1913, Wilson Papers.

26. Chargé O'Shaughnessy to Secretary Bryan, October 25, 1913, *Foreign Relations 1913*, p. 850.

27. Secretary of State to American Embassy, Mexico, October 24, 1913, Bryan Papers, and Secretary Bryan to Chargé O'Shaughnessy, October 13, 1913, *Foreign Relations 1913*, p. 838.

28. J. B. Moore to Ambassador Page, October 8 (?), 1913, Wilson Papers.

29. Harley Notter, *The Origins of the Foreign Policy of Woodrow Wilson*, Baltimore: Johns Hopkins University Press, 1937, p. 274.

30. Denny, *op. cit.*, p. 386, citing Burton J. Hendrick, *The Life and Letters of Walter H. Page*, 3 vols., Garden City: Doubleday, 1922-25. Compare Ambassador Page to Secretary Bryan, October 28, 1913, *Foreign Relations 1913*, p. 852.

31. Major Ryan to Tumulty, July 25, 1913, Wilson Papers; Secretary of State to American Embassy, Mexico, October 24, 1913, Bryan Papers; Ambassador Page to Secretary Bryan, October 28, 1913, *Foreign Relation 1913*, p. 852.

32. Link, *op. cit.*, p. 120.   33. Cline, *op. cit.*, p. 151.

34. Annual Message of the President, n.d. (December, 1913), *Foreign Relations 1913*, p. x.

35. Cline, *op. cit.*, p. 157.   36. *Ibid.*, p. 160.

37. Special Commissioners to Secretary of State, May 20, 1914, *Foreign Relations 1914*, p. 502.

38. Secretary of State to Special Commissioners, June 3, 1914, *Ibid.*, p. 523.

39. Special Commissioners to Secretary of State, June 12, 1914 enclosing Memorandum of the Mexican Delegation to the American Delegation, *Ibid.*, pp. 527-528.

40. Notter, *op. cit.*, p. 108.

41. Josephus Daniels, *The Wilson Era, Years of Peace, 1910-1917*, Chapel Hill: University of North Carolina Press, 1944, p. 180.

42. Cline, *op. cit.*, pp. 140, 145.   43. Notter, *op. cit.*, p. 228.

44. *E.g.*, letters of: Haff, July 22, 1913; Braniff, July 11, 1913; Fall, August 14, 1913; Wilfley, September 3, October 22, 1913; A. B. Hart, April 5, 1914, Wilson Papers.

45. James M. Platt, Mexico City to U. S. Representative Seldomridge, June 23, 1913, enclosed in Seldomridge to Bryan, July 11, 1913, enclosed in J. B. Moore to Tumulty, July 21, 1913, Wilson Papers.

46. Lind to Bryan, September 19, 1913, Bryan Papers.

47. Lind to Bryan, August 28, 1913, Wilson Papers. Lind to Bryan, September 19, 1913, Bryan Papers.

48. Lind to Wilson, January 10, 1914, Wilson Papers.

49. Lind to Bryan, May 29, 1914, Bryan Papers; Lind to Bryan, April 16, 1915, Bryan Papers.

50. Cline, *op. cit.*, pp. 163, 173; Link, *op. cit.*, p. 127.

51. Special Agent Carothers to the Department of State, September 26, 1914, *Foreign Relations 1914*, p. 605, contains Villa's pronunciamento.

52. Link, *op. cit.*, pp. 128-133.

53. *Foreign Relations, Lansing Papers*, Vol. II, p. 547.

54. Secretary Lansing to Mr. Parker, Representing American interests in Mexico, October 19, 1915, *Foreign Relations 1915*, p. 771. It is interesting to note that when Carranza was overthrown and killed in 1920, the Mexicans sought U. S. recognition on the basis of the "irreproachable popular election" of the new government. Secretary Hughes withheld recognition for three years not on this ground, but because "the fundamental question at issue has been the safeguarding of American property rights in Mexico, especially as against a confiscatory application of the provisions of the Mexican Constitution of 1917."

Chargé Summerlin to Secretary of State, June 10, 1921, *Foreign Relations 1921*, Vol. II, p. 411, enclosing Memoranda from the Mexican Foreign Office; Memorandum of interview with Adolfo de la Huerta, Minister of Finance of Mexico, July 18, 1922, Hughes Papers. Hughes to United States Commissioner Warren, May 8,

1923, *Foreign Relations 1923*, Vol. II, p. 537.

55. Cline, *op. cit.*, p. 183.

56. Wilfley to Wilson, September 3, October 22, 1913; Lind to Bryan, September 19, 1913; Lind to Wilson, January 10, 1914, April 16, 1915, Wilson Papers.

57. Madison: University of Wisconsin Press, 1960.

CHAPTER V

1. Samuel F. Bemis, *A Diplomatic History of the United States*, Revised ed. New York: Henry Holt, 1949, p. 528.

2. George T. Weitzel, *Nicaragua and the Bryan-Chamorro Treaty*, (speech), 1927, p. 4; Secretary of State to Minister Northcott, January 20, 1911, *Foreign Relations 1911*, p. 651.

3. "Memorandum of the Dominican Situation", submitted to the President by the Department of State, September 17, 1912, contained in Huntington Wilson to Taft, September 19, 1912, Taft Papers.

4. Unless otherwise noted the contents of this chapter are based upon information drawn from the volumes of *Foreign Relations* for 1912-1924.

5. Chargé Curtis to Secretary of State, September 3, 1913; Secretary of State to American Legation, Santo Domingo, September 11, 1913, Archives.

6. Minister Sullivan to Secretary Bryan, October 7, 1913, Archives.

7. Sumner Welles, *Naboth's Vineyard; the Dominican Republic, 1844-1924*, 2 vols. New York: Payson and Clarke, 1928, p. 725.

8. Notter, *op. cit.*, p. 279; Bryan to Sullivan, December 7, 1913, *Foreign Relations 1913*, p. 443.

9. "Santo Domingo Investigation, Copy of the Report, Findings and Opinion", by James D. Phelan, Chas. H. Strong, Counsel, Washington, 1916, Wilson Papers, *passim;* Walker W. Vick, Receiver General, Dominican Republic to Tumulty, April 14, 1914; Vick to Wilson, December 1, 1914, Wilson Papers.

10. Welles, *op. cit.*, p. 745.

11. Fort to Tumulty, November 16, 1914, Wilson Papers.

12. "Santo Domingo Investigation", *op. cit.*, p. 21.

13. Secretary of State to American Legation, Santo Domingo, June 3, 1916, Polk Papers.

14. The President of the City Council to the People of Santo Domingo, May 14: "The American Minister added that the purpose for which that force is entering is to guarantee the free election of the new President . . .," enclosed in Vice Consul von Zielinski, Santo Domingo, to Secretary of State, May 17, 1916, *Foreign Relations 1916*, p. 229.

15. General Receiver Baxter to Joseph P. Tumulty, April 10, 1919, Wilson Papers.

16. Welles, *op. cit.*, p. 836; Harold P. Davis, *Black Democracy*, New York: Dial, 1928, p. 336.

17. United States, 67th Cong., 1st and 2nd Sess., Senate Hearings before a Select Committee on Haiti and Santo Domingo, pursuant to S. Res. 112, authorizing a special committee to inquire into the occupation and administration of the territories of the Republic of Haiti and the Dominican Republic, Washington: U. S. Government Printing Office, 1922. Joseph R. Juarez in "United States With-

drawal from Santo Domingo", *Hispanic American Historical Review*, XLII, 2 (May 1962), 152-190, argues that the withdrawal was brought about by the islands diminished strategic value after the war, the conversion of the intervention into a partisan political issue in the 1920 election and the effectiveness of Dominican anti-occupation propaganda both in the United States and Latin America.

18. Welles, *op. cit.*, p. 814.

19. Snowden to Secretary of the Navy, May 8, 1919 enclosed in F. D. Roosevelt to Polk, May 31, 1919, Polk Papers; and Snowden to Minister Russell, December 2, 1919, *Foreign Relations 1919*, Vol. II, p. 142.

20. Welles, *op. cit.*, p. 850.

21. *Ibid.*, p. 820-822, Welles says Snowden expected military government to last "until the generation of Dominicans then in the cradle had reached adult age."

22. *Ibid.*, p. 927.

23. *Ibid.*, pp. 852-855 and Welles to Secretary of State October 2, 1922, *Foreign Relations 1922*, Vol. II, p. 64.

24. Welles, *op. cit.*, p. 906; Minister Russell to Secretary of State, October 10, 1923, *Foreign Relations 1923*, I, 903.

25. Welles, *op. cit.*, pp. 903-931. Welles' experiences with military paternalism and free elections in the Dominican Republic had an important bearing on the policy of nonintervention called the "Good Neighbor" policy in the next decade when he was first Assistant Secretary of State (1933-1937) and then Undersecretary of State (1937-1943) in the administration of Franklin D. Roosevelt.

CHAPTER VI

1. Ludwell L. Montague, *Haiti and the United States, 1714-1938*, Durham, N. C.: Duke University Press, 1940, pp. 210-211; Memorandum of Boaz Long of the Division of Latin American Affairs, January 23, 1914, Wilson Papers. There is a striking parallel to this period in the chaos of 1957 in Haiti when about seven presidents followed one another within a year.

2. Bryan to Wilson, January 21, 1914, Wilson Papers; Bryan to Wilson April 2, 1915, Bryan Papers.

3. Bryan to Minister Blanchard, August 28, 1914, Archives; Acting Secretary of State Lansing to Blanchard, October 29, 1914, *Foreign Relations 1914*, p. 355.

4. Where not otherwise indicated the material in this chapter is drawn from *Foreign Relations* Volumes 1914-1930 and *Foreign Relations, the Lansing Papers*.

5. Bryan to Wilson, January 7, 1915; Wilson to Bryan, January 13, 1915, Wilson Papers; Bryan to Wilson, March 23, 1915, Bryan Papers.

6. Commissioners Fort and Smith and Minister Blanchard to Secretary of State, March 13, 1915, Wilson Papers.

7. Latin American Affairs Division Memorandum, June 22, 1915, on Paul Fuller's report of June 14, 1915, Archives.

8. Bryan to Wilson, April 2, 1915, Bryan Papers.

9. Secretary Bryan to Wilson, February 25, 1915, Bryan Papers.

10. When Dartiguenave later reneged on his promise, Lansing called his bluff by threatening that if the Haitian President did not accept the treaty, the United States would set up a military government, "until honest elections could be held." Montague, *op. cit.*, p. 220.

11. Montague, *op. cit.*, p. 239.   12. Davis, *op. cit.*, p. 210.

13. Montague, *op. cit.*, p. 229.

14. W. Cameron Forbes Journals, Vol. III, 1930-1934, p. 68. Juarez, *op. cit.*, attributes the longer occupation of Haiti than Santo Domingo to: existence of a treaty legalizing the American status in Haiti, the absence of comparable bonds of sentiment with Hispanic America, the continuance in office of Haitian executives who benefited from Marine protection, racial prejudice which rendered American public opinion indifferent to the Negro republic's fate, and the failure of withdrawal from Nicaragua in 1925.

15. Montague, *op. cit.*, p. 278.

CHAPTER VII

1. Memorandum on "The Overthrow of the Government of Costa Rica by the Minister of War, Federico Tinoco, January 27, 1917," by Jordan Stabler, Division of Latin American Affairs, Department of State, February 6, 1917, Archives.

2. Unless otherwise noted the contents of this chapter is from the 1917 to 1920 volumes of *Foreign Relations* and the *Lansing Papers* published in the same series.

3. The Agent of the De Facto Government of Costa Rica (R. Fernandez Guardia) to the Secretary of State, March 12, 1917, *Foreign Relations 1917*, p. 313; Samuel E. Piza to Tumulty, August 1, 1917, Wilson Papers; Hollins N. Randolph, "In Re: Case of Costa Rica," November 1, 1917, Wilson Papers; John M. Popham to Wilson, February 28, March 23, May 29, 1918, Wilson Papers.

4. Samuel Untermyer to Secretary of Treasury McAdoo, February 28, 1917, Archives.

5. Wilson to Bryan, July 23, 1918, Wilson Papers.

6. Stabler for the Division of Latin American Affairs to Secretary of State, March 3, 1917, Archives.

7. Report of John Foster Dulles, May 22, 1917, U. S. National Archives.

8. General E. H. Plummer, Commanding General Panama Canal Zone to Adjutant General, U. S. Army, May 22, 1917, Archives.

9. Wilson to Senator Joseph E. Ransdell, March 5, 1918; Wilson Papers.

10. Wilson to Lansing, May 28, 1917, Archives.

11. Undersecretary Davis to Wilson, June 25, 1920, July 13, 1920, Wilson Papers.

12. Luis Anderson, "De Facto Government," *Inter-America*, Vol. 8, 1923, pp. 503-534.

13. Division of Latin American Affairs Memorandum, signed H. J. (Hallett Johnson?) to Polk, attached to Polk to Wilson, July 18, 1919, Polk Papers.

14. C. P. Anderson Diary, December 12, 1924, Anderson Papers, re talk with Munro.

CHAPTER VIII

1. *Foreign Relations, 1907*, Vol. II, pp. 601-605. This case has been related on the basis of Honduran sources by William S. Stokes in *Honduras: An Area Study in Government* (Madison: University of Wisconsin Press, 1950).

2. *Foreign Relations, 1911*, pp. 299-307.

3. General Máximo B. Rosales to President Wilson, Feb. 4, 1916 with appended note by J. Butler Wright, Acting Chief, Division of Latin American Affairs, Archives.

4. J. Antonio López G. to Hallett Johnson, Chief of Division of Latin American Affairs, July 7, 1919, Archives.

5. Lansing to Wilson, Aug. 29, 1919, Archives.

6. *Foreign Relations, 1919*, Vol. II, p. 376.

7. Minister Jones to Hallett Johnson, April 21, 1919, Archives.

8. Acting Secretary of State Phillips to Minister Jones, July 20, 1919, *Foreign Relations, 1919*, Vol. II, p. 379.

9. Minister Jones to Secretary of State, July 28, 1919, Archives.

10. Lansing to Wilson, July 25, 1919, Archives.

11. Hallett Johnson to Phillips, Sept. 4, 1919, Archives. Acting Secretary Phillips to Minister Jones, Sept. 5, 1919, *Foreign Relations, 1919*, Vol. II, p. 383.

12. Commanding Officer, U. S. S. *Baltimore*, Amapala, Honduras, to Secretary of Navy, Oct. 13, 1919, Archives.

13. Minister Jones to Secretary of State, Sept. 16, 1919, *Foreign Relations, 1919*, Vol. II, p. 386.

14. *Conference on Central American Affairs, Washington, December 4, 1922-February 7, 1923* (Washington, 1923) p. 287.

15. Memorandum, Division of Latin American Affairs, Munro to White, Feb. 19, 1923, Archives.

16. Secretary of State to American Legation, Honduras, Feb. 26, 1923, Archives.

17. Memorandum, Division of Latin American Affairs, Munro to White, April 4, 1923, Archives.

18. Secretary of State to Minister Morales, April 28, 1923, *Foreign Relations, 1923*, Vol. II, p. 426. Emphasis added.

19. Division of Latin American Affairs, White to Phillips, April 26, 1923, Archives; Minister Morales to Secretary of State, May 13, 1923, *Foreign Relations 1923*, Vol. II, p. 429. Unless otherwise indicated, the rest of this case is based on this volume and those for 1924 and 1925.

20. Minister Morales to Secretary of State, July 12, 1923 cited in Secretary of State to American Legation in Honduras, August 4, 1923, Archives.

21. Hughes to Coolidge, April 9, 1924, Archives.

22. Secretary of State to Commissioner in the Dominican Republic (Welles), April 10, 1924, *Foreign Relations, 1924*, Vol. II, p. 303.

23. Secretary Hughes to American Legation, Honduras, May 23, 1924, Archives.

24. Frederick R. Gibbs to Joseph R. Baker, Assistant Solicitor, Department of State, April 5, 1924; enclosed is a memorandum by H. V. Rolston, General Manager of the Cuyamel Fruit Co. dated April 4, 1924, Archives.

25. Sumner Welles to Secretary of State, Report, June 2, 1924, Archives.

26. Stokes, op. cit. pp. 251, 255; Minister Lay to Secretary of State, Sept. 14, 1932, *Foreign Relations, 1932*, Vol. V, p. 713.

CHAPTER IX

1. Wood, *op. cit.*, pp. 153-155.

2. See J. Lloyd Mecham, *The United States and Inter-American Security 1889-1960*. Austin: University of Texas Press, 1961, *passim*.

3. Hans J. Morgenthau, *Politics Abong Nations*. New York: Knopf, 1949, p. 440.

4. Herbert Feis, *Churchill, Roosevelt, Stalin; the War They Waged and the Peace They Sought*. Princeton: Princeton University Press, 1957, pp. 3, 7.

5. *Ibid.*, p. 202, citing Fitzroy Maclean, *Escape to Adventure*, p. 309.

6. Louise W. Holborn (ed.), *War and Peace Aims of the United Nations 1939-1942*. Boston: World Peace Foundation, 1943, p. 2.

7. William L. Neumann, *Making the Peace, 1941-1945, The Diplomacy of the Wartime Conferences*. Washington: Foundation for Foreign Affairs, 1950, p. 20.

8. Robert E. Sherwood, *Roosevelt and Hopkins*. New York: Harper, 1948, pp. 709, 782.

9. Feis, *op. cit.*, p. 60.

10. Cordell Hull, *The Memoirs of Cordell Hull*. New York: Macmillan, 1948, II, 1266.

11. Feis. *op. cit.*, p. 24.   12. *Ibid.*, p. 275.

13. See the accounts of Edward Taborsky in *Foreign Affairs*; "Benes and the Soviets," XXVII (January 1949), and "The Triumph and Disaster of Eduard Benes," XXXVI (July 1958).

14. Louise W. Holborn (ed.). *War and Peace Aims of the United Nations from Casablanca to Tokyo Bay, January 1, 1943-September 1, 1945*. Boston: World Peace Foundation, 1948, p. 7.

15. Hajo Holborn has argued that the fate of Eastern Europe was really decided at Munich in 1938: "The year 1938 was also the last in which the western European powers could have cooperated with the Soviet Union without paying a heavy price for her assistance. . . . Out of the wreckage of the European state system, American participation in World War II helped salvage only Western Europe and the larger part of Germany and Austria." Hajo Holborn, *The Political Collapse of Europe*. New York: Knopf, 1951, p. 158. Viewed this way, the western democracies came out of the war with no more than they "earned."

16. Sherwood, *op. cit.*, pp. 836-37.

17. Stephen D. Kertesz, *Diplomacy in a Whirlpool, Hungary Between Nazi Germany and Soviet Russia*. Notre Dame: University of Notre Dame Press, 1953, p. 107.

18. Feis, *op. cit.*, p. 123.

19. Winston S. Churchill, *Triumph and Tragedy*. Cambridge: Houghton Mifflin, 1953, p. 422.

20. Harry S. Truman, *Memoirs*. Garden City: Doubleday, 1955, I, 86.

21. Sherwood, *op. cit.*, p. 709.   22. Neumann, *op. cit.*, p. 98.

23. Louise W. Holborn, *op. cit.*, e.g., speech of Premier Wladyslaw Sikorski, February 24, 1942, in Vol. I, p. 472 and address of Premier Stanislaw Mikolajczyk, July 27, 1943, in Vol. II, p. 1069.

24. Richard Hiscocks, *The Rebirth of Austria*, New York: Oxford University Press, 1953, p. 42, and Kertesz, *op. cit.*, p. 140.

25. Philip E. Mosely, "Hopes and Failures: American Policy Toward East Central Europe, 1941-1947," *Review of Politics*, XVII, October, 1955, 481. After the Hungarian uprising in 1956 in which one of the principal demands of the revolutionists was for free elections, Communist Premier Janos Kadar is said to have told a visiting delegation: "The workers' power can be destroyed not only by bullets but also by ballots. We must reckon with the fact that we might be

thoroughly beaten at the elections." U.S. Department of State *Bulletin*, XXXVIII, No. 969, January 20, 1958, pp. 108-109.

26. U.S. Department of State, *Foreign Relations of the United States: The Conferences at Malta and Yalta, 1945*, Washington: Government Printing Office, 1955.

27. Neumann, *op. cit.*, p. 95.

28. Henry L. Stimson and McGeorge Bundy. *On Active Service in Peace and War*, New York: Harper, 1957, p. 610, and Truman, *op. cit.*, p. 79.

29. *The Conferences at Malta and Yalta, op. cit.*, p. 98.

30. Kemal H. Karpat. *Turkey's Politics: The Transition to a Multi-Party System*. Princeton, N.J.: Princeton University Press, 1959, p. 239.

31. *The Conferences at Malta and Yalta, op. cit.*, p. 805.

32. Hajo Holborn, *op. cit.*, p. 182.

33. Edward J. Rozek, *Allied Wartime Diplomacy; a Pattern in Poland*, New York: Wiley, 1958, p. 335.

34. Chester Wilmot, *The Struggle for Europe*, New York: Harper, 1952, p. 656.

35. Isaac A. Stone, "American Support of Free Elections in Eastern Europe," *Department of State Bulletin*, XVII (August 31, 1947), 320.

36. *Ibid.*, p. 315.

37. Vernon Van Dyke, *American Support of Free Institutions in Eastern Europe*, Yale Institute of International Studies, Memorandum No. 28 (August 10, 1948), pp. 9-10.

38. Redvers Opie, *et al.*, *The Search for Peace Settlements*, Washington: Brookings, 1951, p. 79.

39. This account is drawn largely from L. S. Stavrianos, *Greece: American Dilemma and Opportunity*, Chicago: Regnery, 1952, pp. 162-75.

40. James F. Byrnes, *Speaking Frankly*, New York: Harper, 1947, p. 73.

41. Frank Smothers, William H. McNeill and Elizabeth Darbishire, *Report on the Greeks*, New York: Twentieth Century Fund, 1948, p. 29.

42. Joseph and Stewart Alsop, "How Our Foreign Policy Is Made," *Saturday Evening Post*, CCXXI (April 30, 1949), 30.

43. E.g., "Soviet Violations of Treaty Obligations," *Department of State Bulletin*, XVIII (April 4, 1948), cited in C. E. Black (ed.), *Readings on Contemporary Eastern Europe*, New York: Mid-European Studies Center of the National Committee for a Free Europe, 1953.

44. Hugh Seton-Watson, *The East European Revolution*, New York: Praeger, 1956, pp. 46, 406, 411.

45. For others see Seymour M. Lipset, "Some Social Requisites of Democracy: Economic Development and Political Legitimacy," *American Political Science Review*, LIII (March 1959), 69-105.

46. Hans P. Krosby, "The Communist Power Bid in Finland in 1948," *Political Science Quarterly*, LXXV (June 1960), 229-43.

47. Kenneth Ingram, *History of the Cold War*, London: Darwen Finlayson, 1955, pp. 83-95.

48. Robert D. Tomasek, "British Guiana: A Case Study of British Colonial Policy," *Political Science Quarterly*, LXXIV (September 1959), 402.

49. Herbert L. Matthews, "Diplomatic Relations," in *The United States and Latin America*, New York: The American Assembly, 1959, p. 162, citing Philip

B. Taylor, Jr., "The Guatemalan Affair: A Critique of United States Foreign Policy," *American Political Science Review*, L (September 1956), 787-806.

50. Sherwood, *op. cit.*, p. 702.

51. Leslie B. Bain, "How We Failed in Hungary," *Reporter*, XVI (January 24, 1957), pp. 26-28, and Franz Spelman, "What the Hungarians Say about Western Propaganda," *Harper's*, CCXIV (April 1957), 70-74.

52. Dr. Jan F. Triska is one of the few American scholars working on the problem of discovering under what conditions the Soviets will *not* violate a treaty. See his preliminary studies, "Model for Study of Soviet Foreign Policy," *American Political Science Review*, LII (March 1958), 64-83, "Treaties and Other Sources of Order in International Relations: The Soviet View," *American Journal of International Law*, LII (October 1958), and with Robert M. Slusser, *A Calendar of Soviet Treaties*, Stanford: Stanford University Press, 1959, and by the same authors *The Theory, Law and Policy of Soviet Treaties*, Stanford: Stanford University Press, 1962.

53. George F. Kennan, "Disengagement Revisited," *Foreign Affairs*, XXXVII (January 1959), 187-210.

54. For an interpretation of Soviet motives in terms of national interest, see Samuel L. Sharp's contribution to *Soviet Conduct in World Affairs*, edited by Alexander Dallin, New York: Columbia University Press, 1960, pp. 46-58.

55. Stephen G. Xydis, "The Secret Anglo-Soviet Agreement on the Balkans of October 9, 1944," *Journal of Central European Affairs*, XV (October 1955), 248-71, and "Greece and the Yalta Declaration," *American Slavic Review*, XX (February 1961), pp. 1-24.

CHAPTER X

1. The substance of this chapter was delivered at the panel of the American Political Science Association on "Building Democratic Institutions Inside Foreign Countries," New York, Sept. 9, 1960.

2. For shorter periods and with greater limitations on our control, we occupied the home territories of our allies in Western Europe and Greece and contributed to the restoration of democratic institutions there after World War II.

3. See John D. Montgomery, *Forced to be Free: the Artificial Revolution in Germany and Japan*, Chicago: University of Chicago Press, 1957.

4. Robert G. Scigliano, 'The Electoral Process in South Vietnam: Politics in an Underdeveloped State," *Midwest Journal of Political Science*, May 1960.

5. Leon Gordenker, "The United Nations, U. S. Occupation and the 1948 Election in Korea," *Political Science Quarterly*, LXXIII (Sept. 1958), 426-450.

6. U. S. Statement on Korea, Secretary of State Herter to the Korean Ambassador, April 19, 1960, *New York Times*, April 20, 1960, p. 6.

7. *The Lewiston* (Maine) *Sun*, May 16, 1961, p. 1.

8. Garel A. Grunder and William E. Livezey, *The Philippines and the United States*, Norman: University of Oklahoma Press, 1951, *passim*.

9. Jorge R. Coquia, *The Philippine Election of 1953*, Manila: University Publishing Co., 1955; H. B. Jacobini, "Western Political Forms: Their Adaptation to the Philippines," *Southwestern Social Science Quarterly*, XL, 2 (September 1961), 173-180; Harold F. Gosnell, "An Interpretation of the Philippine Election of 1953," *American Political Science Review*, XLVIII, 4 (December 1954), 1128-1138.

10. See: W. J. M. Mackenzie, *Free Elections*, New York: Rinehart & Co., 1958; by the same author, "The Export of Electoral Systems," *Political Studies*, III (Oct. 1957) 240-257; and T. E. Smith, *Elections in Developing Countries*, London: St. Martin's Press, 1960.

11. J. S. Coleman, "Togoland," *International Conciliation*, No. 509 (Sept. 1956), 1-91.

12. Karpat, *op. cit.*, p. 241.

13. William O. Douglas, *Freedom of the Mind*, Public Affairs Committee, 1962. I am not concerned here with the effects of American policies on the elections of allies like Canada in 1963 where the freedom of the ballot is unquestionable.

14. U. S. Department of State *Bulletin*, Vol. XL, No. 1038 (May 18, 1959) pp. 726-727.

15. J. L. Mecham, "Democracy and Dictatorship in Latin America," *Southwestern Social Science Quarterly*, XLI (December 1960), 294-303.

16. This account is drawn from O. Edmund Smith, *Yankee Diplomacy, U. S. Intervention in Argentina*, Dallas: Southern Methodist University Press, 1953.

17. Herbert L. Matthews, ed., *The United States and Latin America*, American Assembly, 1959, p. 165.

18. David Lawrence, "Cuba's Tragic Era," *U. S. News and World Report*, XLVI, 4 (Jan. 23, 1959).

19. Adolf A. Berle, Jr., "Latin America: the Hidden Revolution," *Reporter*, XX, 11 (May 28, 1959), p. 20.

20. *New York Times*, July 19, August 2, 1962, p. 8.

21. Rowland Evans, Jr., "First Steps in Dominican Democracy," *Reporter*, XXVIII, 1 (Jan. 3, 1963), pp. 21-23.

22. *New York Times*, February 10, 1960, p. 13. A purportedly verbatim record of the conversation is in Jack Anderson's column, "Washington Merry-Go-Round" *Lewiston* (Maine) *Daily Sun*, February 23, 1960.

23. M. Margaret Ball, "Issue for the Americas; Non-Intervention v. Human Rights and the Preservation of Democratic Institutions," *International Organization*, XV (Winter 1961), 21-37; Mecham, *The United States and Inter-American Security 1889-1960, op. cit.*, pp. 420-421.

CHAPTER XI

1. See John H. Herz, "The Problem of Successorship in Dictatorial Regimes: A Study in Comparative Law and Institutions", *Journal of Politics*, XIV, 1 (February, 1952).

2. Jessup, *op. cit.*, p. 332.

3. E.g., President Wilson refused to intervene in a Peruvian electoral dispute in 1914.

4. George F. Kennan, *American Diplomacy, 1900-1950*, Chicago: University of Chicago Press, 1951, pp. 95, 100.

5. Joseph C. McKenna, *Diplomatic Protest in Foreign Policy; Analysis and Case Studies*, Chicago: Loyola University Press, 1962, arrives at a more optimistic conclusion as to the efficacy of diplomatic protests by the United States, but he does not deal with any cases involving free elections.

6. E.g., Secretary of State (Colby) to Italian Ambassador, Aug. 10, 1920, *Foreign Relations 1920*, Vol. III, pp. 463-468.

7. Press Release issued by the Department of the State, on March 21, 1923, containing Secretary Hughes' statement to the Women's Committee for Recognition of Russia, and letter to President Gompers of the A.F. of L., July 19, 1923, *Foreign Relations 1923*, Vol. II, pp. 755-764.

8. *Conference on Central American Affairs*, Washington, *op. cit.*, pp. 164, 363.

9. Press Release by the Department of State on September 17, 1930, *Foreign Relations 1930*, Vol. I, pp. 387-389.

10. The most prolific writer on the conditions of democracy in Latin America in recent years has been Russell H. Fitzgibbon.

11. See Merle Kling, "Toward a Theory of Power and Political Instability in Latin America", *Western Political Quarterly*, IX, 1 (March 1956), 21-35.

12. Letter from John Keith enclosed in Minister Hale in Costa Rica to Secretary of State, March 14, 1917, Archives.

13. See Edwin Lieuwen, *Arms and Politics in Latin America*, New York: Praeger, 1960.

14. Before the December, 1962 election in the Dominican Republic, a housewife told a reporter, "I don't know who I'll vote for because I don't know who will win." *Washington Post*, Dec. 16, 1962.

INDEX